DANGEROUS BORDER CROSSERS

Guillermo Gómez-Peña has been variously described as "among the most significant of late-twentieth-century performance artists" *(The Village Voice)*; "a peacemaker in the world's culture clash" *(Vanity Fair)*; and a "wizard of language" *(Chicago Tribune)*. He is without doubt a unique outsider-artist who crosses borders and "talks back."

In *Dangerous Border Crossers*, Gómez-Peña continues his epic artistic journey through globalization, the commodification of identity, and the continuing culture wars. His writings, like his performances, point towards a borderless future and a poetics of hybridity.

This latest anthology of his performance chronicles, diary entries, poems, essays and texts, sheds an extraordinary light on the life and work of this migrant provocateur. He documents and illuminates his brilliantly inventive collaborations with Roberto Sifuentes and other artists, and reveals, for the first time, what it's like to be a Chicano on the road.

DANGEROUS BORDER CROSSERS
is at once sexy, scary and inspiring.
Prepare to be provoked.

When not on the road with his troupe, La Pocha Nostra, **Guillermo Gómez-Peña** divides his time between San Francisco and Mexico City. His previous books include *Warrior for Gringostroika* (1993), *New World Border* (1996), *Friendly Cannibals* (1997) and *Temple of Confessions* (1997).

"*Through the performance ritual, the audience vicariously experiences the freedom, cultural risks, and utopian possibilities that society has denied them. Audience members are encouraged to touch us, smell us, feed us, defy us. In this strange millennial ceremony, the Pandora's box opens and the post-colonial demons are unleashed.*"

FROM GÓMEZ-PEÑA'S PERFORMANCE DIARIES

GUILLERMO GÓMEZ-PEÑA

DANGEROUS

BORDER CROSSERS

• • •••••••The Artist Talks Back

ROUTLEDGE
Taylor & Francis Group

LONDON and NEW YORK

First published 2000 by Routledge
11 New Fetter Lane, London EC4P 4EE

Simultaneously published in the USA and Canada by Routledge
29 West 35th Street, New York, NY10001

Routledge is an imprint of the Taylor and Francis Group

Designed and typeset by Sutchinda Rangsi Thompson
Printed in Great Britain by Bell and Bain Ltd., Glasgow

British Library Cataloguing in Publication Data
A catalogue record for this book is available from the British Library

Library of Congress Cataloging in Publication Data

Gómez–Peña, Guillermo.
    Dangerous Border Crossers: the artist talks back / Gómez–Peña, Guillermo.
        p. cm.
    1. Gómez–Peña, Guillermo. 2. Performance art–United States. I. Title.
NX512.G66 A35 2000
790'.2–dc21

99-052962

ISBN 0-415-18236-0 (hbk)
ISBN 0-415-18237-9 (pbk)

Para la Leona, el zut, y la Reina de Cocoteros
my millennial trinity; my reason to continue . . .

"*True . . . my performance work has kept me from getting a job and has alienated me from sectors of my community. But it has also prevented me from ending up in jail, in a mental institution, or in the cemetery.*"

FROM GÓMEZ-PEÑA'S PERFORMANCE DIARIES, 1994

Contents

Illustrations and Sources

Preface and Acknowledgements

My case is unique. Although I studied Linguistics and Literature at the UNAM (Mexico City) and Post Studio Art at the California Institute of Arts, I am not a product of academia. For sixteen years I have been an independent artist and writer. The fact that I don't depend on any educational or cultural institution grants me some extra freedoms which I always try to exercise to their fullest. I have no formal job to lose. I've got no boss, director, or patrons.

This, my fifth book, is perhaps my most ambitious enterprise as a performance writer. It is a conscious attempt to bridge many gaps, both in my life as an interdisciplinary artist and in the field of performance, including those between cultural identity and performance persona, practice and theory, art and activism, transgressive aesthetics and radical politics, and the somewhat private realm of the creative process and the public realm of distribution and presentation. Like my performances, the (conscious) impulse behind my writings is the desire to speak as a public intellectual and a socially committed artist in a time and place where this appears to be a lost battle, and to attempt to do so in an innovative way, using every possible medium to which I have access: performance, installation art, film, radio, journalism, theory, the Internet, and when necessary, direct political action. In my work, all of these overlapping territories are interconnected through an intricate system of veins and wires. They feed one another, translate into one another, project shadows into all directions.

This eclectic book is composed of selected writings that span from 1994 to 1999, including chronicles of performance adventures; reflections and essays on performance, culture, identity and politics; conversations with like-minded colleagues; texts written for National Public Radio; and excerpts from my diaries and my performance scripts. Like my psyche, some of these texts suffer from a logical case of identity crisis. Chronicles and essays originally written for radio or newspaper eventually became part of a performance script or a public discussion in a town meeting, or vice versa. Excerpts from some of these texts eventually found their way into one of my videos or installations, or were used as "techno-placas" circulated in virtual space. It's just the way I work, the way my performances and books get made. I believe in the border culture of recycling and recontextualizing. The combination of materials included here has its own logic and structural integrity, but divisions between sections and categories are intentionally open and porous. I encourage the reader not to regard the structure of the book as a linear itinerary; if you would prefer, feel free to choose your own reading order, your own route across my conceptual topography.

Like my performance work, this book would not have been possible without the selfless help of so many people. First and foremost, I wish to acknowledge my adored compañera and soulmate, Carolina Ponce de León, "La Leona de Chapinero," who not only read each and every draft and gave me invaluable suggestions on how to improve them, but also firmly protected me from the demands of my public life so that I could have the necessary time and solitude (in between projects and tours) to rework existing texts and come up with new material. Carolina, you are it! Loca, soy tuyo hasta la muerte. Somos.

I also wish to thank my dear colleague, Lisa Wolford, who edited the manuscript with her laser scissors, patiently correcting my Chiconics, and who challenged me to be a better, more complex and more valiant writer. Talia Rodgers, senior editor at Routledge for literature and performance, originally conceived of this project. She extended herself beyond the limits to develop a more personalized relationship with an artist who is needy, complicated and insecure. She challenged me to be both more personal and more rigorous, and to write a book that is simultaneously theoretical and accessible. I hope I didn't disappoint you, Talia.

My incredibly loving familia must also be acknowledged, because the time I spent writing this book (in the scope of my crazy life) was certainly time away from them. Especially my mother, doña Martha, and my son, Guillermo "zut" Emiliano, who patiently suffered my intermittent absences absorbed in front of my laptop without ever complaining. Queridísimos, I hope I can make up the missing time in the coming months.

And of course I need to acknowledge the valor and compatible pathologies of my closest performance accomplices, who are always ready to jump into the flames with me, especially my main partner in crime, Roberto "CyberVato" Sifuentes; Nola Mariano, holy protector of my back against insensitive producers, conservative critics, and ferocious IRS agents; and Sara Shelton-Mann, "La Clepto-Mexican Gringa."

Other endearing lunaticos who informed and shaped this book with their ideas, their support, and their love include the Washington Cartel (Kim Chan, aka "La China Chola," Cristina "La Breck Girl" King, Abel López, B. Stanley and Sylvanna Straw), the San Francisco Cartel ("El Capo" René Yañez, "El Chueco" Gustavo Vázquez, Rona Michele, Eugenio Castro "El Mapplethorpe de Acapulco," Lorraine Bautista, Elaine "La Sesos" Katzenberger, Alice Joanou, Allison Delauer, Enrique Chagoya, Joe Lambert, Miya Masaoka, Lynn Hershman, Jeff Jones, Andrea Suess, Suzanne "La Zorca" Stefanac, Isis Rodriguez, Guillermo Galindo, Liz Lerma, Josh Kun, Greg Morozumi, and the SOMAR squad), the Motown Mafia (Nancy Jones and Isabella Basombrio), the Crow Cartel (Susan Stewart and Tyler Medicinehorse), the Wales Cartel (Richard Gough, Judie Christie, Rachel Rogers, Ian Morgan, Alex Alderton, Misha Myers, Adam Hayward, Heike Roms), the New York cartel (Richard Schechner, Diana Taylor, Barbara Kirshenblatt-Gimblett, Peggy Phelan, Javier Martíñez del Pinzón, Pilar Cano), the Mexico City Clan (César Martíñez, Juan Ybarra, Josefina Alcázar, Roger Bartra, Felipe Ehrenberg, Violeta Luna, Yoshigiro Maeshiro), the Latino MacArturo Ombudsmen Mafia (Baldemar Velázquez, Sandra Cisneros, Ruth Behar, Joaquín Avila, Hugo Morales, Hippolito Roldán, Maria Varela, Luis Alfaro), the LA Cartel (Rubén Martinez, Elia Arce, Tim Miller, Leilani Chan, Beto Arcos, Josefina Ramírez, Peter Sellers, Dorcas Roman, Rubén Guevara, José Antonio Aguirre), the Arizona Tribe (Norma Medina, Kathie Hotchner, and Michelle Ceballos), the Chicago Cartel (Encarnación Teruel, Nena Torres, Marcos Raya, Achy Obejas, Carlos Cumpian, Carol Becker, Iñigo Manglano-Ovalle), the National FLOC Cartel (the Cuevas family, Silvia Muñiz-Mutchler, and many others), and the bloody clans Culture Clash, Chicano Secret Service, and Los Delicados. Other nomadic Mafia members include James "el Shame-man" Luna, Miguel Algarin, Danny and Maruca Salazar, Isaac Artenstein, Robert Sánchez, Juan Felipe Herrera, Juan Tejeda, David Schweitzer, Susan Harjo, Leticia Nieto, Laurie Beth Clark, Sandy Stone, Penny Remsen, Raymond Bobgan, Leslie Bentley, Norman Frisch, Marietta Bernstoff, Antonio Turok,

Rafael Lozano-Helmer, Susie Ramsey, Anne Pasternak, George Emilio Sánchez, Roberta Uno and of coursísimo, my grungero nephews Ricardo, Carlitos, Iana and Cristóbal, who fortunately decided not to follow in my footsteps. Thanks to all of you vatos and chucas for believing in my saliva, in my Spanglish knives, in my black leather and studded heart.

During the two years it took me to put together this book, I lost several relatives. My tender uncles Manuel, Eugenio, Rubén, and Nacho, and my cousin Juanito departed unexpectedly to the other side to gather with my father and grandparents, but I hope with all my heart that they will get to read this finished book wherever they are (the Aztec Mictlán or the Catholic heaven), because without the love and attention they gave me while growing up in Mexico City, I couldn't possibly be the person I am, this pinche locote pero somewhat together borderólogo. The performance begins . . . y la zozobra.

> *Dear foreign reader:*
> *welcome to my conceptual set*
> *welcome to my performance universe*
> *welcome to my borderzone*
> *welcome to the cities and jungles of my language*
> *las del inglés y las del español*
> *kick back*
> *light up your conceptual cigarette*
> *& breath in, breath out,*
> *breath in, breath out,*
> *rreelllaaaxxxx*
> *now, reach over,*
> *grab your crotch*
> *or the crotch of your neighbor*
> *& massage gently . . .*

I would like to thank the following publishers for giving permission to reproduce previously published material:

Deported to the North and The Psycho in the Lobby of the Theater originally appeared in *New World Border*, City Lights Books 1996.

The Subcomandante of Performance originally appeared in *First World, Ha Ha Ha!: The Zapatistas Challenge*, anthologized by Elaine Katzenberger, City Lights Books, 1995.

The Two Guadalupes originally appeared in *Goddess of the Americas: Writings on the Virgin of Guadalupe*, anthologized by Ana Castillo, Riverhead Books, 1996.

Virtual Barrio originally appeared in *Clicking In: Hot Links to a Digital Culture*, anthologized by Lynn Hershman, Bay Press 1996.

INTRODUCTION

2 El Naftaztec, 1998.

1 Border Brujo, 1988.

1492 Performances

I choose to continue remembering
the singular journey
that led me to this stage
five centuries of foreign domination
total
1492 performances
in which
I've cut my hair
sliced my wrists
farted & eaten on stage
danced on fire & ice
recreated my birth
invoked my ancestors
conspired against the government
asked for a job
sold my identity
deported myself back to Mexico
repositioned my soul within my body
reshaped my body to accommodate
    your whims
or to confirm your fears
aquí, tu miedo encarnado
en mi cuerpo
my body elastic

mi cuerpo celluloid
my body passional
mi cuerpo folkloric
my body cartographic
mi cuerpo cyber-punk
my body rupestre
mi cuerpo ceremonial
my body militant
mi cuerpo metaphorical
my bloody body
cuerpo adentro
me interno
en un concierto
de adioses
me amortajo
hacia el futuro incierto.

FROM "THE 1992 TRILOGY"

3 In the Altar of Love, 1999. Gómez-Peña and Carolina Ponce de León.

Love Poem

Carolina:
since I met you
my endemic rage against the world
slowly turns to melancholy
as I witness the partition of my heart
into 2 hemispheres:
a) the world with you, in you
in between the 2 Carolinas
– la del norte y la tuya –
b) y el otro
el de afuera,
digamos, el resto del universo
& if I think too much about it on the road
I just get enormously sad
& then my only consolation
is the memory of your last words
(tu poema # 14)
and the longing for our next embrace
pa' cuando, mi loca? y dónde?
Nueva York again?
San Francisco or Mexico City?

JULY 17, 1998

. . . thus the road was my salvation
& performance meant the possibility of connecting
all these places and facts in a somewhat coherent manner
meeting people with slightly similar concerns:
performance, language, activismo, geografía,
phony tribal artifacts, aficionado archaeology & shit
therefore I parted again
this time to the sierra Tarahumara, in Northern Mexico
Raramuri, Mater Dei Dolorosa
amén
twenty years later...
I am still writing & performing, de milagro.

FROM "THE LAST MY-GRATION,"1995

"Journalist: What do Mexicans and Americans share across the border?

Gómez-Peña: Crisis, pure crises, displacement, fear...and reciprocal sexual
    desire.The rest is geography, man...and TV of course."

La Migrant Life

I

I hate diaries and autobiographies. I have always found the "confessional" tone a bit foreign. The spectacle of my own pain and (anti)heroism is strictly reserved for my beloved ones. Why? I am not Protestant, nor do I come from an exhibitionist culture of public confession, like Anglo-America. I am an ex-Catholic pagan, and I only write or make art about myself when I am completely sure that the biographical paradigm intersects with larger social and cultural issues. Thus it is quite a challenge for me to write a book about my life and tribulations as a performance artist, taking on the risk of "confessing" what no one needs or wants to know, and/or romanticizing the already over-romanticized life of a nomadic artist and ending up with a corny book. But since I like challenges (my life and art have often been propelled by irrational challenges), I have decided to undertake this somewhat "autobiographical" project, in the hope that some readers will see their lives, faces and ideas reflected here and there in the multiple shifting (and cracked) mirrors of these texts. I hope to avoid describing my cultural, sexual or political adventures in order to create a place for myself in an Olympian pantheon of anti-heroes. I don't want to heroize/eroticize my oppression as a post-Mexican in racist USA, or as a "Chicanized" Mexican in nationalist Mexico; I have already done enough of that in my earlier books and performances. Instead, I want to reveal what lies behind and beneath the making of performance art, particularly when crossing extremely volatile geographic and cultural borders. It is important to me to discuss the conflicts that surround and inform both the content of my writings and performance work, and the process of development. To do so, I have to chronicle the innumerable border crossings, political *broncas* and crosscultural misencounters that constitute the raw matter of my art, the pulsating flesh of my performance actions and poetical/theoretical writings. These elements, so central to the life and experience of an artist, paradoxically go unremarked by performance critics and historians.

The conflicts and challenges that shape my work (and that of other artists working on similar fronts) increase exponentially when one considers the historical and cultural context of my work: the militarization of the US/Mexico border, the savage globalization of economy and culture, the millennial culture of apocalypse and despair, and the resurgence of virulent neonationalisms, parochial moralities and spiritual fundamentalisms. It is also important to remember that Chicano and Mexican artists traveling around the world, especially the much-touted "First World," have a radically different experience than, let's say, German or Australian artists traveling in Latin America. Our experience as "Third World" nomads in the ever-shrinking "First World" is marked by political violence and cultural misunderstandings. Perpetually viewed through the mythical projections of the dominant culture, we face endless confrontations if we attempt to correct misreadings of our (phantasmic) identities.

Touring the overlapping cartographies of Anglo- and Latino-America, Europe, Asia, and North Africa, my performance accomplices and I have crossed many dangerous borders. In doing so, we have risked our identity, our dignity, and occasionally even our lives. We have been harassed by cops and border patrolmen put off by our "Latino hipster" look, stalked by lunatics attracted by our foreignness and flamboyant clothing, blasted by right-wing evangelists and essentialist academicians, and once even chased out of town by self-righteous patriots who found our work "un-American." I don't regret any of these encounters. In fact, they have taught me a great deal about human behavior, life, culture and even performance. Fortunately, with a few exceptions – hey, everyone loses it now and then – my performance collaborators and I have been able to avoid responding to these threatening situations with anger or agression. Instead, we use humor, multilingualism, and surprising performance strategies to fight back. Most of the time, we win, or at least get (temporarily) even.

II

Performance as an artistic "genre" is in a constant state of crisis, and is therefore an ideal medium for articulating a time of permanent crisis such as ours. Performance is a disnarrative and symbolic chronicle of the instant which focuses mainly on the "now" and the "here." Performance is about presence, not representation; it is not (as classical theories of theater would suggest) a mirror, but the actual moment in which the mirror is shattered. The act of creating and presenting a performance carries a sense of urgency and immediacy that does not exist in other artistic fields. We experience life, therefore we perform – or rather, we perform as we live, love, travel and suffer, everything woven together into a complex, multi-hued tapestry. Traveling, both geographically and culturally, becomes an intrinsic part of the artistic process, particularly for those of us who see ourselves as migrants or border crossers.

Since my early work with the Border Arts Workshop (1984-1990[1]) I have defined myself as a migrant provocateur, an intercultural pirate, a "border brujo," a conceptual coyote (smuggler), and, more recently, a "web-back," zigzagging the ever-fluctuating borders of the dying "Western Civilization." My life as a border crosser has been an intricate part of my political and aesthetic praxis. Again, I am, therefore I travel, and vice versa. I travel in search of the many other Mexicos, my other selves, and the many communities to which I belong; while traveling, I make art, write, theorize and edit my memories.

I first left Mexico City in 1978. Since then, I've spent almost twenty years traveling from South to North and back – from city to city, country to country, English to Spanish. I travel from myth to social reality, always returning to my origins (by now mythical as well), retracing the footprints of my biological family and revisiting the many overlapping communities of which I am a part: the diasporic Latin Americans, the deterritorialized citizens of everywhere and nowhere, the inhabitants of the so-called "margins" and crevices, *los vatos inter-sticiales*, the hybrids, exiles, and renegades. This partly conscious desire to retrace the footprints of these peoples and communities is precisely what compels me to keep moving. This objective is perhaps what separates my own personal road

---

1   The Border Arts Workshop was a binational collective of artists and activists which utilized the Tijuana/San Diego border region as "a laboratory of social and aesthetic experimentation."

movie from the standard American genre, which is largely about finding oneself on the road. I wish to clarify: I don't aspire to find myself. I wholeheartedly accept my constant condition of loss. I embrace my multiple and incomplete identities, and celebrate all of them (or to be more precise, most of them, since there are aspects of my multiple repertoire of performance personae that I truly hate, and that sometimes frighten me).

I've spent many years writing and making art on the road, from Mexico City to San Francisco, from Buenos Aires to central Canada, from Tijuana to Vladivostok, and all the spaces in between. But "the road" to me means something more than a neo-romantic, rockero "lifestyle." It's a strange form of home, a sort of moving Bermuda triangle inhabited by a floating community of trouble-making travelers like me – the Tribe of the Inflamed Eyelids, my extended *familia*. I find them wherever I go, and the routes we travel belong to a different cartography than those outlined on the hegemonic maps of the chi-chi "international" art world. As part of our political and aesthetic praxis, my colleagues and I have always made a point of performing not just in the hip art spaces of major cultural centers like New York, Mexico City, or Los Angeles, but also venturing into places where people might never have seen, as one perplexed audience member in Kansas City once put it, "intelligent Meskins" who actually talk back, or in our own words, "mariachis with big mouths." Whether martyrs of Chicanismo or stupid cultural kamikazes, we feel a certain pride in having survived backwoods Georgia, rural Florida, and the American heartland of Iowa, Ohio and Indiana, "exotic" places where people often don't know what the word "Chicano" means, and the only existing references to Mexican culture are the Taco Bell chihuahua, "Cheech and Chong," and Cuervo Gold. In our sui generis performance cartography, a typical tour schedule for myself and my performance accomplices might read something like this: *San Francisco, Washington, Montana, Lintz, San Sebastian, Denver-Boulder, Tijuana, El Paso, New York, Alberta, Los Angeles, Mexico City, Chiapas, Aberystwyth, Detroit, then back to San Francisco.*

Home? San Francisco has been my most recent "physical home," meaning my current point of departure and return. The physical home, *la casa*, is the place where my computer, books, videos, and archives happen to be, and most importantly, the place I share with my beloved Carolina. It is also the place where I rehearse and pack before returning to my other home, the conceptual one – the road, *la jornada*, my personal Bermuda triangle. My Mexican home, my small family house located in a nineteenth century working-class neighborhood in Mexico City, is quite mythical to me. It is the place to which I return once every couple of months in search of political energy, tender memories, maternal love, and good food (and occasionally to perform). Sadly, in recent years, Mexico City has become the capital of the great continental crises, a resonance box where all violence (political or cultural, directed or random) gets amplified to a point of absurdity. The echoes of this violence are heard all the way to the Latino barrios of the US, as well as in my performance scripts.

4 Gómez-Peña's family at the old house. Mexico City, 1953. Left to right: **brother Carlos, mother Martha, father Guillermo, and sister Diana.**

III

Nomadism and migration have become central experiences of millennial post-modernity. As our (cultural) continents collide and overlap in the rapid process of "globalization," the ongoing migration of South to North and East to West redefines not only geopolitical borders, but also language (the currency of *lingua francas*), identity (national and personal), activism, art and popular culture. My performance accomplices and I have sailed the troubled waters created by this strange "continental drift" in the hope that we might someday find a coastline.

I have never been alone in this enterprise. I have been blessed with many friends and colleagues who have shared portions of this endless journey to the end of Western civilization and the outposts of Chicanismo. My most frequent companion on these journeys has been Roberto Sifuentes (aka CyberVato), who since 1991 has collaborated and toured with me in different capacities: technical director, lighting designer, performer, co-director, and "cyber-disc-jockey." We jokingly describe ourselves as "the Lewis and Clark of the Chicano movement" always charting the Mexican *terra ignota*. Two important borders separate

Roberto and I: cultural and generational. He is a Chicano in the process of Mexicanization (which means that he is looking South) and I am a Mexican in the process of Chicanization. (Will I ever become a "real" Chicano? Will I ever "arrive"? Will "they" – the border guards of identity – ever let me?) Roberto is also eleven years my junior. These borders have become raw material for our performance adventures and fractured memories.

I remember. I remember in English, Spanish and Spanglish. I remember Roberto being stripped down and frisked by Australian customs agents at Sydney airport. I remember going through the border checkpoint at JFK with our mariachi hats in hand, and being welcomed by a smiling INS agent who thought we were a duo of "amigo entertainers." I remember countless times when Roberto and I were pulled over by the cops driving home after a performance, still in full robo-raza regalia, what a hard time they had dealing with our flamboyant performance personae. Or how many times drunk jocks have come up to us as we were chilling out in a bar after a street intervention to ask whether what we were wearing was our (folkloric) "national costume." I remember being besieged by white supremacists during a residency in Providence, Rhode Island, and having to get police protection. I will never forget the faces of the skinheads in Helsinki who threatened Roberto for dancing salsa with a Finnish girl. Nor will I forget the acute disappointment expressed by the Madrilenian producers of a chic arts festival when they first saw our brown faces at the Barajas airport: "We thought you were . . . American." Or Roberto's bewilderment when an Italian critic was dismayed to discover that he was not a "real" gang member. I will always treasure the memory of the US ambassador in Brussels, who flipped out when he realized that I (a Mexican) was "representing" the US at the Time Festival. I can't count how many times people have come up to Roberto and me after post-performance discussions to tell us how good our English is, and how surprisingly "articulate" we were. Many other memories wander around my psyche and into this book. They are mischievous, strangely familar, and at times sad, but all have contributed to shaping my political understanding of art and identity.

IV

Contrary to some people's perceptions, the life of a migrant performance artist isn't entirely glamorous. It is true that we sometimes get put in five-star hotels

5 Exhausted after a day of street interventions. Gómez-Peña, Sifuentes and local artist.

and invited to exclusive places to which few other Chicanos have access. But it is also true that at times, "touring" means cheap motels, bad food, and run-ins with weirdos and the local authorities, not to mention fifteen-hour work days. Sometimes our only consolations are friendship, humor, the surprise of a new cultural or geographic discovery, and of course, phone calls from loved ones (provided, that is, we're staying in a place where we even have a phone). It's impossible to imagine what will be waiting for us at the next stop along the way. Glamorous-sounding places are often cruel, while "provincial" ones can be quite exciting. Performing in New York or London can be dispiritingly isolating, if not properly planned, whereas with the right producer or organizer, Aberystwyth, Wales, or the Crow Reservation in northern Montana can turn out to be a strangely ideal context for the work. In allegedly conservative parts of rural America, where we have expected violence and misunderstanding from our audiences, we have instead encountered deep tenderness and profound solidarity, while we have faced potentially serious danger and blunt *pendejismo* (stupidity) in snobbish, sophisticated enclaves of (allegedly) progressive thought and culture. Our mental stereotypes topple by their own weight as we travel.

My friends, those who stay in one place, often ask me to describe a typical day on the road. Each day is different, but a few constants remain: no matter how late Roberto and I went to sleep, the next morning begins early. We work out (if you don't exercise daily, you inevitably get ill). If we choose to jog, it is clearly an atypical jogging ritual; with me in my cowboy boots and chili pepper shorts, we hit the streets of a new city, stopping at cafes for cigarettes and shots of espresso. At the hotel, we usually brainstorm with our laptops for an hour or so before being picked up by our hosts, who often take us either to a press conference, or to the local NPR affiliate or community radio station to talk about politics and art. (If we are in a place where people are not familiar with our work, we often have to try and answer questions such as "Guerrmou, what can you tell us about your new album?" or "Yiguermou, can you describe the plot of your new play?" In such cases, we have to help the uninformed interviewer save face, and still have a decent and informative interview. It's a real challenge). Then, we have a short lunch and either go to the local university or community center to give a talk, or directly to the theater or museum to make all the technical preparations for the show. By the time we finish, it's already dark, and we're ready to chill out. In the evenings, we meet at a bar or cafe with local artists and activists, who tell us about their political dramas. Latinos and other members of diasporic communities are particularly eager to tell us their story and ask us for advice. Often, immigration activists or bilingual teachers want to show us the dark side of the city – the site of the most recent driveby shooting, or the place where the last demonstration was broken up by the cops. Late at night, our hosts take us out to dinner. Naive presenters offer to take us to "the only Mexican restaurant in town," or serve unrecognizable imitations of Mexican food in their own homes. We politely inform them that we prefer "truly exotic food, you know. . . German, Russian, Southern . . ." Some presenters have heard stories of our alleged "wild lifestyle" and want to contribute to the mythology by taking us on a "special tour" to a sleazy or dangerous part of town. Ocassionally, they introduce us to local eccentrics, party animals, or collectors of the bizarre. I empathize with their dilemma: how to entertain two Mexican guys who once crucified themselves in the name of art, and who often live for three-day periods inside Plexiglas boxes as "endangered species" or "ethno-cyborgs"? Is the city interesting enough for these *locos*? What do they eat? What kind of people do they want to meet? Do they only hang out with other Latinos? Are they into shamanic drugs or bizarre sexual practices? The fact is that reality isn't nearly as strange or colorful as myth. We certainly don't want to meet every outlaw in town, nor are we expecting to get busted or have a transcendental experience in every city we visit. But neither do we want to be left alone in the hotel. We want to engage thoroughly in the local cultural and political life (the civic dimension of our work is extremely important to us), but at the same time we need a little privacy. Once the project is over, we love to go crazy and exorcise the demons of the performance.

People sometimes get disappointed when they meet us: either we aren't as wild as our performance characters in the photos, or as outrageous in our daily behavior as gossip and preconceptions (whether about Mexicans or performance artists) might lead them to expect. In fact, we tend to be rather . . . polite. We are often fragile and melancholic, and we sometimes get sick as a result of so much travel and work. Late at night at the hotel, if there isn't a party to go to or the city is not conducive to walking, it's easy to fall into a spiderweb of loneliness – a very particular kind of loneliness, produced by constant deterritorialization and intensified by distance. No matter where we are geographically, we are conceptually equidistant from our "home(s)" and our beloved ones. At such times, CNN becomes important, and old American movies are suddenly interesting. At other times, the extravagant energy of the work attracts wonderful locos, misfits and visionaries, and suddenly you find yourself dancing country & western at a barn in Saskatchewan at 4 a.m., or howling at the moon in the Rockies. Besides, after fourteen years of touring, I have many dear friends wherever I go who make sure to provide me and my accomplices with enough tenderness and chiles to continue our trek to the mythical North, and our inward journey to the bottom of our identities.

Meanwhile, as we travel from San Antonio to Seattle and then to Toronto, the e-mails pile up in cyberspace and the letters in the mail, and angry or guilt-tripping phone messages accumulate back home. It is only thanks to the grace and intelligence of my super-assistants, "Allisonica" Delauer ,and more recently Lorraine Bautista, and my "holy agent/political bodyguard," doña Nola Mariano, that the menacing "real world" doesn't collapse over my head.

V

Even travelers have some cast-iron rules. If there is enough of a budget, I try to invite my lover to visit for a week. If she can't, no matter where I am, no matter how short the time between projects, I either go to meet my lover, wherever she is, or take the time to visit with my mother or my son. If you lose touch with your beloved ones, you can also lose touch with yourself, and then you begin believing that what you do is somehow heroic and revolutionary. That's when you know you're fucked.

The saddest aspect of touring is that the world does not stop back home. Your loved ones miss you and need you, and you need them as well, but there is not much you can do about it. Your closest friends, with a few exceptions, don't give you any slack. "Hey *loco*, it's about time that you called. How is the Marco Polo of Chicanolandia? Will you have a few minutes to spend with me this time, or are you too famous?" People really tell you this shit. They may be teasing, but they don't understand that the needle goes straight through your heart and opens the biggest wound of all – the one produced by not entirely belonging anywhere. Only those friends who have equally complicated lives understand why you disappear so often without leaving traces; they learn to accept you as an ephemeral being, a ghost-like presence who appears and disappears from other people's lives, just like they do. Your friends and relatives eventually learn that the rare times you are able to spend together must be lived as intensely as possibly, because there's no way of knowing when you'll see each other again.

The dilemma of love and touring is particularly traumatic. For a relationship to work, your lover must be tough, supportive, and equally consumed by his or her own complex, professional life. If not, no matter how strong s/he might be, s/he will eventually get tired of waiting. Nomad artists must make special efforts to nurture love in the storm and chaos of their daily lives. When a separation becomes unbearable, it's important to get on a plane and go to be with one's lover for a few days, no matter how long the journey or how expensive the plane ticket. Meanwhile, like Americans say, we need to give each other a lot of slack, write e-mails and love poems to each other, and when we are together, live every moment with absolute passion.

My mother is definitely more demanding than my beloved Carolina, especially since my father and grandmother died. Her demands for me to be more present in her life, to be a more responsible son, fill me (an ex-Catholic Mexican) with guilt, but I am extremely grateful to her. No matter where I am calling from, she reminds me of the basics in life: have you been brushing your teeth? Do you have clean underwear? Do you have the right clothes for that weather? Have you seen a doctor lately? Did you phone your son today? Your uncle Pepe is ill; when are you going to visit him? Have you paid your bills? Is the IRS still breathing over your shoulder? When can I expect you back in Mexico? At first, her advice and gentle nagging give me vertigo, since there isn't much I can do about them on the road, but ultimately they ground me and give me a sense of perspective, reminding me that the demands of ordinary human life and connections with family are in many ways more important than my adventures on the road.

Losing someone you love madly while touring is one of the worst experiences in life. I have lost many beloved ones this way, starting with my father. When I received the dreaded call from my mother telling me that he had just died by falling down the stairs, I took the first plane I could and arrived that night for the funeral. It took me years to reconcile myself with the fact I couldn't say goodbye to him. With my grandmother Carmen, I was luckier. I was performing in New York when I got the phone call from Mexico City telling me that Grandma Pipa might die at any moment. On the phone, I begged her to wait for me. After the show, I went straight to the airport and caught the next plane, arriving in Mexico City three hours before she died. Over the years, many relatives and friends have died while I was touring, and my mother chose not to tell me until after the tour was over. Blackout. I returned to a different Mexico, an unfamiliar landscape with fewer emotional citizens inhabiting my inner city. I felt much lonelier and more deterritorialized. Now these relatives and friends exist only as ghost-like images in my personal road movie, sepia photos from my family album, tender memories of a lost world – the so-called "homeland," the one I once left for good.

This mournful loss is a familiar sensation in the everbleeding heart of a migrant, and it never goes away. But you take a deep breath, put on your cowboy hat, snakeskin boots and some killer make-up, grab your hand-carved "tribal" cane and hit the streets again. You walk North. You look great. You look more like yourself – like one of your many selves . . . You are ready to continue living, performing, causing trouble . . .

JUNE 1999

Returning to America (1997)
Radio Chronicle

I fly back to the US
a few days after "black Tuesday"
the sad April first when the new anti-immigration legislation
came into effect.
its Thursday night at a hectic LAX
as I wait for my luggage
I am sniffed by 2 humongous police dogs
a border guard approaches me.
no big deal
I always get stopped 'cause I've been told
I just have this archetypal "suspicious" look
a cross between a border dandy, and a generic Latino outlaw.
"excuse me sir, where are you coming from?"
"Mexico City" I reply.
"why?" he asks
"what do you mean?
why Mexico City as opposed to Hong Kong?
or why am I coming back?
'cause since I live here in California,
I am condemned to always come back."
he finds no humor in my logic
"what do you do?" he asks.

"I'm a performance artist, and an occasional commentator for NPR."
"no, I am asking you what do you do," he insists
"you mean, you want me to describe my aesthetics & cosmology?
or you are simply implying I am lying to you?"
he is now visibly upset & demands to see an ID.
I show him an Art press card.
"what do you write about?"
"crossing borders, US/Mexico relations,
immigration, situations like this one."
he pauses and then continues more aggressively:
"so what do you think about your country's government
being so involved with those big-time drug dealers from Juarez?"
"It's bad" I say
"but what about the fact that there is evidence
to suggest that the drugs coming from the contras a decade ago
were introduced to communities of color via the LAPD?"
he takes a step back "where did you get that crap?"
"it was international news last year" I reply.
"but nowadays the drugs are mainly coming from Mexico"
his insistence in demonizing Mexico sets me off
"sure," I answer
"precisely because there is a market here in America;
or are you so naive as to think that the production of drugs
creates the market?"
he doesn't get my point.
neither do I
instead
he writes a mysterious note
& sends me to secondary inspection
where I spend the next two hours
watching a bored customs agent
inspecting every inch of my suitcases,
including toiletries, props, costumes,
performance scripts, my phone agenda,
and all because of my big mouth and my thick mustache.

6 El Pre-Industrial Cannibal. From a CD-Rom project in progress in collaboration with Lynn Hershman.

CRIMINAL IDENTITY PROFILE
(Highly Classified/Not For Publication)

COMPLETE NAME: Guillermo Lino Gómez-Peña

ENGLISH TRANSLATION: Guermo, Guiliermou, Yiguermo, Giguamo . . . Comes-Penis or Piña

NATIONALITY: Since early 1999, dual: Mexican and USian

SELF IDENTITY: Mexican in process of Chicanoization

RACE Non-specific, probably mestizo

LANGUAGES SPOKEN FLUENTLY: Spanish, English, Spanglish, Gringoñol, Franglais, Robo-esperanto & fake Nahuatl

DISTINGUISHING FEATURES: performance scars on both arms, stomach and right knee; hyper-Mexican mustache; loungy side burns; pinto tattoos on chest, right arm and left shoulder; melancholic gaze

OCCUPATIONS in order of importance: Performance artist, writer, videoasta, journalist, activist, borderólogo, reverse anthropologist, experimental linguist, media pirate, bad actor

MAIN PERFORMANCE ALIASES in chronological order: Mister Misterio, El Existentialist Mojado, Border Brujo, El Warrior for Gringostroika, El Untranslatable Vato, El Mariachi Liberachi, El Aztec High-Tech, El Quebradito, El Naftazteca, El Mad Mex, El Mexterminator, Information Superhighway Bandito, El Web-back

WEAPONS USED TO FIGHT BACK in order of importance: Language (spoken & written), live performance, radio, the Internet, theatricalized madness, humor, silence, a "Mexican survival kit" (contents: fake press cards, assorted chiles, hang-over relief medicine, make-up, shamanic artifacts of sorts, a mariachi hat to look "friendly," etc.), and as a last recourse, my fists

ALIASES, NICKNAMES & TERMS OF ENDEARMENT
In chronological order, with identity of perpetrator

Guillito and **mijo**	my mother
Guille	my aunts
Memo	my sister-in-law
Manga	my childhood football/soccer friends
El Pirata	my Mexico City neighbors
GP and **loco**	close friends
ese and **homes**	street Chicanos
Go-Mex and **Mexty**	close friends
amorcito and **mi pechocho**	my wife

DEROGATORY NAMES
In chronological order, with identity of perpretrator

naco	upper-class Mexican
hippioso	conservative Mexican
chilango	anti-centrist Tijuanense
wetback	border patrolman
greaser and **meskin**	rural Americans
beaner	art producer
taco boy	transvestite
"Cheech & Chong"	drunk US businessman and Russian taxi driver
pseudo-Chicano or **fake Chicano**	Chicano nationalist
fake Indian	ex-girfriend
sexist	Chicana essentialist

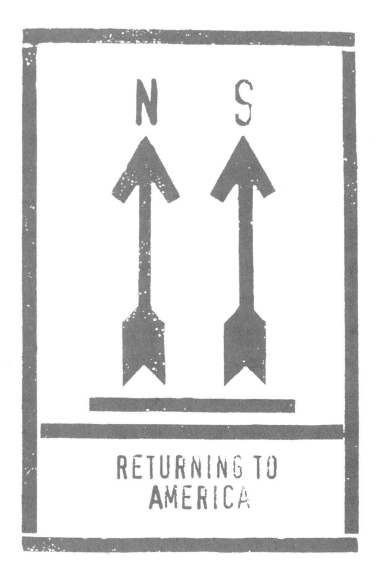

PERFORMANCE DOCUMENTS

PART 1

"Performance is the most flexible language I have found. I utilize it to analyze our social crises and cultural misplacement; to articulate my desires and frustrations in the overlapping realms of politics, sexuality, art and spirituality. Performance is a vast conceptual territory where my eclectic and ever-changing ideas, and the ideas of my collaborators, can be integrated into a coherent system and be put into practice. It's radical theory turned into praxis though movement, ritual, gesture, sound, light and spoken text."

FROM GÓMEZ-PEÑA'S PERFORMANCE DIARIES, 1990

7 El Veteran Survivor.

Supernintendo Ranchero
excerpt from *BORDERscape 2000*

(Opera singer sings Mozart intertwined with a soundbed of Japanese techno music. Roberto Sifuentes stands on top of a metallic pyramid. He wears a laboratory coat and teched-out glasses, and speaks in a computer-processed, mechanical voice. Guillermo Gómez-Peña enters dressed as El Mad Mexterminator, riding a motorized wheelchair. He moves across the stage in a mechanical, video-game-like pattern, responding to gestural commands from Sifuentes.)

RS   San Francisco, March of 99. Dear Chicano colleagues, welcome to *BORDERscape 2000*, part three of a performance trilogy. Allow me to introduce to you the very first prototype: a beta version of an imperfect Mexican. This cyborg still has a sentimental mind and a political consciousness. He failed the test for robotic migrant workers, and still longs for his homeland. Eventually when we manage to get the Mexican bugs out of him, we will create a Chicano, the vato uberalis, the next step on the evolutionary scale. Speak Mexi-cyborg!! Repent yourself!! Use voice #53 and please stick to the script.

GGP   *(processed voice #1)*: No, I won't cru-ci-fy myself to protest la migra no more.

RS   You can't repeat a performance or it would become theater.

GGP No, I swear,
I won't box with a hanging chicken for art's sake . . .
nor will I exhibit myself inside a gilded cage
as an endangered species or an androgynous wrestler/shaman.

RS Why Mad Mex Frankenstein?

GGP I'm just gonna be a poet for a while.

RS Then be a poet. Stick to the spoken word material. Go!! Go North!!

GGP So I continue my trek north
like a compulsive explorer
El Marco Pollo de Tijuana,
El Vasco de Gama de Aztlán
ever looking for a new island, a new performance stage
to spill my beans, my bleeding tripas,
expose my crevasses, my wounded penis
in the name of ex-pe-ri-men-ta-tion.

RS Now you wish to be a performance artist again?

GGP Not exactly.

(GGP intersperses "no's" through following text)

RS So Vato, give us some blood,
show us your piercings, your prosthetics,
eat your green card or burn your bra
but get fuckin' real!

GGP no, no, ni madres.

RS Why?

GGP Cause I'm giving up, right now, in front of you.

RS Oh god, you fuckin' martyr!

GGP I willingly turn myself in to my inner border patrol
three agents are present tonight
come on, get me!!

this is your golden chance culeros
I su-rren-der to my own darkest fears.

RS   You're not responding to my performance commands. You were much better when you were just trying to be a poet. Go back to poetry. Synthesize an entire cosmology into one burning sentence. Go!

GGP   Fear is the foundation of your identity *(he points at someone in audience)*.

RS   What a fuckin' assumption.

GGP   To be Mexican is a felony not a misdemeanor . . .

RS   Hey better, chido, punchy.

GGP   versus ser pocho es still una afrenta binacional.

RS   You are using Spanish unnecessarily. Shift accent.

GGP   *(Texan accent)* I'm fully aware that your ears are tired of listening to so many foreign languages
(He speaks in "gringo tongues," interspersed with recognizable English words)

RS   Stop! Next dialect!

GGP   Hey, that's how English sounded to me when I was a kid.

RS   So upgrade yourself!

GGP   Such linguistic vertigo you have to endure daily
I mean, you can't even communicate with your maid
or your gardener,
and then you come to California
(gringoñol)
& carrramba mamazita!
the artist speaks Spanglish and gringoñol
(mispronounced Spanish)
io hablou el idiouma del criminal, il drogadictou y la piuta
e' cuandouu io hablou tu muérres un poquitou mas.

RS   English only, pinche wetback!

GGP I mean, 23 states in America have embraced English only
California just abolished bilingual education
and I dare to talk to you in Spanglish? Que poca ma . . .

RS Good boy . . . you are assimilating.
What is your prime directive? Explain yourself.

GGP To you or to the audience?

RS To the audience.

GGP Dear citizens of nothingness:
this is a desperate attempt by a dying performance artist
to recapture the power of the spoken word
in the year of virtual despair and victorious whiteness.

RS Stop! Now, do something more kinetic, more defiant.
Don't you have a fuckin choreographer?

GGP Sara!!!

RS Music!!

GGP Sara!!!

RS We need some hip music
cd #3; track 2, take 1: Japanese tea house lounge. Go.

(Lights transition to lounge look.)

RS Yeah! Now, stand up & dance. (Repeats three times.)

GGP stops wheelchair and attempts to stand up but fails. He eventually succeeds in standing. GGP dances cheesy disco & twist, then falls down on his knees.

RS Stop the music. This is terryfying
Who do you think you are? an MTV Latino?

(GGP crawls back onto the chair while speaking. Lights return to normal and sound goes back to techno music.)

GGP El Mariachi with a biiiiiig moooouth.

RS Not anymore carnal.

GGP Mexi-cyborg el extra-extra-terrestre.

RS Not quite yet. You wish.

GGP El immigrant bizarro con su mente explosiva y expansiva
al servicio de la fragmentación político-poética.

RS State your function or lose your greencard.

GGP To you or to the audience?

RS To the audience.

GGP My normal state of being, carnal,
is to die for you, cause after all these years
I'm still imprisoned inside this historical purgatory.

RS Still obsessed with history in the year 2000?

GGP *Yes.*

RS That's cute.

GGP Do you remember the terms of the Guadalupe-Hidalgo treaty?
do you fuckin' remem . . .

RS Can anyone answer this pathetic poet?

GGP Est-ce que vous êtes illégal?
L'illégalité est à la mode, n'est-ce pas?

RS OK, you win this time. Let's talk about illegality...Go!

*(GGP moves to extreme downstage and looks into audience. House lights come
up. After each question, RS intersperses improvised replies.)*

GGP Are there any illegal immigrants in the audience?
People who once were illegal?
What about people who have had sex with an illegal alien?
Can you describe in detail their genitalia?
Are there people here who have hired illegal immigrants
for domestic, or artistic purposes?
Yessss! To do what exactly?

How much did you pay them?
How did you feel about that?
Thanks for your sincerity . . .
Now, have any of you ever fantasized about being from
another race or culture?
Which one?
Black, Indian?
Native American? Mexican?

RS   Boring. Cambio de canal: give me burning sentence #2.

(House lights down)

GGP   Ser emigrante en América ya es un acto ilegal.

RS   Translation please?

GGP   Just to be different is potentially an illegal act
one strike & you're out!
punishable with deportation without trail,
and retroactive to 10 years.

RS   That's too . . . technical

GGP   I mean, to be excluded from a national project
at a time when all nation states are collapsing
is not an extraordinary act of heroism
or literary fiction, ask the Welsh or the Irish, man . . .

RS   That's too fuckin' heavy to deal with right now.
This is the year 2000;
it's all about style without content.

GGP   You mean radical actions without repercussions?

RS   Right!

GGP   Tropical tourism without Montezuma's revenge?

RS   Global nada . . . rien

GGP Nothing-ness, really?
Just style, anonymous sex, weird trivia?
So, if that's what defines your values and your identity,
let's fuckin' engage in trivia.

RS Good! But bring down at least 10 decibels the level of your drama.
Remember: pc est passé, and so is rage, Supermojado.
Now, give me some burning trivia. Go:

GGP Madonna defeated Argentina & got to play Evita
Gooooo Madonna!!

RS Dated material. Next!

GGP Selena died precisely during the crossover.
(Looking up.) Selena, we luv you diva, auuu!!

RS What's so fucking special about Selena?

GGP Her whiny voice, her liposuctioned nalgas.
Besides, she is all we have, since we've got no real leaders
o que? Do you think we have any true Chicano leaders?

RS Kind of.

GGP Can you mention one?

RS Eddie Olmos *(GGP reacts)*, El Haniachi Two *(GGP reacts)*, the Taco Bell
Chihuahua.

GGP Fax you, man! Marcos! He is not a Chicano but he is certainly a leader . . .

RS He's just a fading myth. Back to our search for burning trivia. Go!

GGP Zappa is resting in the Olympus of Americana
(me persigno)
per ipsum, ecu nip zzzum Zzzzappa!

RS And so is Sinatra.

GGP Sinatra?

(Sings) "When I was 35, it was a very good year"
ese mi Frank
your absence hurts much more than that of Octavio Paz.

RS Hey that's a great trivial line.
Do you have some of this shit on disc?

GGP No. I no longer have a laptop. I am a Neo-Luddite.

RS A luddite with a mechanical wheelchair?

GGP Yes.

RS You fuckin' ro-man-tico! Shift 348X-13 Trivialize race. Go!

GGP OJ was a cyborg constructed by your own fears & desires.

RS But was he guilty?

GGP Yes, he was guilty & not that interesting a character

RS But we cared about him, cause he was (GP intersperses "¿Que?") . . . cause
he is a...a...a...black cyborg.

(Pause)

GGP I didn't say it. You did!!

RS These are the issues that truly matter

GGP Sure . . . in a time & place
where nothing significant truly matters.

RS What you consider trivia is my raison d'être.
Give me a headline that truly captures our times.

GGP Clintoris & Linguinsky: the great millennial soap opera.

RS Elaborate...elaborate...elaborate.

GGP Monica finally described in detail the genitals of your President.

RS Don't elaborate.

GGP She said, she said:
"it's pink, about three inches long, and it never gets hard
but there is something endearing about it."

RS You are diverging from our subject matter. We are begining to sound like
bad experimental poetry. Neruda meets Jello Biafra.
What are we really here for?

GGP Tonight?

RS Tonight

GGP Tonight?

RS Tonight

GGP *(to the audience)* There is too much turmoil in your private life for me to
bother you with the truly heavy issues like racism, homelessness or police
brutality.

RS Right! That was the 80s, ese.
We've heard that pop song so many times
but tonight, your audience is understandably tired.
They suffer from . . . repeat with me:
com-pa-ssion fa-tigue, yeah.

GGP com-pa-ssion fa-tigue, yeah.

RS Just to hear you say it makes me want to slash you in the face.

GGP Thank you.

*Lights up on Sara Shelton-Mann SL. dressed as Mariachi Zapatista. She breaks
into fast-paced, Chaplinesque movements with a gun, dancing to Mexican punk.
Strobe light. Music stops abruptly and video cuts out at end of her dance. Juan
Ybarra as Green Alien enters. Beginning of Nintendo Ethnic Wars.*

"Performance, like religion, is about faith . . . and deception."

SAN POCHO AZTLANECA TO A JOURNALIST

"North American and European visions of Latin America are fascinating. It is entertaining to observe the shadows Western thought casts on the walls of the Mexican equivalent of Plato's cave. There are two recurrent visions: Americans and Europeans think they can see their own alter ego in the Latin American mirror in the form of a savage but paradisiacal alternative. What they also see, however, is radical, Oriental otherness."

ROGER BARTRA, "MEXICAN REFLECTIONS ON DISTORTED IMAGES," TELOS, 1995

"I believe in the power of decorating and aestheticizing the body in order to exaggerate, challenge and problematize mythical notions of the Mexican Other. In the American imagination, Mexicans are allowed to occupy two different but strangely complementary spaces: we are either unnecessarily violent, hypersexual, cannibalistic and highly infectious; or innocent, "natural," ritualistic and shamanic. Both stereotypes are equally colonializing."

FROM GÓMEZ-PEÑA'S PERFORMANCE DIARIES, 1997

Mexican Beasts and Living Santos

I

In early 1994, Roberto Sifuentes and I premiered in Arizona our most ambitious collaborative art project to date, a performance/installation titled the *Temple of Confessions*[1]. We combined the format of the pseudo-ethnographic "diorama" (as in my previous "living diorama" projects with Coco Fusco and James Luna[2]) with that of the dramatic religious "dioramas" displayed in Mexican colonial churches, exhibiting ourselves inside Plexiglas boxes as both cultural "specimens" and "holy" creatures. The piece was based on a religious metafiction; we became the last two living *santos* [saints] from an unknown border religion, in search of sanctuary across America. People were invited to experience this bizarre "pagan temple" and confess to the saints their intercultural fears and desires. Roberto and I were completely unaware of the Pandora's box we were about to open. Partly due to the profound spiritual and cultural crisis afflicting US society, and partly perhaps due to America's obsession with public and private confession, people stormed into the Scottsdale Center for the Arts (Arizona) on opening day and expressed to our end-of-century santos their innermost feelings, fantasies and memories of Mexico, Mexicans, Chicanos, and other people of color. That first performance adventure proved to be quite intense. The gallery experienced record attendance, an angry patron decided to withdraw her support from

---

1   The *Temple* toured the US for two and a half years. During its last stop at the Corcoran Gallery of Art in Washington DC, we added a techno version of the *Temple*, incorporating confessions sent via the Internet (http://www.mexterminator.com). Once the project was over, sharing the actual confessions with our readers was perhaps the best

the institution after witnessing "Mexicans, chickens and other vulgarities," and the staff was forced to engage in a healthy debate about the institution's priorities, its mission, and the very role of contemporary art.

II

For over two years, the *Temple* was presented in extremely diverse contexts – "high art" museums, experimental art galleries, populist city festivals, university campuses and even a seventeenth-century convent in Mexico City. In every site, the project was slightly transformed to incorporate some local issues and iconographies. However, most visual and performative elements remained. There were three main "ceremonial" spaces: the Chapel of Desires, the Chapel of Fears, and a sort of mortuary chamber in the middle.

In the main altar of the Chapel of Desires, Roberto posed as "El Pre-Columbian Vato," a "holy gang member" engaged in slow-motion, ritualized actions. His arms and face were painted with intricate pre-Columbian tattoos, and his tank-top was covered with blood and perforated with holes from gunshots. He shared the restricted space inside the Plexiglas box with fifty cockroaches, a live, four-foot-long iguana, and a small table holding useless technological gadgets – a spray can, a whip, and what appeared to be real weapons and drug paraphernalia, items often associated with Chicano youth culture. Behind him stood an "authentic"-looking façade of a "pre-Columbian temple" made out of Styrofoam. As visitors got closer to the tableau, the artificiality (and "inauthenticity") of the image became more apparent, and the original visual shock slowly turned into fascination and curiosity. "El Pre-Columbian Vato" incarnated the fears and desires that Americans feel toward youth of color living dangerously, who are perceived simultaneously as scary and sexy. Their ephemeral but intensely

---

way we could contribute to the understanding of the dangerous territory of intercultural and interracial relations in contemporary America. This led us to the creation of various documentary projects: a radio documentary (New American Radio Series, NPR), a book, *The Temple of Confessions: Mexican Beasts and Living Saints* (powerHouse, New York, 1997), and a film documentary produced by PBS as part of their series *Works in Progress*. Analysis of the Internet confessions will be part of an upcoming book which I am co-authoring with performance scholar Lisa Wolford.

2 These projects are chronicled in my book *The New World Border*, City Lights, 1996.

8 Performing the *Temple* at a seventeenth-century desacralized convent. X-Teresa Arte Alternativo, Mexico City, 1995.

lived lives become irresistible to a society which has so effectively protected itself from impassioned physical and emotional experiences. Right in front of Roberto, there was a church kneeler with a microphone for the audience to confess. He never answered back, and rarely did he acknowledge the presence of the confessor (unless she or he was verbally abusive to him).

Opposite Roberto's altar was the altar of the Chapel of Fears, where I sat on a toilet (or a wheelchair) costumed as "San Pocho Aztlaneca," a hyper-exoticized curio shop shaman for spiritual tourists. I literally wore my composite identity. Dozens of tourist souvenirs and tribal talismans from different parts of the Americas hung from my "Tex-Mex Aztec" outfit. I shared my Plexiglas box with live crickets, stuffed animals (a rooster and assorted reptiles), fake "tribal" musical instruments, and a small table filled with artifacts that suggested associations with witchcraft. In the Anglo imagination, Mexico is frequently associated with pagan rites and preindustrial wisdom. A ghetto blaster, which I often manipulated as a musical instrument, played melancholic music from various parts of the world, including Gregorian chants mixed with rap, circus music, Mexican waltzes and

Indian blues. An elegant, lavender neon light framed my altar, providing it with a sleek, modern look.

Just as in Roberto's case, from a certain distance, I looked "authentic" (I could have been an indigenous shaman in a diorama sponsored by *National Geographic*). But as viewers got closer to my box, they began to be aware of the artifice, and I started to look like a generic Benetton primitive – a designer shaman created by the wizardry of MTV. Despite this, the archetype of the Mexican as wise witch doctor remained intact. Visitors attempted to establish a personal "spiritual" connection with me. Their eyes looked desperately for mine. If I decided to engage in a personalized relation with them (mainly through eye contact, symbolic hand motions or subvocalizing), emotions began to pour from both sides: sadness, vulnerability, guilt, anger, tenderness. Some people cried, and in doing so, they made me cry. Some expressed their sexual desire for me, and I discreetly reciprocated. Others spewed their hatred, their contempt and their fear, and I willingly took it. At least a third of the visitors eventually decided to kneel and confess.

In the middle gallery, visitors encountered an enigmatic vignette: a six-foot-tall Cigar Shop Indian standing across from a female mannequin wrapped in fake leopard skin and tied with rope. The mannequin sat on an old church pew. Both characters seemed to be mourning the contents of a body bag stamped with the letters INS (Immigration and Naturalization Service), while a stuffed rooster hung over the "corpse." Velvet paintings hanging on the red and black walls of the gallery depicted other hybrid saints: El Transvestite Pachuco, Santa Frida de Detroit, La Yuppie Bullfighter, La Neo-primitiva, El Maori Lowrider, etc. A small table beneath each painting held votive candles and a symbolic object: a World Cup soccer ball, a miniature "Tex-Mex accordion," a plaster figurine of Bart Simpson wearing a poncho, etc. People were encouraged to light a candle or deposit "personal offerings" on the tables. We often got photos, expired credit cards, tampons, condoms, cigars, flowers, and coins.

Two "nuns" (actress Norma Medina and dancer Michelle Ceballos)[3] performed the dual roles of caretakers of the Temple and living icons. Norma was dressed as an expectant "chola/nun," with two tattooed tears running down her left cheek (one for each murder she committed, according to Pinto [Chicano

---

3   In Providence, dancer Michelle Ceballos was replaced by Iranian-American dancer Carmel Kooros. In the Mexico City performance, there were no nuns.

prison] culture). Michelle was costumed as a "dominatrix nun" with a lowrider goatee and a garter belt under her habit, which she ocassionally flashed to perplexed men. At times, the nuns were frozen effigies that displayed themselves conspicuously in the aestheticized environment. Their tableaux referenced imagery from classical painting, Catholic icons, porn and movie stereotypes. At other times, they walked through the gallery in silence, discreetly approaching audience members and encouraging them to "confess." They also chanted religious songs, and cleaned the Plexiglas boxes, the body bag, and the shoes of visitors with their veils. Unexpected encounters with extravagant or sociopathic visitors demanded improvised, performative reactions.

After spending an average of two hours meticulously exploring the *Temple*, visitors were finally ready to confess. They had three options. They could confess into the microphones placed on the kneelers in front of the Plexiglas boxes (in which case their voices were recorded and later altered in post-production to protect their anonymity). If they were shy, they could either write their confessions on a card and deposit them inside an urn, or call an 800 number when they left the gallery. At night, after the performance, Roberto and I went to a sound studio and listened to all the confessions made that day. The most revealing ones were then incorporated into the installation soundtrack for future performances. By the end of the third day, Roberto and I left the boxes and were replaced by human-size effigies – a sado-masochistic lowrider with holographic "skull" glasses and a "sleepy Mexican" with a gas mask tenderly holding a taxidermied rooster. The live performance ended, and the *Temple* remained as an installation for several weeks. Written and phone confessions continued to be accepted.

The project functioned simultaneously as an elaborate set design for a theater of mythos and "cultural pathologies," and as a melancholic ceremonial space for people to reflect on their own racist attitudes toward other cultures. The meaning of the space shifted in relation to the cultural baggage and racial or ethnic background of the visitor, and on his or her particular relationship to the symbols and performance characters. To some it looked like "a Catholic temple from a cyber-punk novel," where they were made to assume the unpleasant role of "spiritual tourists." To others it seemed more like "an interactive anthropology museum of the future," where they were placed in the position of cultural voyeurs. People also defined the *Temple* in written confessions as "a stylized Indian trading post," "an ethnographic porn shop," "a haunted house on acid," and "a post-modern dime museum of Apocalypse culture." This ambiguity was crucial to the piece, since it allowed for the coexistence of multiple interpretations, reactions, and forms of interactivity.

III

I'm convinced that the kind of recorded and written confessions we received in the course of this project couldn't possibly have been obtained through field work, direct interviews, or talk radio. The extremely seductive yet threatening imagery, as well as the considerable amount of time that people stayed in the space, helped bring to the surface forbidden or forgotten zones of the psyche. Because of this, the confessions tended to be quite emotional, intimate and revealing. They belonged to the realm of myth, archetypes, dreams, pure sentimentalism, and raw passion. Although some people tended to exaggerate and behave in a disingenuously performative manner out of insecurity or their desire to challenge us, most were truly sincere. The range of confessions went from extreme violence and racism toward Mexicans and other people of color, to expressions of incommensurable tenderness and solidarity with us or with the cause we were perceived to represent. Some confessions were filled with guilt, some with archetypal American fears of cultural, political, or sexual invasion, or of violence, rape, and disease. Others were fantasies about escaping one's race or ethnicity and wanting to be Mexican or Indian. Conversely, Mexicans and Latinos suffused in self-hatred confessed their desire to be Anglo, Spanish or "blond." There were also many explicit descriptions of (real and fictitious, but equally revealing) intercultural sex encounters. Many of these explicit confessions of desire were directed toward us. People invited us to join them in acting out hardcore sexual fantasies, or expressed their desire to hurt or even to kill us. Since our job as artists was not to analyze or moralize, but merely to open a Pandora's box and release the colonial demons, we never expressed approval or disapproval to the confessor. Nor did we ever absolve them. After all, the *Temple of Confessions* was more about America's cultural projections and its inability to deal with cultural othernesss than about the Latino "other." In this sense, it was an exercise in reverse anthropology, rather than a forum for uncovering and indicting racist behaviors.

"The North stereotypes the South. In turn, the South internalizes these stereotypes and either reflects them back, commodifies them to appeal to the consumer desire of the North, or turns them into 'official culture'. Meanwhile, national identity gets lost in this display of reflections and refractions. It's like being inside a House of Mirrors."

GÓMEZ-PEÑA INTERVIEWED IN REFORMA, MEXICO CITY, AUGUST 25, 1996

A Selection of Audience "Confessions"

(The following selected "confessions" were obtained during the various performances of "Temple of Confessions". Some were made directly to the "performance saints", and others were either written on cards and deposited in urns or made via an 800 phone number.)

FEAR

"When I go on vacation to the Yucatan this winter, I don't want to get kidnapped or killed."

"I had a tough day in Juarez, my one day in Mexico. I was nearly mugged, got approached by many prostitutes. I hope I have not mixed this experience into my prejudices. I fear that I may have."

"Please don't shoot me. I'm afraid of getting shot...by Mexicans, simply for being white."

"Chicanos scare me. The men, they scream at me. When I see them, I think 'rape.' I feel this is wrong, but I can't help it."

"My smart, sensitive, attractive, vivacious 17 year old daughter is attracted to Latin boys . . . She now has herpes. These Latin boys need to learn some respect."

"When I see a Mexican or a Mexican-American man, I cringe because I assume he's going to make a sexual comment to me."

"I am scared shitless of women from other cultures talking to me."

"I fear that Mexican gang members will break in one night and rape my grandmother."

"I fear that there will be drive-by shootings in our quiet, white, middle-class neighborhood in Scottsdale, Arizona." Signed: A Spanish teacher.

"You people treat your women like slaves and your pets like shit."

"I am afraid that we will soon be outnumbered citizens."

"I hate Mexicans. All they are is babymakers."

"I fear Mexicans getting medical services and Americans having to wait."

"I hate you precisely because I understand you."

"Stop cleaning your gun with our flag, Wet Back!"

"Why the voodoo in your work? Many things in your culture scare people visually. Can't you be more positive, more sensitive towards us?"

DESIRE

"I want to be seen as a true advocate of your culture; as righteous and not as a 'white liberal' & to make love to a Latina with a firm body."

"I want to be rich and still have an identity."

"I am all for cultural diversity as long as it doesn't raise taxes."

"I don't have any fears about Mexico. I would like to travel there and eat at the Cafes and see Incan Ruins and shit."

"I confess to listening to the real lives of Mexicans as if they were movies because they are so foreign to me that they don't seem real."

"My desire right this moment is for the cholo's crotch. Is it stuffed or the real deal? look hot, hot, hot!!

"My desire is to taint my white blood with the blood of another race. I desire to become a woman of foreign origin to overcome the shame of my heritage and mingle with the world of secrets."

"I want to become a woman; a big, robust, black woman with a ghetto accent."

"I am insulted by the assumption that all white women want to get fucked by Latino men or women. Fuck you! You want to fuck me? Jerk off on some other white girl. My phone number is (410) . . ."

"I desire to fall in love with a Hispanic and be mistreated."

"I love to fuck hot Nogales whores!"

"I desire freedom from you people following me."

9 Audience member confesses his intercultural sins to San Pocho Aztlaneca, The Corcoran Gallery of Art, Washington, DC.

"El Mad Mex"

(Homo Fronterizus. Replicante #187)

As seen in the film "Natural Born Matones"

Habitat: the American Borderlands

Features: Illegal border crosser and cultural invader, defender of immigrants' rights, drug and jalapeño pusher, practices boxing, Tex Mex rock and narcoshamanism, seduces gueras and abducts innocent Anglo children. Sponsored by the Gulf Cartel and the Zapatista movement. Wanted by the DEA, the FBI, the INS and the Smithsonian Institution. Indestructible!

Prosthetic extensions: Jalapeño phallus & robotic bleeding heart

"CyberVato"

(Homo Chicanus. Replicante # 209)

Habitat: The US Inner Cities

Aliases: Cholo, pinto, chuco, homie, "at risk" youth, "information super-highway bandit" and "Calvin Klein vato"

Features: Techno-savvy, neo-nationalist, monolingual, drug addict, experiences permanent social resentment and self involvement, surviver of innumerable cultural drive-by shootings. Wanted by MTV and the Los Angeles Police Department. Considered Endangered Species

"La Cultural Transvestite"

(Femma Gringotlanis)

As seen in the film "La Novia del Mariachi"

Habitat: Mexican colonial towns, border cantinas, beach resorts and California ashrams.

Features: Self-destructive, escapist, master impersonator of cultural otherness, adopts a different "pet culture" every year, devours mestizos and Indian dandies, experiences permanent identity crisis, spiritual vertigo and cultural nymphomania.

"Today, I'm tired of ex/changing identities in the net.
In the past 8 hours,
I've been a man, a woman and a s/he.
I've been black, Asian, Mixteco, German
and a multi-hybrid replicant.
I've been 10 years old, 20, 42, 65.
I've spoken 7 broken languages.
As you can see, I need a break real bad,
just want to be myself for a few minutes.
ps: my body however remains intact, untouched, unsatisfied,
unattainable, untranslatable"

FROM "FRIENDLY CANNIBALS," 1997

Ethno-cyborgs and Genetically Engineered Mexicans

Recent Experiments in "Ethno-Techno" Art

I

In the mid 90s, when the artworld went high-tech overnight, the debates about the human body and its relation to new technologies dramatically polarized the experimental arts community and particularly the performance art milieu. There were those in the "machine art" movement who advocated the total disappearance of the body and its replacement with digital or robotic mechanisms; others believed that the body, although archaic and "obsolete," could still remain central to the art event if physically and perceptually enhanced with technical prostheses. The artists of "Apocalypse Culture" responded viscerally to these proposals by adopting a radical Luddite stance, attempting to reclaim the *body primitive* as a site for pleasure, penance and pain, and to "return" to a fantastical and imaginary neotribal paganism, very much in the tradition of US anarchist "drop out" culture. None of these options were viable, however, for Chicano/Latino performance artists and other politicized artists of color interested in new technologies. Roberto Sifuentes and I tried to explore other possibilities by infiltrating virtual space as "cyber-immigrants" (Web-backs) and smuggling subversive ideas as conceptual *coyotes*. Our original goals were to politicize the debates around digital technologies and to infect virtual space with Chicano humor and *linguas polutas* (such as Spanglish). We also wanted to employ new technologies to enhance mytho-poetical interactivity between performer and live audience, and as a tool for researching fundamental expressions of inter-cultural fear and desire.

In 1994, Roberto and I began to incorporate *in situ* digital technologies in our "diorama" work. The project premiered at Diverse Works Gallery in Houston, Texas, under the rambunctious title of "The Ethno-Cyberpunk Trading Post & Curio Shop On The Electronic Frontier." We invited our compadre Native American performance artist James Luna and some local artists to join us. Part of our goal in the project was to make visible to the audience the types of transformation that performance artists go through as they move from the realm of the personal to the public, and from ritual space to cyberspace. Visitors entering the gallery found a visible "dressing room" area, where we applied make-up and changed costumes. They passed through a "high art area" where our props and personal objects (along with various folk artifacts and pre-Columbian figurines) were carefully displayed as aestheticized museum pieces, contextualized by fictional labels. They finally came to a "human exhibition area" where we displayed ourselves as "exotic specimens" and "performance artists at work." The exhibition area also featured stuffed animals (a puma, a horse, etc.) and curiosity cabinets containing ironic post-modern or pseudo-primitive "archeological artifacts" that commented on the hybrid nature of contemporary culture and our dying "Western civilization." Computer screens, video monitors, neon signs and digital bars flashing taxonomic descriptions of the "ethnographic specimens" (ourselves), added a sci-fi flavor to our techno-tribal environment.

Part of our project included the construction of a website that featured images of our performance characters, along with our first version of an "ethnographic questionnaire" asking Internet users to share their projections and preconceptions about Latinos and indigenous people. Though we were still not fully aware of the implications of what we were doing, we hoped partially to surrender our will and allow both gallery visitors and Internet users to collaborate with us in determining the nature and content of our performance.

Roberto was costumed as CyberVato, a "robo-gang member" consumed by techno-gadgetry, including a computer keyboard which he used to communicate with Internet users during live performances. Each day, James and I transformed ourselves into different performance personae, including "the Shame-man," "el Postmodern Zorro," "El Cultural Transvestite," and "El Natural Born Asesino." Roberto in his diorama environment conspired with a filmmaker who moved through the space, capturing the details of these transformations and transmitting them live onto the Internet via video teleconferencing. People who saw the webcast or visited our Internet site were invited to send us images, sound files, or texts that expressed how they felt Mexicans, Chicanos and Native Americans of the 90s should look, behave, and perform. Responses were displayed on gallery monitors manipulated by techno-disc-jockey Cyber-Vato, and influenced the ever-changing personae created by James and myself. We also accepted performance "commands" verbally from live audience members, as well as directives submitted by fax or by phone. As "replicants on call," James and I were a bit nervous about the unpredictable nature of the experiment and the outrageousness of some of the responses which arrived (especially from people sitting at the other end of a modem or fax machine, who were thus able to protect their anonymity and distance themselves from the possible implications of live interaction). We clumsily tried to incorporate as much as possible of the material we received. Much of our performance was (unavoidably) improvised, but audience members seemed to enjoy their perceived power over us. James, Roberto and I only performed live for one week, but the installation and artifacts remained in place, allowing local artists and gallery visitors to continue playing in our virtual house of mirrors and labyrinth of ethnic projections.

II

The success of this initial "ethno-techno" art experiment marked a radical change in the direction of our work. Roberto and I decided to mantain our "techno-confessional" website as an ongoing source of performance material. In the first year, we received over 20,000 "hits" (visitors to the site) according to the counter, and a large percentage of them answered our pseudo-anthropological questionnaire. The responses were of a uniquely confessional nature, decidedly more graphic and explicit than those gathered during live performances of the *Temple of Confessions* (the other major project we were working on at the time). Why the differences? Perhaps the distance and total anonymity offered by the Internet, along with the indirect invitation to discuss sensitive matters of race, sexuality, and identity in an artificially safe environment, provided people with

10 El Mad Mex is betrayed by his robotic hand.

the necessary courage to reveal their most secret fears of cultural invasion and their most explicit interracial desires and sexual fantasies in ways they would never be willing to do face to face. During the mid-90s, when we began these projects, the US was in a collective state of repression and denial regarding matters of race and gender. The virulent backlash against "political correctness" was at its peak, and so were the anti-immigration sentiments promoted by ultra-nativist politicians like Pat Buchanan, Jesse Helms and (thankfully now ex-)California governor Pete Wilson. The marginalization and silencing of progressive views, combined with the openly xenophobic trend in national policies and conservative rhetoric, may have been taken by many as a tacit endorsement of prejudice and Mexiphobia.

Roberto and I decided that the next logical step in our ongoing project of reverse anthropology would be to use the confessional material submitted by our live and virtual audiences to design visual and performative representations of the new mythical Mexican and Chicano of the '90s. The most recurrent and emblematic responses from live audiences and Internet users became the inspiration for a series of performance personae or "ethno-cyborgs" co-created (or rather "co-imagined") in dialogue with gallery visitors and anonymous net users. Since a majority of the responses we received portrayed Mexicans and Chicanos as threatening Others, indestructible invaders, and public enemies of America's fragile sense of coherent national identity, we titled our new performance project *Mexterminator*, referencing the superhuman, robotic assassins of the Schwarzenegger movies. Our intention in this new project was to allow Internet users and live audience members to help determine the physical and psychological profiles of our "ethno-cyborgs," thus influencing both the design and content of our living diorama performances. We relied on their input to decide how we should be costumed, what kinds of music we should listen to, what sorts of props and objects we should handle, and most importantly, what types of ritualized actions we should perform and how we should interact with audience members. Our goal was to incarnate the intercultural fantasies and nightmares of our audiences, refracting fetishized constructs of identity through the spectacle of our "primitive," eroticized bodies on display. The composite personae we created were stylized representations of a non-existent, phantasmatic Mexican/Chicano identity, projections of people's own psychological and cultural monsters – an army of Mexican Frankensteins ready to rebel against their Anglo creators.

The results of our experiment in anti-colonial anthropology turned out to be much stranger than anything we could have imagined on our own. The "sleepy Mexican" was banished from the colonial unconscious of contemporary America, deported back to Hollywood. The exotic border "señorita," who populated folk songs, movies and poems for decades, was nowhere to be found (except as incarnated in the more overtly eroticized figure of Salma Hayek). Neither were Frito Bandito, Speedy Gonzalez, Juan Valdez, the "greaser" bandit or the suffering Frida Kahlo. They had been replaced by a new pantheon of mighty robo-Mexicans. Armed with mysterious shamanic artifacts and sci-fi automatic weapons, their bodies enhanced with prosthetic implants and their brown skin decorated with Aztec tattoos, these hyper-sexual "ethno-cyborgs," clothed in high Tex-Mex/gangster-rap regalia, both defied and perversely incorporated every imaginable Hollywood and MTV stereotype, every fear and desire secretly harbored in the fragile psyches and hearts of contemporary Americans. "We" were perceived to be unnecessarily violent, yet fashionably seductive; techno-literate, yet primeval. Politically strident yet gifted with inexplicable shamanic powers and spiritual awareness, these mythical Mexicans were contradictory, unpredictable – and strangely familiar. After reading thousands of pages of Internet submissions, my colleagues and I concluded that a perverse dialectic of intercultural violence and interracial desire was central to America's perception/projection of cultural otherness.

My performance accomplices and I created complex personae that reflected these constructs, refracted through our own particular "robo-baroque" aesthetics. Sponsored by Mexican drug lords, the Zapatista comandancia, Chicano radicals, and MTV, "we" – the indestructible cyber-mojados – had already succeeded in occupying the US of Aztlan. Our new mandate was to seduce, abduct, possess and take control of our audience's psyche, language, country and institutions. We were the flesh and blood incarnation of America's millennial fantasies about immigrants from the South, Latinos from the inner cities, pagan sexuality, indigenous witchcraft, and the Spanish language. What the audience ended up experiencing during the performance was a stylized anthropomorphization of its own post-colonial demons and racist hallucinations, a kind of crosscultural poltergeist. While my collaborators and I were fully responsible for the aesthetic realization of the performance, the unusual creative process we employed to generate material, making (involuntary) collaborators of thousands of anonymous Internet users, meant that we were by no means the only ones accountable for the content of the piece. Like it or not, our audiences (both live and virtual) were unavoidably implicated in our panic worldview.

"Are you into tattoos, jalapeños, and ethno-porn? Are you into sexy Tex-Mex art that does not question your privilege? Do you wish to experience a political peepshow? Do you desire to smell or touch a live Mexican?"

CONCEPTUAL CLASSIFIED AD

III

El Mexterminator premiered in Mexico City in March 1995 under the working title of *The Museum of Frozen Identity*. Experimental dance choreographer turned performance artist Sara Shelton-Mann appeared with me in that piece, and eventually became a central member of the collaborative team. Different versions of the *Mexterminator* performance have been presented in Canada, Puerto Rico, Spain, Austria, Italy and the UK, as well as throughout the US. Although the composite personae we portray reference contemporary Anglo constructions of Mexican identity, the context for our performance has become strangely internationalized due to the global dissemination of US pop cultural images of Latinos, rather than because audiences in other countries initially perceive genuine connections to the situation of their own subaltern communities.

The scope and magnitude of the project shifts dramatically in relation to the characteristics of the sites where we perform, taking into account such factors as available budget and technological infrastructure, along with the physical possibilities and limitations of the venues where we perform. Roberto and I have toured a low-tech version of the project that requires only two performers (ourselves), a soundtrack and a film that can either be projected onto a screen or (worst case scenario) played on a standard video monitor; this relatively low-budget version has been popular with small college campuses and marginally funded alternative art spaces. More technically ambitious versions of the piece incorporate as many as eight collaborating performers, along with sophisticated visual projections and digital technologies. One of our most elaborate productions of *Mexterminator* took place in a giant warehouse in San Francisco and ended up looking like a kind of techno-rave, with six ethno-cyborgs on display and sound mixed live by audio-diva Rona Michele. When we are invited to present

Mexterminator in more traditional "high art" museum settings, we try to mimic the presentational style of the institution, incorporating "post-Columbian codexes", archeological artifacts from "the Second US–Mexico War," and velvet paintings of border superheroes, masterpieces in the genre of Tijuana tourist art. The modular and ever shifting nature of the project permits us to adapt to very different types of venues, and to appeal to a broad range of audiences.

Though many visual, conceptual and performative elements of the piece change from site to site, a few constants remain. When the audience arrives in the lobby or entrance of the performance space, they encounter a written or prerecorded text outlining the metafictional premise of the performance.

> **The nation-state has collapsed. The ex-US of A has fragmented into a myriad micro-republics loosely controlled by a multiracial junta, and governed by a Chicano prime minister named Gran Vato. The Tortilla Curtain no longer exists. Spanglish is now the official language. Panicked by the New Borders, Anglo militias are desperately trying to recapture the Old Order. Our border heroes, El Mexterminator, CyberVato, and La Cultural Transvestite have deserted from the newly formed government to join a strange hybrid militia opposing the reverse authoritarianism and radical essentialism of the ruling party. The new government of Aztlan Liberado sponsors interactive ethnographic exhibits to teach the perplexed citizenry how things were before and during the 2nd US/Mexico war. This performance/installation is one example of these official projects.**

As audience members enter this fictional "Museum of Experimental Ethnography," they are met by performance docents in laboratory coats who "guide" them through the menu of possible interactions with the performers. The performance space is filled with fog and dramatically lit to suggest a Blade Runner-in-Tijuana type of world, inhabited by hyper-racialized replicants and ethno-cyborgs. Dead feathered chickens hang from the tall ceiling at different heights. A (fictional) black and white documentary of "the Second US/Mexico war" is projected onto a large screen. A loud, high-energy soundtrack includes

11 CyberVato Prototype #227

documenting the visual and performative evolution of the replicants, both during live performances and in staged photos shot at his studio. Many of his evocative, stunning images have been used as conceptual postcards, posters, and illustrations for magazines and books. Selected photos will also be incorporated into a new website currently under construction, allowing Internet users to see some of the hybrid creatures and cultural chimeras created on the basis of their original suggestions.

In early 1998, after we had been immersed for some time in this multifaceted process of creative investigation, my collaborators and I felt that it was time for the ethno-cyborgs to be given voice. In dialogue with Roberto and Sara, I wrote a proscenium piece titled *BORDERscape 2000*, which incorporates the personae of the ethno-cyborgs, providing them with texts delivered in a range of computer-processed voices. The soundscape for the piece, a montage created by Rona Michele, combines prerecorded rap and rock en español with live arias by opera singers. Roberto shifts from his robo-gang member persona to a Rastafarian preacher announcing the arrival of a "new, post-democratic era," and a martyred, transgender Christ, while I alternately embody a kind of cybernetic Stephen Hawking, a hermaphrodite shaman (aka Gran Vato, President of the US of Aztlan), and an S&M Zorro. In addition to the various manifestations of her "Clepto-Mexican Gringa" cyborg, Sara also appears in *BORDERscape* as a schizophrenic Southern Belle transvestite/essentialist Chicana academician, satirically commenting on sensitive issues of race and gender. Dancer and performance artist Juan Ybarra, as the Butoh Alien, also performs a central role in the piece.

The ethno-cyborgs have also invaded the realms of video and radio. They have made cameo appearances in our recent films, *Borderstasis*[2] and *The Great Mojado Invasion*.[3] Some of my commentaries for the National Public Radio programs *All Things Considered* and *Latino USA* have been delivered in the computer-processed voice of "El Mexterminator." These strategies of recycling and recontextualizing ideas, images and texts continue to be a central aspect of our performance methodology, consistent with the techno-rascuache nature of our aesthetic.

For the past two years, theater historian and performance theorist Lisa Wolford has quietly conspired in our project of reverse anthropology, observing and documenting the outrageous behaviour of our audiences in different cities and institutional contexts. She has gathered voluminous fieldnotes including conversations with audience members who initiated unusual or paradigmatic interactions with us, or who seemed to be strongly affected (positively or negatively) by what they witnessed in our performance. She has helped us sort out, categorize, and make sense of the ongoing responses to our conceptual websites and ethnographic questionnaires. Drawing on Lisa's research and analysis, and always in dialogue with her, Roberto and I continue to add layers of complexity to our palimpsestic replicants, designing new "ethno-cyborgs" and creating new scenarios and scripts. Lisa's participation in this project as researcher, informant, and dramaturg has become so intricately woven into our creative process that the borders between scholar and artist, creator and observer, have been completely re-defined. In the past few months, we have begun to experiment with co-writing. The fruits of this unique collaboration and multi-leveled dialogue will become the basis for an upcoming book tentatively titled *Mexterminator: Ethno-Techno Art*, which we hope to publish with Routledge in the year 2002. The content, structure and style of the book, as well as the still-emerging process of its creation, will hopefully model a new and more engaged form of dialogue and collaboration between artist and theoretician, as well as a new, multi-centric way of writing about performance.

2   *Borderstasis* is a "video diary" commissioned by German TV Arte. The idea was to select fifteen artists working in politically sensitive "border zones" throughout the world. My "diary" combines staged interviews, skits developed for the camera, excerpts of Mexican B-movies, documentation of past performances, and old family films. The structure of the film is very much like the structure of my live performance work. The video aired in seven European countries in 1998.

3   *The Great Mojado Invasion* was made in collaboration with Mexican filmmaker Gustavo Vazquez. This "Chicano sci-fi mocumentary" uses found footage from multiple sources (racist ethnographic films, border B-movies, marginal sci-fi movies from the 50's, and "historical" archival footage) intertwined with staged performance narrative by one of my personae. The film is contextualized within the meta-fiction of the "Second US/ Mexico War," and purports to recount the history of Mexico from pre-Columbian times to the year 2001. Different versions of *The Great Mojado Invasion* have been projected (without sound) as part of the Mexterminator performance, as well as in productions of *BORDERscape 2000*.

*"If our personae survive the involuntary audience of the street, they
will probably survive the meanness of the art world."*

GÓMEZ-PEÑA TO A JOURNALIST FROM THE DETROIT FREE PRESS

DURING A "STREET INTERVENTION."

When Our Performance Personas
Walk out of the Museum

Three Public Interventions

Introduction

My colleague and I see the ever changing performance art world as a moving
laboratory in which to develop and test radical ideas, images and actions, a
conceptual territory that grants us special freedoms (aesthetic, political and
sexual) often denied to us in other realms such as academia, political activism,
grassroots organizations and certainly the media. One of the ultimate goals of
our work, however, is to step outside the art world and venture into unfamiliar
territory, specifically into socially and politically sensitive locations. Our ideas
and performance personas acquire particular weight, dimension and density
when presented in populist contexts such as public squares or streets, monuments
and historically charged buildings. Our work continually shifts back and forth
among these different contexts, returning to the sanctuary of the artworld in
search of complicity and the space, tools, and infrastructure that allow us to
develop new work, then turning again toward populist venues where our ideas
and the accessibility of our work are tested in a very different way. In this
sense, we are privileged border crossers, temporary insiders (or rather "insiders/
outsiders") in many worlds. Within the art world, our work gets developed
and presented in optimum technical conditions, but often for audiences primarily
interested in style, form, and highly specialized theoretical matters. Our involuntary audiences in populist realms tend to be less theoretically sophisticated,

but more demanding in terms of clarity and
spectacle – and quite often, more sincere
and compassionate. Our best work results
precisely out of the friction created by
these overlapping worlds.

The following text chronicles three
public interventions that took place in
various sites and contexts. "The Cruci-
Fiction Project" was staged with an
invited audience, but designed largely
with the intention of generating media
coverage. "Ode to a Dying Barrio"
was created first and foremost for an
"involuntary audience" on the streets
of the Mission, but documented by a
PBS television crew. The objective of "Ellis
Island y que?" was to generate photographic images that would later be distributed in multiple formats and venues. In all three cases, the distribution of
the documented images, whether through photos or video, consolidated the
symbolic meaning of the work. Though these types of performance interventions
are central to our performance praxis, they often go unnoticed to critics and art
historians, who concentrate almost exclusively on work that takes place within
the strict confines of the art world.

13 Kneeling in front of a Van Gogh painting
before leaving the museum and hitting the streets.
DIA, Detroit, 1995.

PUBLIC INTERVENTION #187: "THE CRUCI-FICTION" [1]

On the evening of April 10, 1994, one week after Easter Sunday, an unusual
"end-of-the-century performance ritual"[2] took place at Rodeo Beach in the
Marin Headlands Park across from San Francisco's Golden Gate Bridge. My
accomplice (or rather "co-penant") Roberto Sifuentes and I crucified ourselves
for three hours on two sixteen-foot by twelve-foot wooden crosses dressed as the

---

1   An earlier chronicle of "The Cruci-Fiction Project" appeared in the book *Temple of
Confessions*, PowerHouse, 1997.
2   All the words and sentences in quotation marks are direct quotes from the flyer
handed to the audience during the "Cruci-Fiction Project".

running down our faces, our arms and legs sore from the pressure of the metallic prostheses. Overwhelmed by the experience, we contemplated the myriad implications of our actions.

That night, I engaged in a very intense and personal conversation about America's current paranoia about immigration with a gorgeous Colombian immigrant named Carolina Ponce de León, a curator of Latin American art living in New York at the time. We compared notes on "our permanent condition of deterritorialization." We found out that we were born on the same year, within six days of each other, that we are both single parents of blond Latino kids, and that we both work in the jagged terrain of transnational cultural exchange and hybrid identities. We talked about the fact that both our countries (Mexico and Colombia) are undergoing an accelerated process of political and cultural fragmentation. Two orphans of two nation-states drinking tequila in a Manhattan lounge bar. I was completely unaware that months later, she would become my lifetime compañera.

Performance Memory
Tijuana, 1994

I sit naked on a wheelchair
wearing a NAFTA wrestling mask
my chest is covered with pintas
shit like:

> *"los chucos también aman"*
> *"me dicen el jalapeño pusher"*
> *"Aztlán es pure genitalia"*
> *"the bells are ringing in Baghdad"*
> *"greetings from Ocosingo"*
> *"too blessed to be stressed"*
> *"don't worry, be Hopi"*
> *"burritos unidos hasta la muerte"*
> *"no one can like a Mexican"*
> *"la ganga no morirá"*
> *"New Orleans ain't my barrio"*
> *"Selena, forever reina"*
> *"to die is to perform the last strip-tease"*
> *"mwan vit u creve"*

enigmatic pintas, may I say
say, say, say...
(I try to speak but I can't)
I can barely speak tonite
(I whisper into the mic)

dear audience
ease my pain
lick my chest, my sweat, my blood
500 years of bleeding . . .
from head to toes
& all the way down to the root
I bleed
from Alaska to Patagonia
y me pesa un chingo decirlo
pero sangro
de inflación, dolor y dólar
(merolico)
de inflamación existencial
y mexicanidad insatisfecha
sangro
de tanto vivir en los United
de tanto luchar contra la migra
de tanto y tanto crossing borders
sangro, luego existo
parto, luego soy
soy
soy porque somos
we are un fucking chingo
the transient generation acá
from Los Angeles to the Bronx & far beyond
(including Canada for protocol reasons)
we, the mega "WE,"
we cry

(20 second pause. Mexican waltz begins. Cameras one and two rolling. Five naked Zapatistas mop the floor in slow motion. Eight wax figurines stand motionless on the binational chessboard. Continúo.)

15 *Facing page:* **Minutes before the audience enters, Gómez-Peña finishes his "tribal make-up".**
X-Teresa, Mexico City, 1995.

therefore the moon . . .
demanding restoration
tonight . . .
the moon . . .
is . . .
cracking . . .
up . . .
and you,
whoever you may be
are looking for an angry lover

FROM "THE LAST MY-GRATION" 1995

My Third Tattoo
Radio essay, 1998

I've always taken tattoos seriously. As a performance artist, my body is my laboratory of experimentation, my canvas and diary. In this most personal book, scars are like imposed inscriptions, whereas tattoos are the words and phrases consciously chosen by me. Whatever happens to my body inevitably affects my art and sense of self; my social and sensual relationship to the world, and vice versa.

Like most visible scars, each of my tattoos reveals a dramatic shift in my accidental and nomadic biography. Verbigratia: the bold pre-Columbian snake etched on my left shoulder by Mexican artist Doctor Lacra celebrated my arrival in early 1995 to San Francisco, my most recent hometown. In mid-1996, tattoo master Don Hardy and I collaborated on the design of a huge tattoo on my right arm and shoulder: a detailed map of Mexamerica made up of intricate computer circuits. Migrant Aztec god Quetzalcóatl, the giver of culture and agriculture, is seen departing from the Yucatan peninsula on a lowrider motor boat, while to the north, Zorro bursts out of the US on his rearing black stallion. This one-of-a-kind tattoo functions as a biographical/historical map of my journey as a Mexican immigrant, one that goes from south to north and from pre-Columbian America to high-tech Chicanismo. (Believe me, dear reader, El Zorro's appearance on my skin was definitely not inspired by Antonio Banderas.) Being the largest and most visible of my tattoos, it is the one that most affects my social interactions. With the exception of places like New York or San Francisco, where tattoos have become commonplace, no matter where I am, bikers, lowriders, rockers, ex-prisoners, and apocalypse hipsters are always ready to bond with me; whereas cops and conservative people observe me with suspicion. Why? A tattooed brown body has very specific connotations for US law enforment agents. It is a bold act of social defiance, and signifier of a criminal past.

In July 1998 I got my third and most painful tattoo, this time right over my heart: an intricate skull with a rattlesnake wrapped around it. A crown of electric thorns frames the head. Its forehead bears a romantic sign written in barrio calligraphy, "Sin Fin," which in Spanish means "without end." Unlike my prior tattoos, this one was done in the purest Chicano prisoner style, with delicate renderings and soft fading grays. The artist is Rubén Franco, a 23-year-old sureño ex-gang member from East Los Angeles who resides in the Watsonville area. His main clientele are migrants who work the strawberry fields of Northern California. They go to him to get tattooed on their backs and chests as a permanent reminder of their dangerous US adventure, right before returning to their homeland. The favorite designs of the migrant workers are Virgins of Guadalupe, bucolic landscapes populated by gorgeous cholas and muscular vatos locos . . . and skulls, just like mine.

The reasons behind my third tattoo are many. Since I turned 43, I am becoming hyper-conscious of my own mortality. Two of my uncles died recently. I separated from a three and a half year long relationship. And if this weren't enough, someone stole my laptop with the manuscript of my new book (this one), and a grumpy border patrolman decided to invalidate my green card when I was coming back from Mexico. As you can imagine, these incidents clearly marked the end of a chapter in my life, and the beginning of a new era.

Rubén believes that the skull on my heart is just the beginning of what will eventually be a whole mural inscripted on my chest symbolizing my new life, or rather the birth of a new self, my fourth one. It's like Chicano Buddhism. I know it will be painful, but to tell you the truth, every tattoo becomes yet another act of defiance to pain, as well as a ritual affirmation of life on the edges of a dying Western civilization.

"Americans cross the border South in search of identity and history. Mexicans cross the border North as if coming into the future. Since we suffer from an excess of identity, deep inside what we really want is to get rid of it . . . We cross the border to reinvent ourselves . . ."

FROM THE FILM "BORDERSTASIS," 1998

"In the 70s performance was about authenticity. The blood was real blood, so to speak. In the 90s, it's all about artifice. Chicanos and other so-called "artists of color" understand artifice 'cause the hardships of everyday life are so intense that they demand to either be forgotten, satirized or stylized."

FROM GÓMEZ-PEÑA'S PERFORMANCE DIARIES, 1997

The Art of Camouflage
Performing in extremely unusual contexts

The following text chronicles four collaborative performance projects which took place in unusual contexts: cable TV, a Natural History museum, malls and an opera house. Each of these contexts presented particular challenges to me and my collaborators, and demanded that we adopt different tactics and strategies. These otherwise highly diverse projects are unified primarily by a goal of destabilizing and subverting problematic notions of "racial" and cultural authenticity. I am well aware that my wonderful collaborators would probably construct very different accounts of these experiences, and I deeply respect their diverse experiences and interpretation of events, but the narratives I present here are as "true" as memory allows.

1 Information Super-highway "bandits" Performing for Cable TV

On Thanksgiving Day, 1994, the evening news of over 3.5 million American households was suddenly interrupted by two "cyber-Aztec TV pirates," transmitting their bizarre views on American culture and identity direct from their underground vato-bunker, somewhere between New York, Miami and Los

Angeles. In actuality, what the viewers were watching was an experiment in interactive television via satellite. Roberto Sifuentes and I had teamed with film-makers Adrienne Jenik, Philip Djwa and Branda Miller from Eye-Ear Studio at Rennselear Polytechnic, New York State, to broadcast a simulacrum of a pirate TV intervention to hundreds of cable television stations across the US. Our amazing publicist had managed to persuade over 400 program directors from all over the country to advertise the time slot under a fictional title. Initially, as far as the viewers were concerned, what they were witnessing was a "true" pirate TV intervention, though they slowly became aware of the artifice behind our performance strategies.

The style of the broadcast was influenced by MTV, with five hand-held cameras in constant motion. The content was a unique blend of radical politics, autobiographical material, "Spanish lessons for xenophobic Americans," and outrageous parodies of traditional TV. Roberto and I spoke in English, Spanglish, Franglais, and an invented "Nahuatl." During the broadcast, we demonstrated a "Chicano virtual reality machine" by means of which the viewer could (in the context of the fiction) request "instant visualization of personal and historical memories;" these were in fact pre-produced segments utilizing home movie footage and videos from past performances. The broadcast also featured a "Chicano virtual reality bandana," that would allow (Anglo) users to vicariously experience racism. We also received "live" reports from writer Ruben Martinez via PictureTel (video telephone) from the Electronic Cafe in Santa Monica. Footage of other types of broadcasting intercut with our performance video were meant to suggest to the viewer that the "legitimate" broadcasters were attempting to regain the airwaves, but we ultimately managed to maintain control.

For an hour and a half, the "TV pirates" invited perplexed viewers to call in and respond to the broadcast. We encouraged them to be intelligent, poetical, and performative in their responses. The performance was also transmitted over computer networks via "M-Bone," and those watching in cyberspace could interact with us (and each other) by posting images and written comments. We received dozens of phone calls and computer messages, and probably broke many FCC rules.

Roberto and I were scared shitless of the possible legal repercussions of our TV experiment. For weeks after the event, we waited in dread for the arrival of a mythical FCC inspector in a trenchcoat. But instead of the scary repercussions we expected, it turned out that the experiment was so successful and "hip" that many cable stations who originally refused to go along with our fictitious premise decided to air the broadcast a few months later. When this happened, we were flattered, but uneasy. What did it mean to re-broadcast a supposed pirate TV intervention that was a simulacrum in the first place? We became obsessed with this dilemma. Our unexpected success could mean two entirely different things: either we had managed to find "a crack in the system" and accidentally kicked ass, or the system was completely immune to radical content, and only concerned with the high production value and aesthetic hipness of the project. If this was the case, we asked ourselves, wasn't this the ultimate paradox of contemporary "radical" performance? Our perplexity continued to increase. After the national re-broadcast of *Naftazteca:Cyber-TV for the year 2000 AD*, a one-hour, edited version of the project won first prize in the category of "best experimental video" at the Guadalupe Film Festival in San Antonio. At that point, I could only conclude that American culture has always had a place for the anti-hero, the accepted iconoclast, and that nowadays perhaps some performance artists occupy that place.

2 "The Shame-man meets El Mexican't at the Smithsonian Motel and Golf Course." Performing in Museums of Natural History

Native American performance artist James Luna and I have known each other since the mid 1990s. Our work is stylistically very different; James practices an aesthetic of simplicity, whereas (according to critics) the style of my performance work is "excessive" and "neo-baroque." But we share similar political and theoretical concerns: we both theorize our own artistic practice; we are both critical of the way indigenous and ethnic identities are portrayed by mainstream cultural institutions and commodified by pop culture, tourism and self-realization movements; and we both utilize melancholic humor and tactics of "reverse anthropology" as strategies for subverting dominant cultural projections and representations of Mexicans and Native peoples.

My friendship and conceptual kinship with James has engendered many projects. From 1993 to 1996, he and I engaged in one collaborative project per year under the title "The Shame-man meets El Mexican't at [name of the host organization]." One project in particular stands out for me . . .

16 Performance "re-enactment" of the Smithsonian Bust. Living diorama by Gómez-Peña and Luna.

From my performance diaries:

"It's Friday morning. Luna and I share a diorama space at the Smithsonian's Natural History Museum. We are inside an ethnographic prison cell. I sit on a toilet costumed as a mariachi in a straitjacket with a sign around my neck that reads 'There used to be a Mexican inside this body.' I attempt unsuccessfully to get rid of my straitjacket in order to 'perform' ('entertain' or 'educate' my audience). A Mexican waltz mixed with rap contributes to the pathos of my tableau. Meanwhile, James paces back and forth, changing personas. At times he is an 'Indian shoe-shiner', offering to shine the shoes of audience members. At other times, he becomes a 'diabetic Indian,' shooting insulin directly into his stomach. He then transforms into a 'janitor of color' (like most of the janitors in this, and other US museums) and sweeps the floor of the diorama. Hundreds of visitors gather in front of us. They look very sad . . . Next to us, the 'real' Indian dioramas speak of a mute world outside of history and social crises. Strangely, next to us, they appear much less 'authentic'. The visibly nervous museum staff makes sure the audience understands that 'this is just performance art . . . and they are famous artists.'**"**

"James and I have been rehearsing our next 'intervention' at the Natural History Museum. The piece consists of a selection of irreverent monologues, songs, dances, and staged conversations that problematize our bittersweet relationship with mainstream cultural institutions. This time the performance will take place in the main auditorium. It's 10 p.m., and James and I decide to take a break in our dressing room. Roberto and our producer, Kim Chan, are with us. James lights up some sage. I light up a Marlboro. Minutes later, several security guards break in and try to bust us for 'smoking dope.' When they finally realize it's just sage, they feel embarrassed and leave. I write in the margins of my script: *'The performance is never over for us. No matter how much we understand that ethnic identity is a cultural and ideological construction, and that as performance artists we have the power to alter it at will, nevertheless, we are always confronted in the most unexpected moments by the guardians of fetishized identity and the enforcers of stereotype.'*

When Aleta Ringlero, the curator of Native American art, finds out what happened, she gets furious, calls each and every Smithsonian undersecretary, and lets them have it. James, Roberto, Kim and I prefer to have a drink at a bar. It's just another day in our neverending pilgrimage towards the end of Western civilization.**"**

3 **Ethnic Talent for Export** Performing in Malls

When the controversial North American Free Trade Agreement (NAFTA) was finally approved in January, 1994, the side effects of the rapid globalization of economy and culture became an important subject in the work of many Mexican, Chicano and Canadian artists. Cultural institutions on both sides of the two borders began to engage in a depoliticized exchange of what, at the time, I termed

"Naftart." As a direct response to the pervasive trans-cultural hype, Cuban–American writer and artist Coco Fusco and I decided to invent a (fictional) post-NAFTA multinational corporation to market and distribute ethnic talent worldwide. We named it "Mexarcane International (Ethnic Talent for Export)." We decided that the logical location for this fictitious enterprise would be trendy shopping malls, the ultimate space for performance in globalized commodity culture. We placed our exhibition stand and temporary "office" in highly visible mall locations, usually next to the food court. This project was first presented at the National Review of Live Arts (Glasgow), and then taken to Dufferin Mall in Toronto and to Whiteley's Mall in London as part of LIFT '95.

Persuading mall administrators to let us stage an experimental performance art piece was not a problem, especially if we were backed by a prestigious art organization or festival. The management couldn't care less about the content of the project. All they wanted to know was if the *show* would bring in more people. We answered affirmatively. Our original idea was to mimic the "friendly tribalism" of corporations like Benetton, Banana Republic and The Body Shop. For this purpose, our presentational style and overall design needed to be sleek and yet ambiguous enough to generate a doubt in the viewer's mind: "Are they for real?" (whatever "real" meant in such a context) "Maybe it's an interactive advertisement for a new store or an upcoming product." We quickly discovered our presentation needed to be hyperstylized so as not to be to be engulfed and erased by the lush environment of consumer entertainment and fake tolerance.

For the performance, we set up a corporate-style backdrop (created by a professional corporate designer), complete with "explanatory" texts written in imitation corporate jargon, and images of "happy natives" from around the world. Coco was seated at a desk in front, dressed as the Aztec girlfriend of Mr. Spock. Across from her, approximately 20 feet away, was my cage. For four to six hours a day, over three-day periods, I exhibited myself seated inside a tiny gilded or bamboo cage as an exotic "multicultural Frankenstein." Each detail and element of my costume came from a different culture in the Americas. I was "a living sample of Mexarcane's products for export," a composite "primitive" ready to fulfill the consumer's desire for exotica. Mall visitors were encouraged to "activate" me in order to experience my "incredible ethnic talents." My "live demonstrations" included: commercials for chile shampoo, "Ancient Grains" cereal, and other organic products; modeling tribal wear (in hopes that someone would hire me "for a rock video shoot or a kinky catering service"); posing in attitudes of martyrdom, despair, and poverty "for German documentary photographers"; doing shamanistic rituals and playing new age tribal music concerts (on toy instruments) "for confused suburbanites"; and (the most popular of all) demonstrating "pre-Columbian condoms," using a clay dildo as a proxy. During these demonstrations, Coco conducted interviews and surveys to determine the "ethnic desires" of the audience. After each interview, she would decide which "demonstration" was most appropriate for a particular consumer, who was then instructed to approach the "composite Indian" and ask me to "perform". Since I was not supposed to speak English (after all, I was an "authentic primitive"), the person who approached me had to mouth their request slowly and carefully, one syllable at a time, as if talking to an infant or a trained animal.

Contrary to our original expectations, our presence in the mall was not considered particularly outrageous. An eerie kind of "normality" and cool indifference seemed to surround the event. People participated very actively, acritically and without self-consciousness, in much the same way they were used to participating in other interactive displays in the mall. Those who expressed strong feelings about the piece were primarily immigrants and people of color, but these emotional reactions never went beyond shedding a tear, or leaving us a supportive written note. Usually, by the third day of a performance, the management finally figured the real implications of a piece, and was extremely happy to see us leave for good.

4 The first, the last, the only "Lowrider Spanglish Opera."
"There Goes the Opera House . . ."

When Los Angeles producer Michael Milenski first contacted me in late 97 to ask if I wanted to direct an opera for the Long Beach Opera House, I truly thought he was kidding. The proposed piece was *The Indian Queen,* a seventeenth-century British baroque opera with text by Dryden and music by Purcell. Before accepting, I asked him two things: to fax me the libretto, and to become more familiar with my work by reading some of my books.

Dryden's text is filled with outrageous racist stereotypes and Eurocentric constructions of otherness. Set in an imaginary pre-contact Mexico, it describes a fictional conflict between Aztecs who behave like British royalty, and Incas who behave like mythical Scots. (In the seventeenth-century British imagination,

17 The high-tech Aztec set of La Indian Queen.

Scots were perceived as savages.) The Indian Queen herself is the personification of *America salvaje*, an oversexed, gluttonous female primitive, hungry for war and quick to betray her family and people.

The thought of "inverting" the script was so seductive that I couldn't resist. I got so nervous I developed acute insomnia. My initial proposal to Milenski was as follows. I wanted to rewrite the libretto in Spanglish, set it in a contemporary Californian mediascape, work with both symphonic and Mexican pop musicians, and create a cast using mainly Chicano performers and experimental artists, including many of my close collaborators. My demands were so outrageous that I felt sure they would be rejected (maybe deep inside that's precisely what I wanted) but Milenski reluctantly agreed. Just to make sure he really knew what he was getting into, I invited him to a performance of *Mexterminator* in San Francisco. After seeing the performance, he still insisted that he wanted to go forward with the project.

Since I didn't know much about opera, my very first task was to assemble a team of collaborators whose work I knew well and whose aesthetic vision was compatible with mine. City Lights editor Elaine Katzenberger agreed to be dramaturg for the project and work with me in writing the new Spanglish version of the libretto. Sara Shelton-Mann was hired to choreograph the ritual dances of the "primitives" (in our "inverted" version, the Aztec dancers were depicted as "blue savages" out of Celtic legend). Chicano filmmaker Gustavo Vázquez was commissioned to make a film including excerpts of B-movies, Mexican soap operas, and racist ethnographic documentaries, that was intended to comment on the live action and create a sort of ongoing "meta-reality." Milenski approached conductor Andreas Mitisek from the Salzburg Philarmonic, who got a kick out of the idea of directing an orchestra dressed á la "Chippendale's Aztec," and agreed to be part of our adventure for very little money. We knew that we also needed a staging director with experience in opera, someone with the skills to handle the difficult challenge of bringing together the work of actors, musicians, singers, and dancers, and who would agree to carry out our aesthetic and political vision rather than imposing his own. Los Angeles Maestro David Schweitzer was a logical choice.

Elaine, Sara and I had already shared a number of professional adventures and knew each other well. We clicked with David from day one. We shared an irreverent sense of humor and a fascination with perverse pop culture, high kitsch and sharp-edged politics. Perhaps the hardest task facing us was the need to create a new collaborative model with an unusual division of labor specific to the project. We had to learn to trust each other's sensibilities and decisions. Though Elaine and I did most of the rewriting and conceived the main concepts for the production, it was David who eventually had to work out most of the actual details of the staging and assemble the whole enchilada. For my friends and I, this was a radical exercise in ceding authority. The situation was made even more complicated by the fact that Sara and I were already committed to another project that overlapped with the rehearsal period for the opera: an extremely intensive, month-long residency in New York, which included performances of *Mexterminator* at Museo del Barrio and a number of performative events and interventions produced by Creative Time. Whenever Sara and I could manage a couple of days off from our multiple projects and commitments in New York, one or both of us flew back to California to work on the opera. It was an extremely chaotic and nerve-wracking experience, and our sense of ourselves as "trespassers" in the high-cultural, Eurocentric domain of opera made matters even worse. The unusual collaborative structure and fragmented working conditions made us fear that we could lose aesthetic control and end up with a project so eclectic that it would be an epic flop.

Auditions came. The team agreed that Moctezuma needed to be cast as a Chicano wrestler. Since Dryden's Indian Queen was a cultural transvestite, we decided to cast the role as a "clepto-Mexican" Anglo (not a Chicana) who purposely mispronounces her Spanish lines. The Queen's confused son, Acasius, became a soft-hearted, liberal Californian surfer. The Queen's arch enemy, an Inca tyrant, became a Miami narco-politico, and his daughter an archetypal assimilationist Indian collaborator – a folkloric "Mexican señorita" sponsored by the Department of Tourism whose job was to welcome the enemy into her culture.

The set was pure Aztec High-tech in Vegas. It involved a huge metallic pyramid, a lowrider car in the shape of a red stiletto shoe (the throne of *our* Indian Queen), and a "pre-Columbian nightclub" made out of Styrofoam that looked kind of like the Mexican pavilion at Disney's EPCOT, a place where yuppie cultural tourists could drink margaritas and enjoy a taste of "exotic Mexico."

While we were finishing revisions of the script and assembling the final company of actors, dancers and singers, the list of restrictions coming from above became increasingly longer. Magister Dixit: The spoken parts of Dryden's text could be rewritten in Spanglish, but all the sung parts needed to remain in archaic English. We couldn't have any musical intervention from outside sources, which meant no mariachi band, rap group, or Tex-mex accordionist – not even special sound effects. Full nudity for the "blue savages" was out of the question (g-strings were OK). Every day we had to (politely and indirectly but firmly) fight to defend and re-conquer every inch of the creative freedom we needed in order to stage an event that would genuinely merge performance art and opera with a strong Chicano sensibility.

Rehearsals began. In the highly specialized hierarchy of Opera, the roles of Sara, Elaine and I were extremely restricted. We weren't allowed to participate openly in the rehearsal process, and were instead restricted to writing notes and passing them on to David in private meetings so as not to undermine his authority in the eyes of the actors and singers. Actors, dancers and singers all rehearsed separately for most of the process, and it was only in the last two days of rehearsal that everything came together, which made it almost impossible to foresee the end result of such an unprecedented collaborative project. This process severely tested my tolerance and creative will, and of necessity increased my blind faith in my collaborators.

Opening night arrived. The Carpenter Center was packed. My colleagues and I were experiencing a combination of childish excitement and acute panic. If the piece didn't work, I knew I would be forced to go into hiding for at least a year. To our amazement, the performance was not only successful, but according to the press, "it shined". At the end of the piece, the audience applauded like crazy. None of us were prepared for what the LA Times reviewer said about the project the following day: "There is something in *The Indian Queen* to offend just about everyone. There is also something in it that should delight and astonish just about everyone as well. It's a mess. But it's a dazzling mess. It utterly, totally, unapologetically undoes just about everything its authors, composer Henry Purcell and poet John Dryden, set out to do in 1695. But it saves a work that probably could survive in no other reasonable way. It brings something new to opera at a time when you might think just about everything imaginable has already been done."

explains to you that the chefs and the waiters were all part of an epic self-deportation program. Since you are fairly apolitical, you still don't quite get it. Many stores and hotels are closed (for obvious reasons) and the banks are going crazy. All across the country, millions of Mexicans, with their suitcases in hand, are lining up at bank counters to withdraw their accounts on their way back to their homelands.

You begin to worry about your family. You decide to go home, walking of course, 'cause your car, remember, is parked somewhere on the other side of town without gas. Your Hispanic wife is devastated. Most of her relatives chose to go back to the old country. She is also furious because Juan, the gardener, and Maria, the babysitter are nowhere to be found. She explains she had to stay home to take care of the kids and missed all of her work appointments. She even had to take the kids to do the shopping, which Maria normally does. They stood in an eternal line at the supermarket, only to find that there was no fresh produce. According to the supermarket manager, there were no truckers to deliver it. Now your kids are crying because they miss Maria.

You go to bed in total perplexity, and you dream . . . in Spanish. Or better said, you have a nightmare in Spanish: you see yourself picking fruit under a criminal sun for ten hours a day, your hands covered with a monstrous skin disease produced by pesticides. You wake up sweating.

Next morning, you turn on the TV. A panicked President delivers the bad news: very few people responded to his desperate call for workers. The unemployed "citizens" were clearly not inspired by the idea of working for minimum wage and no benefits. The nation's tourist, construction, garment, and food industries are all in disarray. San Diego, Los Angeles, Santa Barbara, San Jose, Fresno, San Francisco, Phoenix, Tucson, Santa Fe, Albuquerque, Denver, San Antonio, Houston, Chicago and a myriad other smaller cities have declared bankruptcy. And so have many national banks. And if this weren't enough, the President concludes, within days, crops across the country will begin to rot because there's simply no one to pick them. Luckily Mexico has offered to send some emergency food supplies, and maybe even some Mexicans. In very broken Spanglish, or rather gringoñol, a desperate President Clinton proceeds to beg the remaining Mexicans to stay [misspelled Spanish]: "Queridous amigous: querremos que ustedis recapaciten y nou abandounen sus trabayos mas. Les subireimos el salary y les dareimos muchious benefits y su terjeita verdi instan-tánea. Por favour."

Now, take a deep breath and slowly come back to the present. Nativist politicos and citizen groups across the country are doing everything they can to stop illegal immigration, and to take away the few rights left for immigrants, including access to education and medical services. They conveniently make no distinction between "illegal" and "legal." They blame all immigrants for crime, drugs, and especially the lack of jobs. Their inflammatory rhetoric appeals to your fear of an uncertain future, but not your intelligence. You feel manipulated and angry. If you could ask one question of the political class, what would that question be? "Are you guys truly, truly aware of the logical consequences of your anti-immigrant politics?"

Now, you cool down. Its been a hard day, que no? You sip your delicious coffee, from Chiapas, and turn up your favorite Latin Jazz.

18 Texas Rangers posing with their "Mexican catches" at the turn of the century.

MIGRANT PROVOCATEURS:

FURTHER CHRONICLES

PART 2

From Chiapas to Wales

1 Revolutionary Tourism

Since the mid-80s I have created performances and installations dealing with the commodification and exoticization of ethnicity by the tourist and the pop culture industries. Perhaps because of this I am overly cautious about performing the involuntary role of stupid tourist myself. I particularly distrust the type of tourism which promises a more "meaningful," "fair," and "radical" exchange of political ideas and cultural experiences, which of course, rarely happens.

During my border activist days, many European and US journalists, photographers and critics showed up unannounced at my Tijuana home. They wanted me either to perform the role of countercultural tour guide and show them "the dark side of TJ," or to re-enact for the camera one of my "risky" border performances. Some were quite persistent and insensitive. Once I had a hard time persuading a German TV crew that it wasn't worth it for me to attempt to cross the border check point in costume and without papers – repeating what I had done the year before – and risk my fragile status as a US "resident alien" just so they could get a good shot for their documentary. They were disappointed. They wanted action, danger, and (clearly in their terms and schedule), to make their visit to the conflictive border region worthwhile. And instead, what they got, in the words of the German producer, was "an extremely talkative intellectual" (or better said, a smart Mexican) deconstructing their problematic role as political tourists of the worst kind.

My distrust of political tourism became proverbial. When all my colleagues were going to Nicaragua to experience first hand the wonders of Sandinismo, I politely rejected every invitation. And when Cuba became fashionable, I stopped going there. (In fact my participation in the 1988 Havana Biennial was taken to Cuba by my friend writer Shifra Goldman in the form of a "border time capsule." It contained detailed instructions "to bury this conceptual box under the gallery floor for ten years". The Cuban curators didn't honor my wishes and the box probably ended up disappearing in the hands of some revolutionary art shopper).

In the first two years of Zapatismo, I was one of the few among my politicized friends who didn't attempt to meet *el capo* of political hype, performance artist extraordinaire *subcomandante* Marcos (read "Marcos, the subcomandante of performance"). And not because I didn't worship the man (alongside Cesar Chavez, he is undoubtedly the closest to a sane and imaginative political leader we Latinos have had in years). I truly had to bite my lip, but the hype around Zapatismo, and the cheesy parade of celebrities in the lobby of the jungle waiting to be received by Marcos and Compañía, really turned me off.

Among others, Madam Mitterrand and Regis Debray were there to pass on to the rebels the blessings of the dying European social democrats; Oliver Stone showed up with his entourage but "couldn't take the water and the mosquitoes"; Eddie Olmos also went there . . . for the photo op; Eduardo Galeano's visit to the now legendary *Convención Intergaláctica* was like the last visit of the Pope to Mexico. Many superstar women journalists fought like crazy to obtain an interview with sexy Marcos. They wanted to "unmask" the hero . . . in bed. Even Benetton representatives showed up to persuade the avatar to appear in a photo ad; and Marcos politely rejected the invitation.

Though I was fully aware of the postmodern media strategies of the Zapatistas and of their masterful manipulation of the media, the idea of "El Aztec High Tech" servidor shaking hands (or rather exchanging props and performance tips) with the rebels just seemed too hip and opportunistic for my taste.

However, last August, I finally succumbed to my own curiosity.

≥2 Radical Chic

Invited by Chicana cultural organizer Marietta Bernstoff and her companion Mexican photographer Antonio Turok, a small group of artist friends (including my collaborator Roberto Sifuentes, Mexican performance artist Lorena Wolffer, Puerto Rican photographer Tania Frontera and I) headed for San Cristobal de las Casas, in the central part of the state of Chiapas, in search of the Mexican *welchmertz*. The Woodstock-like *Convención Intergaláctica* which gathered over 3,000

Zapatista supporters from around the world was just over, and Marietta insisted we didn't have to practice political tourism. In fact the original plan for us was simply to chill out, write, walk the town, meet the local artists and activists and hopefully, if we so desired, come up with a future project. Little did we know.

Chiapas has become a major vortex for end of the century political drama. Forty-seven different ethnic groups with a renewed spirit of defiance are attempting to negotiate space, language, cultural difference and political discourse. And these abrupt negotiations are taking place amidst land invasions, undercover military operations, inter-religious conflicts, and racial wars between *Indigenas* and *coletos* (white San Cristobaleños), between politicized Indians and paramilitary groups trained by the army.

San Cristobal de las Casas is definitely the most surreal post-colonial town I've ever visited. Being the obligatory point of entry to the Zapatista-controlled areas, it has also become (against the will of its inhabitants) the new international capital of radical chic (aka: the SoHo of *indigenismo*). Its colonial charm has been eroded by the presence of "Indian" fashion boutiques, and cappuccino bars and fast food restaurants with revolutionary names, to the dismay of both the racist "coletos" and Europeans in search of authenticity. Whenever there is a major Zapatista event, and during vacation season, the streets are crowded with hordes of revolutionary tourists and dilettantes from all around the world: gringofarians, hippitecas, eco-tourists, "radical" anthropologists, macho journalists, and burnt out leftists. They roam around looking for "the most unique" Zapatista souvenirs and bargaining hammocks and textiles from famelic Indians. They are also looking for a (politico-mystico-sexual) recipe to overcome their terminal nihilism. And in the interim, they provide the "Indious"(misspelled) with arrogant solutions to all their problems. At night they go to the cafes which are practically indistinguishable from those of the Mission District in San Francisco, to discuss the perils or wonders of Zapatismo, and to write their heroic diaries. One such diary from a self-proclaimed Canadian "adventurer" (probably an art student) who insisted on reading it to me at a bistro named "Cafe Paris/ Mexico"(I swear to god), began with the following paragraph reconstructed from memory a few hours later:

Dear X. I'm finally here in the heart of the Mexican jungle (false: San Cristobal is not in the jungle). Please tell Yvonne I don't love her anymore. I found myself a beautiful Chia-pa-ne-ca MU-CHIA-CHIA(misspelled) who truly understands

19 Gómez-Peña and Sifuentes posing as "eco-tourists", Chiapas Jungle.

me, and truly listens to me. My Indian lover is pure, very sexy and quite political: She is organizing her "comadres" to be able to sell their artesanias without the need of government intermediaries. Cool. Tomorrow, I'm moving in with her. Next week I will try to meet some Zapatistas.

Each tourist is looking for a contact, the right person to bring them to the jungle; the proper guide for an exciting "zapatour"; and/or the sexiest Indian (or rather Indian-looking) "insider" to exchange (for a week or two) utopian fluids, cultural secrets and ideological recipes.

At the legendary club *La Galeria* everything gets intensified. On Friday and Saturday nights, all those who just came back – re energized or disappointed – from the zapatour, show up to pick up those who are on their way. They exchange stories (political tourism is also about storytelling), cheap tequila and (they hope) sex. The local mestizo dandies are always ready to provide the *gringo* (meaning any foreigner-looking tourist) with whatever s/he needs: a political contact, good dope, tips for the best restaurants or places to buy this or that, or a night of pre-Columbian pleasure.

Paradoxically, this revolutionary fiesta is perhaps one of the main reasons why the Mexican government hasn't exterminated the Zapatistas. In the suspicious eyes of the government (Mexican politicians are very sensitive to international opinion), each tourist, specially those with foreign names and video cameras, becomes a potential witness; a probable reporter.[1] Because of this, although I found the revolutionary fiesta a bit sleazy and pretentious, I support it whole-heartedly . . . and even promote it among my *gringo* friends: "Go to Chiapas. Buy lots of trinkets. Wear a Zapatista mask. Dance and drink. Have lots of sex with an activist. Pay lots of money for the zapatour. Its worth it. You might be contributing indirectly to the survival of Zapatismo."

3 Involuntary Explorers for the Chicano Discovery Channel

Fernando Ochoa is a sweet man with a mission. For five years he's been working with various indigenous communities in the jungle in projects of "organic

---

1   In 1998, the Mexican government began to expel foreigners "participating in domestic affairs." That year, fifty foreigners, many of whom were members of human rights organizations and priests, were deported from Chiapas.

ritual actions, a coherent symbolic system which helps people understand themselves and their circumstances a little better.) And while waiting for *consulta*, his daughter might braid your hair – Chamula style – to make the overall experience more "authentic." She also serves you *posh*, and this time, you just can't say no.

After the braiding ceremony, we looked like Hollywood Indians. We felt extremely self-conscious, especially as we had to go outside and sit on the front porch to wait for our turn to have a *limpia* (spiritual cleansing ritual). In a matter of minutes, we became public spectacle; an involuntary *tableaux vivant*, perhaps the strangest one they had ever seen. Amused by our cheesy "gringo/ Indian" look, the kids and the elders surrounded us, while the shaman's daughter continued to pour more *posh* in our glasses. We were once again on display as yet another kind of ethnographic specimen: "the border cultural transvestite," meaning, a bunch of Mexicans, Chicanos and one Puerto Rican, in Chiapas, all looking like stylish North American Indian bikers straight out of a rock & roll road movie, and sadly beginning to behave as such due to the effects of *posh*. Our impromptu audience spoke to us in Chamula, and we answered back in Spanish. In our metaphysical drunken stupor, we truly thought we were having a deep conversation. But the Chamulas were probably just fucking with our minds.

After we all had gone through the *limpia*, we compared notes. The diagnosis of *El Shanick* was extremely disappointing: we all happened to have the same "spiritual illness": "someone – of the opposite sex – with dark hair was harming us with *magia negra*" and, to cure this problem, we all had been given the same *nahual* (inner animal/protector): a black eagle. Now in retrospect, I tend to believe that perhaps the *brujo* was right and we were all in fact suffering from the same "spiritual illness"; a deadly combination of spiritual nihilism, cultural voyeurism and Chicano irreverence.

By the time we returned to San Cristobal drunk out of our minds, we were all roaming around in hell. We started fighting with one another like capricious children, specially the couples. Out of the blue I began to walk randomly at night, as if some cheesy metaphysical being was guiding me with a remote control. I ended up at a cantina named "La Esperanza"(Hope) befriending the bartender. He told me: "Are you aware that the brujos are using witchcraft to drive the *turistas* out of town? They are making them ill and fight with one another. It's like they have created a shamanistic virus which only affects ladinos." Next day, Marietta confirmed the gossip: Effectively, people in town were talking about "the anti-tourist *brujeria* campaign." She gave me many convincing examples of

Americans and Europeans who in the last month had been going either through some severe psychological crises, or were suffering from a serious disease. It sounded like one of my performance texts.

5 The Journey to Wales

Roberto and I had only three days to get from San Cristobal de las Casas to Aberystwyth, Wales, where we were paradoxically to attend a conference on "Performance, Tourism and Identity" organized by Barbara Kirshen-Blatt Gimlett and Richard Gough.

The hardest and strangest part of my trip began. My colleagues and I first took a cab to Tuxtla Gutierrez (the capital of Chiapas), where we had dinner with my *chiapaneca* family. My uncle Carlos and my aunt Maga were surprisingly sympathetic to our "romantic views on Zapatismo", given the fact that they had just lost part of their ranch (their lifetime project) during an indigenous land invasion. (Since the leader of the invasion knew my uncle, he persuaded the others to let my family keep part of the ranch). After dinner, my colleagues and I took a plane to Mexico City. Next day we had just enough time to have coffee with my mother, re-pack our suitcases and take industrial alcohol baths to get rid of the unbearable ticks we had collected in the jungle. Then we had to separate: Tania and Roberto had airplane tickets to go back to New York where they live, whereas Lorena and I flew to San Francisco. We were exhausted.

Once at home, I re-packed my suitcase for the third time, and then, operating in automatic pilot, I rushed back to the airport, this time to make my plane to JFK where I was to re-encounter Roberto. I did. He looked as burnt out as I was. We took a short nap at a bar and then boarded our plane to Amsterdam. We were so exhausted (there might not exist a word to describe how we felt) that we simply couldn't sleep. We spent most of the time playing (or rather attempting to play) computer chess and trying to make sense out of our intense traveling memories across Chiapas. In fact the first notes of this chronicle were written during those disorienting hours.

At the Amsterdam airport we had a couple of hours to rest in between planes. We had heard about the legendary airport sauna baths, and decided to check them out. After an hour-long sauna in which we almost lost completely our sense of self, we headed to London. During that flight, we didn't know who we were anymore or where exactly we were heading towards. It was as if our primary identities had been deleted. All we could feel was acute deterritorialization (in the geo-cultural sense), psychological disorientation, and strangely, a pleasant form of existential despair: we were constantly cracking up at obscure matters which were not even understandable to us. To waste time, we even made a list of all the stereotypical images that the word "Wales" evoked in our scrambled minds. The embarrasing list was as follows:

> *. . . resistance-but not as hard core as that of Ireland,*
> *working class anti-colonialist politics,*
> *neo-nationalism,*
> *subaltern Europe*
> *dark green fields with immaculately white sheep,*
> *foggy forests with wholesome white campesinos,*
> *a strange language "which sounded Korean",*
> *food slightly better than the British,*
> *thick beer,*
> *sweet folk rock,* etc.

Next morning . . . we were not in Chiapas.

We were picked up at Heathrow by a smiley American student named Sara Brady. She told us we had to drive to an other airport to pick up "a famous anthropologist named Ed Brunner" who was arriving with his wife "Cookie." On the way to Gatwick (the other airport) she explained to us she only had "seventeen hours of driving experience in the UK" (meaning on the right seat of the car). At the time we didn't understand the implications of her statement.

After picking up Ed and "Cookie," our driver got lost. We spent three hours circling London, looking at maps for the right highway to take us to Wales. We were silently furious and frustrated, but too tired to make a stink. Suddenly the comedic notion of Roberto and I being "The Lewis and Clark of the Chicano movement" acquired absurdist and unpleasant dimensions.

A car trip which normally would take five hours, turned out to be twelve hours long. At one point I decided to console myself thinking of the experience as a sort of performance exercise of endurance. My rationale was as follows: if I can make it to London, I certainly can spend three days living inside a plexiglas box, or vice versa.

We got to Aberystwyth at 9:00 p.m. Richard Gough and Judy Christie from the Center for Performance Research had organized a welcome dinner for the ten theoreticians and artists who had already arrived. All Roberto and I could do to reciprocate their kindness was to smile . . . and methodically eat the delicious Columbian food prepared by Richard's family. That night I cried in silence at my minute student dorm room. Who could possibly believe what Roberto and I had just been through in the past three days? Who could possibly understand that it was logarithmically harder to get from Chiapas to Wales than say, from Tennessee to Micronesia via Buenos Aires. The romantic thought of being in Wales for the first time in my life consoled me a bit and I finally fell asleep. I dreamt my skin was completely covered with a rash; some kind of "anti-tourist skin disease." I kept scratching my skin until it began to bleed.

6 Two Live Mexicans on Exhibit in Wales

The next day Roberto and I were ready to "exhibit" ourselves as "ethnographic specimens" and "ethno-cyborgs," as part of the opening events. The idea of "two live Mexicans" being the main attraction during the first day of the conference was irresistible.

Our "show" was an early version of *El Mexterminator*, entitled *Mexican Beasts & Artificial Savages*. (This work-in-progress is based on an "Internet confessional". We have asked thousands of US Net-users to help us "co-imagine the mythical Mexican of the 90s," and express to us their innnermost fears and desires regarding Mexicans, Chicanos, immigration and Spanish language. These anonymous Internet responses have become the basis for the creation of a series of "techno-dioramas" depicting "ethno-cyborgs," co-created collaboratively with anonymous Net-users. Unlike our previous diorama projects, the idea now is to cede our will to the *internautas* in determining the nature and content of the "living dioramas," including how we should dress, what music we must listen to and, most important, what kind of ritual actions we should engage in. What we do then as performance artists is to *embody* this information, reinterpret it and stylize it using our own aesthetic strategies. These "artificial savages" incarnate profound fears and desires of contemporary Americans regarding Latino/ Mexicano immigrants, and hopefully, function as mirrors for people to see the reflections of their own psychological and cultural monsters.)

Our performance started around 5:30 p.m. For three hours, Roberto and I displayed ourselves on black platforms carefully lit as museum pieces. Roberto was CyberVato, a "techno-gang member" engaged in ritualized actions including plunging a horse syringe into his heart and tongue; self-flagellation with an S&M whip decorated with eagle feathers, and various traditional catholic tableaux intertwined with familiar gangster-rap iconography. His face was painted with Pre-Columbian-looking tattoos, and his T-shirt was saturated with blood and holes from implied gunshots. Next to him was a small table covered with "useless" technological gadgets and what appeared to be real weapons and drug paraphernalia. A digital bar over him presented his taxonomic information:

> "CyberVato"(Homo Chicanus: ethno-cyborg # 6935) As seen on The Evening News. Habitat: The US inner cities Aliases: cholo, pinto, chuco, homie, vato loco, lowrider, gang member. Features: Techno-savvy/neo-nationalist/ monolingual/ melancholic/drug addict/ experiences permanent social resentment and identity crises/loves oldies and Post-Columbian rap music. Poster boy for the culture of victimization.Wanted by the Los Angeles Police Department. Considered "Endangered Species."

Opposite CyberVato there I was, seated on an old wooden wheelchair posing as *El mucho macho* "Mexterminator," a ranchero version of Schwarzenegger's famous avenger, wearing my Stetson hat, my Tijuana black leather pants, a fake tiger-skin vest, and a "Hollywood bandolera." The jaw of a bison was strapped to my lower jaw. Fully armed with unloaded guns and "mysterious shamanic weapons," my persona was more defiant, animated, and pathetic than Roberto's. I applied make-up ritually, practiced "Chicano karate" kattas and performed various slow-motion *tableaux vivants* imbued with cinematic nostalgia, stylized violence and symbolic sexuality. My digital bar read:

> "El Mexterminator" (Homo Fronterizus: ethno-cyborg #187) As seen on the Supernintendo video game "Killer Instinct." Habitat: The American borderlands. Features: Illegal border-crosser/highly infectious/ extremely politicized/unnecessarily violent & hyper-sexual/speaks Spanglish only. Indestructible! Multiple identities: karateca; marksman; stuntman; curio shop shaman; Tex-Mex rocker; drug & jalapeño pusher; undercover activist. Wanted by the INS, the DEA, the FBI & the Smithsonian Institution. Political project: To redefine the West and to invade the North.

Besides trying to remain awake for the duration of the performance, our main objective was to make sure that our activist diorama (which is often presented in less controlled environments with much more foot traffic) retained its political spunk and edges. We don't know for sure if we were able to attain this purpose. Our sense was that our colleagues were truly moved, and with us. Their intelligent gaze, tender eyes, and familiar faces made us feel strangely at home (in Wales, posing as ethno-cyborgs?).

By the second hour, I suddenly began to remember Chiapas, the skeptical indigenous faces, the cyborg-like faces of the Mexterminator-like soldiers, the bar scene in San Cristobal, conversations with burnt-out leftists in search of spiritual medication, silently rowing on Miramar lagoon, listening to the ancient howlings of the zaraguato monkeys at night, an old woman breastfeeding a child inside the church at San Juan Chamula, while a drunk was cursing one of the wooden saints, travelers playing roulette at the Amsterdam airport casino. We had gone a long way: from observing and being observed by indigenous rebels and revolutionary tourists to observing and being observed by performance theoreticians, anthropologists and artist colleagues; from attempting to "decon-struct" (what a pretentious term) and failing to do so, our unwanted roles of "radical tourists" to deconstructing the threatening identities forced upon us by the American mainstream.

The morning after, we jumped on an express coach and a new tour began. For the next three days, emulating a typical bus tour, all the participants in the conference traveled thoughout Wales, visiting various historical sites and attending site-specific discussions and performances, dealing with just about everything we had experienced in Chiapas. At Saint Fagans Museum of Welsh Life, I was programmed to read my performance poetry in a nineteenth-century cock pit, the ultimate site-specific context for a Mexican/Chicano/ border performance artist/tourist in Wales, in an incomprehensible Wales, in a mythical Wales.

As I finish this text, it suddenly dawns on me: tourism in a "globalized" world is perhaps an inevitable experience. Thanks to the Zapatistas and to my performance colleagues, I am no longer overly cautious about performing the involuntary role of stupid tourist. In fact the borderline between "involuntary" and "voluntary" actions has dimmed considerably since then.

SAN FRANCISCO, 1997

The Mexican Community Center in Fort Collings

It's 10:00 at night in the lonely streets of Fort Collings, an extremely racist part of Colorado, and not that far from the headquarters of *Soldier of Fortune* magazine. Roberto and I just arrived, driving from Boulder in a rented van. We are here to perform at the local university. An old truck full of rowdy locals begins following us, flashing its lights and honking at us. We stop, not knowing exactly why, perhaps out of fear. Our hearts beat real fast. The passengers look as if they just drove non-stop for two days straight out of *Deliverance*. They ask us the obvious question: are we lost? We answer that we are looking for the university. The driver, a rural hippy with a nasal voice, says he does not know how to get to campus, but he certainly knows the way "to the Meskin cultural center." I cannot believe my ears: a Mexican cultural center in Fort Collings? He volunteers to guide us.

We follow respectfully . . . from a certain distance. Three blocks later they turn left. We enter the parking lot of a Taco Bell. The driver of the truck screams at us from the window: "Hey buddies, welcome to the Meskin' cultural center." They all crack up theatrically, and drive away singing "La Cucaracha." Roberto and I look at one another with a combination of embarrassment, anger, and a desire to laugh. "Ese, we gotta give it to those racists. They were funny," he tells me. We continue to drive randomly in search of the campus, wishing we had been faster and funnier than them. It's one of those cases in which reality is much more interesting and edgier than performance.

PHONE CALL:
"Excuse me sir, can you put me in contact with Guillermo Gómez-Peña?"
"Sorry lady, I don't speak Spanish."
The man at the motel switchboard hangs up.

From Montana to Helsinki

At times, Roberto Sifuentes and I assume the performance roles of "the Lewis and Clark of the Chicano movement," charting unknown territory for the Chicano Discovery Channel. Other times, we're more like Marco Polo de Tijuana and Cabeza de Pollo (not Vaca) in search of a Hollywood mirage known as El Dorado, Inc. With our props and costumes jam-packed inside a pair of trunks, airplane tickets in hand, and a mad *flota* of scouts and collaborators, we venture into the *terras ignotas* of Gringolandia, Europzin y anexas.

Perhaps one of the strangest countries we have ever visited is Montana, which in old gringoñol[1] means "mountain." Roberto and I were both seduced and apalled by the many spooky mythologies surrounding this micro-republic since the emergence of the American militia movement. From Chicanolandia via CNN and Univision, Montana was perceived as the last bastion of hard-core frontier mentality; an indomitable land inhabited by angry Luddites, fundamentalist bikers, lunatic Christian Identity patriots and right-wing extremists with secessionist tendencies – all armed, of course, and each and every one a racist. Though logic and common sense might have dictated caution, we truly wanted to see it for ourselves.

➼ I
Early scouting adventures

My first opportunity to visit the mythical home of the Freemen and the Montana Militia came in April 1995. Producer Laura Millen from the Missoula Art Museum

---

1   Reverse "Spanglish" spoken by Americans.

20 Chief Mondaaye on exhibit in Germany. Photo hand-signed to a German admirer. Late 1800s.

and some colleagues of hers from Billings and Bozeman organized a speaking tour for me around the state. Given that my life on the road is an inventory of dangerous coincidences, I arrived at Billings airport in a small plane on April 19, the exact day that someone, initially thought by the US media and federal authorities to have been "an Arab terrorist," placed a bomb in the Oklahoma Federal building, killing 168 people, and shattering the last vestiges of America's political innocence. Since the bombing occurred precisely at the moment I was changing planes, I knew nothing about it. When I walked out of the plane and into the airport, I was met by dozens of humorless policemen frisking and questioning each and every passenger. I though to myself, "Shit, *ese*, this is the Wild West!" When my hosts told me about the bombing, I suddenly realized why the stewardess had been stuttering and tiptoeing around me during the flight: in the eyes of provincial Anglos, I might easily be taken for an Arab.

During that first trip, I lectured extensively about my performance work and my ideas about border culture in universities and galleries. Slowly the stereotypes in my imagination of Montanans as right-wing extremists began to evaporate. In fact, most of the audiences I encountered were extremely receptive and sociable, and occasionally I came across hardcore eccentrics, whom I adored. Verbigratia: after one of my lectures on "activist performance," during the question and answer period, a woman in her early thirties raised her hand. She stepped to the front of the auditorium and told the audience she had had a terrible motorcycle accident that left her with huge scars on her back. She proceeded to take off her jacket and T-shirt, and showed us her bare torso and back, covered with long, thick scars. She wanted to know "if she could make art with her scars." I took a moment to consider my answer, and finally replied: "There are many things you can do with those beautiful scars. You can make a performance in which you exhibit your back as an art piece while describing your accident in a monolgue. This performance can be live or for video. Or you can tattoo your back using the scars as a visual point of departure." She thanked me shyly and left the auditorium. I finally realized that what she had done was in fact an extremely poignant performance about her scars. I felt a bit stupid.

The Mysterious Connection between Montana and Chiapas

Scene Two. Another time, after giving a lecture in Bozeman, I was invited to a bar by a group of local artists. There I met a huge, bearded guy who had attended my talk. He introduced himself as "a true American anarchist," and immediately (without any organic logic) began to discuss political self-determination and "the sacred right to bear arms," his eyes glowing in a messianic way. He quoted the Bible to support his arguments. He confessed that he was a supporter of the Montana Militia, "the true American revolutionaries." I asked him why, if that was the case, he had attended a talk on experimental art and border culture. He said that since I was a Mexican artist (he had seen a photo of one of my performance personas in the local paper), he assumed I was going to talk about Zapatismo. I asked what he thought was the relationship between Zapatismo and the US militias. He replied that both movements believed in "the holy right to utilize guns to defend themselves from an oppressive government." Blown away by the analogy, I lost my Chicano cool and anthropological distance. I tried to explain to Tom Payne Jr. that there were major differences between the two cases – that the Zapatistas were indigenous peoples waging a centuries-old war against colonial forces, that they were not interested in guns *per se*, not even in armed struggle, and that their true weapons were the Internet and their now legendary and quite poetical press communiqués. He responded with militia-style clichés, saying that "Anglos were indigenous to Montana," and that like the Zapatistas, they wanted their land and their country back. "From whom?" I asked. "From the federal government, or from people like me?" (He didn't understand my sarcasm.) "You know," I elaborated, "non-Christian dark people with foreign accents." He laughed in a fake manner. I continued with my list of obvious distinctions, pointing out to him that the Zapatistas came from a leftist/internationalist perspective and supported coalition politics, whereas the US militias were micro-separatists, fundamentalist Christians and fringe conservatives. He didn't seem concerned with these subtle distinctions; most likely, he didn't understand what I was trying to say. I politely excused myself and returned to another table to join my artist colleagues. I needed some Pepto Bismol; I was experiencing a serious case of ideological vertigo. Two days later I took a plane to meet Roberto in Helsinki.

➺ II
Chicanos in Helsinki

Roberto and I recurrently find ourselves in a surreal situation as the only Chicano/ Mexicano artists ever invited to present work in a particular city or venue. Over the years, we have performed at Indian pow-wows, pan-Caribbean and Filipino art and theater festivals, Butoh performance gatherings, and European cyberart conferences. Once, for reasons still unknown to us, we were invited to perform at an all-Lesbian cabaret. The more unusual or apparently foreign the context, the greater the challenge with which it presents us; therefore, we always accepts these kinds of *sui generis* invitations. Crossfade.

In May 1995, Roberto and I were invited to participate in the Helsinki Performance Festival, an event that featured mostly Northern European experimental theater troupes. The project we presented was *Borderama*, a Spanglish performance[2] dealing with the cultural wars in America at the time. As the only Latino participants in the Festival, we went through excruciating efforts to "contextualize" our material. We stripped the text of its Chicanismos and local references, we translated key phrases into Finnish, and did everything possible to make the show more visual and less dependent on the spoken word. We even added a local "living diorama": a "Suomi" violinist performing Sibelius's *Finlandia* while seated on a stuffed reindeer. Though I cannot be entirely sure that our performance "translated" to a Finnish context, we got standing ovations every night and lots of attention in the press. (Though we were not able to read the features and reviews, according to our new Finnish friends they were all "very positive.") The success of *Borderama* granted us instant celebrity status for a week. Many people invited us to check out "the Mexican cantina scene" in town. (At the time, tequila was the chic drink in popular "Mexilandia" theme bars). A famous rock band scheduled to perform next on the stage we had used asked if they could borrow our trademark crucified skeleton and hanging chickens for their concert set, and we agreed. We were made to feel strangely at home there. Intercut.

➤ III
Mexican Cowboys and Indian Lowriders

A year and a half after my first visit, I returned to Montana with Roberto. This time, we had received an invitation from Crow artist Susan Stewart and arts producer Arnie Molina to collaborate with indigenous artists from Montana

---

2   The script of *Borderama* was published in my book *The New World Border* (San Francisco: City Lights, 1996).

on two parallel projects. One was a performance/ installation for the Helena Museum of Art titled "Mexican Cowboys and Indian Lowriders," a sort of experimental Indian trading Post and Curio Shop incorporating racist pop archaeology (Indianabilia, Mexicabilia, and "Western" souvenirs), "authentic" Cowboy and Indian art, and "stuffed humans" (the team of collaborating performers). We used fictitious museum labels to create an inverted world in which Chicanos and Indians occupy a fictional center, and Anglos are nomadic minorities and tribal peoples with weird customs and costumes. Our other project was a "tribal slam," a ritualized, spoken-word recital that also involved Chicano and Native American writers and musicians. The overall project was hot. It had all the elements which make our work rock: a field trip across the state to gather "pop cultural archaeology," as well as potential collaborators or "involuntary performance artists," the Chicano/indigenous connection so important to Roberto and I, and a superexotic setting (Montana, in the imagination of radical border artists, represents something similar to Chiapas in the minds of French or German leftists).

The timing could not have been stranger. The extravagant band of anti-government militia members known as Freemen were barricaded in a small compound in a standoff with the FBI. Montana was in the international news, and hundreds of militiamen from around the country were arriving daily to show their support of their local co-religionaries. It was a scary time for brown and red artists to be roaming around the fire. Just before our arrival, Susan Steward and her husban Tyler Medicinehorse, a Crow artist and shaman, were driving through Militia Land with a bunch of colleagues, when suddenly their lowrider van was hit by bullets from a nearby training camp. They sped up. When they arrived to the next town, Susan and Tyler told the cops what had happened and showed them the bullet holes in the metal of the van frame. A police sergeant replied, "Hey, that's your fuckin' problem. What the hell are you Indians doing away from the rez?" Susan replied with her elegant humor, "Sorry, I didn't know we were at war again."

"Indian Bikers" without Bikes

We spent our first two weeks in Montana driving around in a "rent a wreck" station wagon. We visited reservations and cities, roadside museums and Indian trading posts, old cantinas and historical sites such as Little Big Horn. As we

"Gómez-Peña. Your Mexican humor was definitely not translatable."

GERMAN PRODUCER

21 Mimicking famous Indian Warrior Geronimo in a living diorama. Diverse Works, Texas.

traveled from place to place, we accumulated an amazing collection of racist pop cultural artifacts (both purchased and borrowed), which we planned to display as part of our installation at the Helena Museum of Art. During this "art safari," more myths toppled by their own weight. Montanans, even those who fit our visual and social stereotypes (complete with outrageous conspiracy theories and extreme anti-government sentiments), were warm and curious people. Our long hair, leather jackets, and silver jewelry granted us an instant romantic identity as "Indian bikers," opening many doors for us.

Montana bar culture was a particularly interesting realm in which to experiment with the performative possibilities of identity. Verbigratia: once in a bar that advertised "Mexican night" (which meant that the local redneck rock band wore mariachi hats and sat on piñatas while playing Charlie Daniels and the Marshall Tucker Band), we were approached by a huge Australian expatriate biker who simply couldn't figure us out. When I told him we were "biker/ anthropologists," he said, "Oh, I've heard of you guys" and proceeded to buy us a round of drinks. He told us that Montana was a lot like Australia used to be, "a place where a man can be free to do whatever the fuck he wants." His concept of freedom included everything from starting "a small wacko business" of your own to carrying any weapon you liked. When he invited us to the bathroom to see his handgun, we politely told him that it was time for us to move on.

Once while driving to Helena, we almost ran out of gas and had to stop in a town with a population of about 109. As we were filling the gas tank, we saw a wooden saloon complete with swinging doors, with a huge sign that read: "Indians and mountain men welcome." To us Californios, it looked like a movie set. We entered to find six drunks at the counter, four of them asleep on the bar. A hand-made sign with a racist drawing of a cowboy making love to a stereo-typical "squaw" stated that "The best affairs are Indian affairs." Roberto and I sat at the counter, while Tyler and Susan went to play video poker in the back. As we asked for coffee, each and every drunk at the bar straightened up and turned to look at us. A few had missing teeth. They each had a look in their eyes that suggested they wanted to kick our leather asses, if only they could manage to stand up. One of them stumbled toward the public phone. Roberto and I had an uneasy feeling. We loudly announced that we wanted the coffees "to go." Minutes later, we heard trucks pulling up.We paid the bill and walked out to find a couple of trucks in front of the saloon with Confederate flag license plates, racks of rifles, and tough-looking locals ready for trouble. We greeted them politely and made a great show of getting into our van, then got the hell out of town as fast as Rent-a-Wreck could carry us. These types of incidents never make it into our performances, but they certainly help us understand the perils and complexities of identity in a much more visceral way than, say, reading theroetical treatises by Edward Said or Gayatri Spivak.

✈ IV
Skinheads and Tropical Music in Helsinki

After the closing night of our performance in Helsinki, Roberto and I needed to party and exorcise the demons of extreme otherness and cultural misunder-standing. Virve, the director of the festival and her hospitable staff invited us to a nightclub which they claimed was the only place in Helsinki where it was possible to see locals intermingling with immigrants. (Finland has the smallest immigration rate of any country in Europe.) It was a wild scene. Every imaginable Finnish counter-cultural type was present: retro-punks and post-punks, skinheads, self-proclaimed anarchists, neohippy bohemians, flamboyant actors, urban Suomis and immigrants of color, mainly Arabs and Black Africans. African men and tall, blond Finnish girls were all over each other on the dance floor.

We hadn't even found a table before a heavy metalera approached me and (without even introducing herself) started to make out with me. I politely pushed her away, and tried to inquire about her perception of us. She told me in very broken English that she was from a provincial area in Northern Finland and that she "had a lot of Suomi blood," which I guess meant that she was kind of like a Finnish *mestiza*. She said that she had never seen sexy, exotic people like us, and that she imagined we were probably very good salsa dancers. Then in the middle of our conversation, she spoted another exotic-looking immigrant and took off. She clearly wasn't there to engage in a conversation on intercultural semiotics.

Another woman who looked like a Finnish "valley girl" asked Roberto to dance. I noticed a group of loud skinheads on the other side of the bar drinking and pointing at Roberto and the local chava, who were dancing terrible salsa and yu-yu. It looked like trouble. I walked up to Roberto and warned him to keep an eye on the skins. Two hours later, as we were leaving the bar, we found five skinheads waiting for us in the lobby. As we were getting our coats, one of them screamed something at us in Finnish. Roberto replied, "Sorry, but we don't speak Finnish." The skinhead got extremely close to Roberto, and screamed in his face in broken English: "You was dancing with our women, OUR women! This our country fuckheads! Go back to yours!" I looked around and saw the other skins, drunk out of their small minds and swelling muscles, laughing psychotically and preparing to jump us. Roberto was so silent and focused that I knew he was about to punch the screaming barbarian. I interceded (pronouncing my words slowly, almost didactically, so as not to leave any room for mis-un-ders-tan-ding): "Listen man, Finland isn't exactly Mexico's utopia. We like it very much, but you guys can keep your country for yourselves. In fact we are leaving in two days. For good!" One of the brutes said something in Finnish to his most aggressive friend, which I can only imagine was a directive to let us go in peace, since we were being reasonable. As we were leaving I turned around and told them: "See you *vatos* one of these days on our continent. We'll continue our dialogue over there."

➵ V
Dante in Montana

"The Oxford Lounge" in Missoula claims "they've never closed the door in 100 years," and one somehow believes them. The decor is puro Montana baroque, every inch of the walls decorated with animal heads, old guns, handwritten placas of "Western wisdom," naive paintings of famous local drunks, you name it. The place exudes the kind of theatrical ruggedness that European travelers love so much when they come to America. There is something almost religious about it, like Dante's nine circles of hell. First there's the restaurant section, where you can eat brains and eggs with lots of gravy while playing live keno. Then you come to "the back room," an Old West saloon where downtrodden locals (who seem like permanent fixtures) play cards in intense silence. The place becomes increasingly more tragic and interesting as you go down the hall. At the very back is a strip joint with "gorgeous cowgirls," famous for mistreating their less-than-sensitive clientele (the bullies seem to love it and keep coming back for more). It reminds me of performance art in the 80s, when white liberal audiences loved to be scolded by "angry artists of color."

One night, after a performance lecture, some local friends of ours invited Roberto and me to check out the strip-joint. When we arrived, the bouncer (a tough, biker-looking guy) told us it was too late for us to get in. Roberto insisted politely: "Man we've come from far away. Just let us watch the last dance." The guy grabbed Roberto by the shirt and pushed him away. We looked around; several smiling locals were ready for action. I was reminded of the Helsinki bar incident. We decided to go back to the first circle of hell to eat "brains and eggs." It was about midnight. Ten minutes later, as the bouncer was on his way out, he noticed the sequined horse on the back of my leather vest, and apologized to me effusively. He said he hadn't realized we were bikers. I told him that the *pedo* wasn't with me and sent him to apologize to Roberto. The bouncer went over to him and hugged him like a teddy bear. He apologized repeatedly, and told us that in fact his wife was the last performer, the one whose dance we had missed, and that he would gladly "arrange a night with her." Roberto told him that wouldn't be necessary. When the dancer came out, the exhuberant biker praised her talents as "the best stripper in Missoula" to a table of Latino performance artists and Missoula intellectuals. We, in turn, praised the hardcore "purity" of Montana biker culture and went on our way. What can I say. Americans are often "basic" people, and language can be a great survival strategy.

Crosscultural Sweating Ritual

At the Crow reservation, Roberto and I visited Tyler's brother, David Medicine-horse, the first Indian ever to become a County Sheriff in Montana. It was the first time we ever visited a "County Sheriff's Department" for purely social reasons – which is to say, without being handcuffed. A true border crosser, David is both a respectable law enforcement agent and a Sun Dance chief, a political leader and a trickster; thanks to him, the rez is protected on two fronts. Roberto and I took great photos, posing with David and his men. David invited everyone (including his Anglo "right arm," who referred to himself as "an honorary Indian") to a sweatlodge at his place.

The men went in first. Roberto and I were the last to enter. As the thick cloth of the sweatlodge closed behind us, we found ourselves in total darkness. Eight naked men, four generations, sweating and thanking the Great Spirit "for one more day of good life." They chanted in the mesmerizing Crow language and told hilarious Indian jokes. (Roberto and I chipped in some Mexican jokes, which luckily did translate.) I thought to myself "America, this other America, is still a good place to be." Later, while the men finished preparing the food, the women went to sweat. David showed Roberto and me his personal (shamanic) artifacts, which I won't describe out of respect, and his collection of flags, "one for every man from a different country who has sweated here with us." We still owe him two flags, a Mexican one, and one from the Farmworkers' movement.

The next morning, we all had breakfast at a 1950s style cafeteria just outside the rez that offers a huge stack of hotcakes piled 12 inches off the plate, a dozen eggs cooked any style, and sausage links or bacon by the pound, all for about $15. Montanans, like Mexicans, are excessive, and indigenous Montanans, also like Mexicans, are great hosts. It is no coincidence that over the years, Mexican migrant workers have found sanctuary on Crow and Blackfoot reservations; many ended up marrying indigenous women and staying. The process of Mexicanization on the rez has been thorough. In fact, one day when Tyler took us for "real Indian food" at a tiny store operated out of an old woman's kitchen, what they served us was a big bowl of menudo and a jar of very good green chile for the road. Yes, we were strangely at home in Montana.

VI
Another Crosscultural Sweating Ritual w/post Data

The day before our departure from Helsinki, a sweet man we had met through our producer invited Roberto and me to a "traditional Finnish bathhouse," located in an unpronounceable working-class hood. After taking off our clothes, we entered a huge steam room with seats at different levels, each one increasingly hotter. Around fifty nude men with sad faces and flaccid, aging bodies stared at us in an unexpressive way. At the highest level sat a skinny, androgynous-looking man in his late sixties with long white hair and hanging tits. Our new Finnish compadre informed us that he was "the king of the bathhouse" and came there every day. Mimicking the other men, Roberto and I grabbed some branches and repeatedly hit our bodies "to open up those pores." We engaged in a strange, repetitive ritual: leaving the steam room for a cold shower, then returning and hitting ourselves with the branches while the old men continued to stare blankly at our brown, tattooed bodies. The fourth time we entered the steam room, the old drag queen started winking at us; we couldn't help cracking up. Later, our host took us to a room with showers and tables and left us there. An old lady came in, took our towels, and started scrubbing our bodies with a raspy cloth. Since Mexican Catholic culture regards nudity as an extremely private act, it was a difficult experience for us to be naked in public, paritcularly in front of people we don't know, and most especially in front of a 70-year-old granny (being naked in a performance is another matter). The old lady didn't give a shit. She handled us as if we were objects or pets that needed to be cleaned, roughly but not impolitely. We then went with our Finnish friend to a lobby where more nude men sat smoking and drinking vodka. We downed two glasses of vodka, and returned to the steam room to repeat the entire strange ritual. By the time we left the bathhouse three hours later, we were high, dehydrated, and unusually happy.

The next stop was a working-class karaoke bar. When the costumers and MC learned that there were two Mexicans in the establishment we were invited to sing some Mexican songs (to say "invited" is euphemistic, since we had no opportunity to refuse). Everyone in the bar was cheering, and tall glasses of beer keep mysteriously arriving at our table. It was like an upside down version of the Leningrad cowboys touring the US. The "Mexican" songs we were supposed to sing were already chosen for us: first "Guantanamera" (which is actually Cuban), then "Cielito Lindo," and finally some Argentine tango. We faked most of the lyrics and danced like mambo stars to the exaggerated aplause of the cheering crowd. It was simply too much. The day we get that kind of audience response for a performance art piece, I'm gonna be ecstatic.

➤➤ VII
"The Smithsonian of the West"

On our way back from the Kootney/Salish reservation in Montana, my performance collaborators and I stopped at "The Miracle of America Musem, the
Smithsonian of the West," an immense roadside attraction created by the fears
and twisted imagination of one lonesome man. (Changing names to protect the
not-so-innocent, we'll call him Dr. Jim.) Every room offers an interpretation
of an aspect of "American culture," arranged in a mythical chronological order
created by the impresario and featuring "important movements" that had impact
on "American values" – or rather, on the bizarre curator's worldview. In Dr. Jim's
fictional timeline, if I remember correctly, an exhibit on "The Indians" stands as
a primeval point of origin, followed by the history of religion, race, then sports,
then the American revolution, ending with a display that praised capitalism
("good") as opposed to communism ("evil"). This vernacular museum is like
the mind of a mass murderer – twisted and encyclopedic, stuffed with all manner
of bizarrely juxtaposed objects. Each room is crammed full of dressed-up
mannequins, posters, figurines, mechanized toys, paintings, airplanes, tanks and
period cars, creating a deranged worldview that a performance artist can truly
appreciate.

Dr. Jim has collected most of his stuff in unethical ways. According to Tyler,
he lends money to poor farmers and Indian families, then confiscates their
belongings when they fail to repay the loan. Since we were the first people to
show up in weeks, Dr. Jim was particularly talkative. We shared an obsession
for collecting and exhibiting strange artifacts, though from diametrically opposed
positionalities. He seemed not to mind our "commie" views, and we cut him
some slack about his paranoid conspiracy theories. At one point, I asked him
to show us the most sensitive stuff in the collection, things he couldn't show to
"normal people." He giggled and told us to wait for his wife to leave the room.
"She doesn't like me making friends with strangers," he said. Minutes later when
she left, he brought out a Grand Dragon's robe with hand-embroidered lettering
stating "Montana KKK." He claimed to have found it accidentally while cleaning
the barn of a friend, and that it had probably belonged to a previous owner of
the barn. "I'm sure," Roberto replied. We told Dr. Jim about our performance
installation in Helena, and asked if we could borrow some objects. "Sure," he
answered, much to our surprise. "Just make an inventory of whatever you want,

and come pick 'em up a few days before the show." We invited Dr. Jim and his family to the opening.

Unusual Celebrations of Border Art away from the Border

Our last week in Montana was undoubtedly the most fun. Many friends arrived from out of town to participate in our two projects. Cheyenne performance artist Bentley Spang came from Wisconsin to perform the role of an "Indian anthropologist" in our living diorama. Producer Kim Chan, aka "La China Chola," flew from New York with Nuyorrican maestro Miguel Algarin, who had agreed to participate in "The Tribal Slam." The hybrid *flota* couldn't be stranger, nor could our social interactions with the place. On his first day in Helena, Miguel, a Nuyorrican elder from the Lower East Side who is unapologetic about his bisexuality, made connections with a Hutterite family, one of Montanas most unusual micro-communities. This sect of radical German Luddites has remained so thoroughly isolated since the seventeenth century that at one point a doctor suggested they bring in outsiders to fertilize the women in order to save the race. On another day, a group of neo-anarchist mountain men we had met at a bar invited us all to a "May pole ritual picnic" at a ranch an hour outside of Helena. To our ethnocentric surprise, most of them were intellectuals whose complex, anarchist critique of society drew on multiple sources: a biker philosophy of freedom, an Earth First type of militant environmentalism, and an emphatic support of Zapatismo and all indigenous causes in the Americas (which, in their eyes, included our particular brand of art). They lived on a "self sustaining" farm powered by solar energy, complete with a tennis court and sculpture garden. I told my friends as we drove away from the picnic that if what we had seen that day wasn't performance art, I wasn't Mexican.

Most of the people we had met on our travels through Montana showed up for the opening of the performance, along with their friends and relatives. The crowded Helena Museum looked like a combination of a high-art "Indian trading post" and a border rave, the gallery walls hung with nineteenth century Western paintings and twisted Monatanabilia. The performance "specimens" were displayed inside plexiglas boxes, Susan as "Hollywood Indian Princess Poke-your-haunches/AIM (American Indian Mother) Activist" and Tyler as a "cigar shop Indian." His taxonomic placard read "Pay-per-view holy man/FBI (Full-Blooded Indian) undercover agent Oosh-Baachewaa, a.k.a. Assberry."

By inserting coins in a slot, he could be activated to perform assorted tasks, including singing an Indian love song or chanting words of wisdom ($2.00), performing an Indian naming ritual ($5.00), or – for the wealthiest and most adventurous patrons – a weekend spiritual retreat at the Crow Reservation for only $1,500. Across from Tyler, Roberto posed as an "Indian lowrider," while I was a kind of Tex-Mex super-cowboy, allegedly "The Original Cowboy," a characterization that wasn't well received by some of the humorless locals.

In addition to the living dioramas, we displayed stuffed animals symbolic of the West (a grizzly bear, a puma, eagles, ducks, etc.) and excavation sites with objects from working-class Anglo Montanans and suburban California families, along with our bizarre collection of Montanabilia, contextualized by fictitious museum labels. While people circulated around the installation, Bentley measured the size of the skull and jaws of "the most peculiar-looking Anglo Montanans."

A few days later, at "the tribal slam," several Indian writers and drummers and a country & western singer jammed with the Latino *flota*. Roberto and I did some excerpts from *Borderama* and jammed with our Indian poet colleagues. Miguel read excerpts from the Turner Diaries[3] and the *Unabomer Manifesto*, interspersed with apocalyptic love poetry. Later that night, he received several death threats phoned to his motel. He couldn't care less. The man loves playing with fire, and he knew there was a lot of combustible material in Montana.

➤➤ VIII
The Last Night in Helsinki

Final scene: 2 a.m. in the freezing cold streets of Helsinki, Roberto and I waiting for a cab at a taxi stand, three people (all Finnish) ahead of us in line. Seventeen minutes later (we counted each and every one), it was finally our turn. A cabbie stopped, but took off as we moved toward the car. We signaled the next one to stop; he passed by without even looking at us. Another cab arrived, immediately speeding away when he got a look at us. By this point we realized what was going on, and started getting pissed at the Finnish cabbies.

When a taxi finally stopped, the driver got out and opened the door. As we approached, he told the Finnish lady behind us in line to hurry up and get in. She

---

3   Considered the Bible of the militia movement, this extreme right-wing novel chronicles an imaginary war between the US government and a group of white supremacists.

looked ashamed for a moment, but took his offer. After the seventh rejection, we were fuming. When the next cab drove past, we opened the door and jumped in before it had fully parked. The driver was taken by surprise. He panicked, as if we were about to mug him. We tried to explain (in English) that we were guests at an International Arts Festival, and that we only wanted to go back to Hotel Such-and-Such. We showed the cabbie a guest card from the hotel. He screamed at us in Finnish, probably telling us to get out of the cab, but this time we were determined to fight back. We kept reciting the name of our hotel and the words "tourists, tourists." He finally agreed to take us, cursing us in Finnish for the entire drive, Roberto and I cursing back in Spanglish. The whole incident reminded me of the way Chicanos had to break into the artworld, one art trend after another ignoring us until finally we decided to hijack a museum. It was our last night in Finland, a country that prides itself for being one of the most monocultural societies on earth.

That night, before going to sleep I wrote in my performance diary: "What do African-Americans in New York have in common with Pakistanis in London, Gypsies in Madrid, Turks in Frankfurt, and two Chicanos lost in Helsinki? Answer: A bittersweet relationship with taxi drivers, skinheads and cops."

As I reread the final draft, I confess to my inability to understand Finnish culture, and therefore to be able to consciously exoticize it in an interesting way. In my imagination, Finland is clearly a more superficial and "other" space than Montana. I don't have informants there capable of filtering back my memories. I am clearly a colonial anthropologist in reverse.

1999

Vladivostok: An Untranslatable Memory
Radio Chronicle

In July of 1990, I traveled to the Soviet Far East as part of a binational human rights commission involving "citizen diplomats" from San Diego and Tijuana. The objective was to exchange information with Soviet groups. It was the stormy year of perestroika, and we were one of the first "Western delegations" to visit the closed city of Vladivostok since the Stalin years. Unlike my colleagues, who presented either straight political data on human rights abuses at the US/Mexico border or decorative art objects as presents, I chose to present my politicized performance art.

I will never forget my first performance in Vladivostok, a true challenge in intercultural diplomacy. The event was to take place at the monumental Convention Center, which to my foreign eyes looked like a Mexican Olympic gym from the 70s. My Soviet hosts provided me with a room to rehearse, sour coffee, hard cookies, and two translators: a 65-year-old physicist who spoke Russian and "British English," and a 20-year-old woman who claimed to have been "Miss Vladivostok" two years before. She spoke Russian, of course, and a very peculiar Spanish "learned with the help of some 1940s records from Spain." Our only rehearsal consisted of a surreal trilingual discussion about what they perceived to be the content of my Spanglish monologue. After two hours, we finally decided on a strategy for translation: I would perform a five minute excerpt from my monologue and freeze, then my two involuntary border art "collaborators" would walk on stage and translate, or rather, attempt a translation. Then I would unfreeze and continue my monologue for five more minutes, then freeze again as the translators stepped on stage to continue translating . . . And so on and so forth. That's precisely what we did. So, a spoken word performance that normally took one hour ended up being three hours long. When my epic performance was finally over, no one knew it was the end. I probably bowed six times to signal the conclusion, but the audience didn't get it. Finally, my involuntary sidekicks came out (for the twentieth time) and applauded. Then, the 300 audience members, many of whom were part of the local political and intellectual elite, all stood up at once and applauded like crazy. Their applause went on forever, I swear. I was totally confused.

My next two performances, one at the local theater school and one at a "dissident" coffee shop, were not much different. After each performance, I experienced a combination of tenderness and embarrassment. I will never know exactly how well my attentive Russian audiences understood my Spanglish art, but they seemed very touched.

Before I left the ex-Soviet Union, I received two flattering offers of marriage – from my translators. The physicist invited me over for dinner. The menu consisted of fried Spam and sweet Hungarian wine. She made me finish the bottle by myself, and then offered me her 32-year-old daughter in marriage, an engineer working in Leningrad at the time. She showed me lots of snapshots and assured me repeatedly that her daughter "really loves Mexicans." Ex-Miss Vladivostok also wanted to marry me. After a function at an art school where I was invested with an "honorary Artists' Union card," she told me in her esperantic Spanish that "she would make a great wife in America." Neither one of them was truly interested in me, but in what I represented at the time: an Aeroflot ticket out of the USSR. Today, I wouldn't be surprised if my potential Russian brides were happily married somewhere in Hoboken, New Jersey, or Santa Monica, California. Of course, there's also the spooky possibility that they might be hooking in the streets of London, Amsterdam, or Berlin. Life in the post-Cold War era is both a dangerous trip and an untranslatable experience.

The "Psycho" in the Lobby of the Theater

(This slightly longer version of the New World Border *poem was rewritten for radio)*

I'm rehearsing at a theater somewhere in the midwest. This psychotic-looking man in a wrinkled suit has been waiting for me in the lobby since 10 a.m. The teckies are flipping out and can't concentrate on the rehearsal. They tell me that the psycho's got a mysterious Samsonite briefcase on his lap. It's spooky! I tend to attract all kinds of locos. But since I've learned that the best way to deal with them is through poetic confrontation, I take a deep breath, go to the lobby and approach him with my full intensity:

"Are you waiting for someone sir?" He looks at me in silence.

"Waiting, merely waiting eh? Waiting for what exactly?" He doesn't answer me.

"Waiting for the economy to improve?" Silence.

"Waiting for your children to leave home and for all the immigrants to leave your country? Waiting for god to come back from India or speak to you on Cable TV? Waiting for the next hysterical talk show to address your most sincere concerns?" He still does not answer. I get increasingly exasperated.

"Waiting for the next bestseller on how to improve the quality of your loneliness? It's lonely out there, que no?" Total silence.

"Come on, you gotta answer me! What are you fuckin' waiting for?! Waiting for the next cheap vacation to Mazatlan? For more vouchers and coupons? For a random bullet perhaps? Waiting insomniac in your underwear to hear from your drinking buddies, while you pick another fight with your desperate wife?" By now, I am totally worked up.

"Come on, answer me!!" Incommensurable silence.

"No Mister, it's pointless to keep waiting. This is the year of the barking dog . . . and I'm afraid your fears are much bigger than your wishes." He finally stands up; his eyes wide open like a fish. I shake his hand.

"You might be wondering who the hell I am?" The man is visibly scared and still unable to reply or comment on my monologue.

"I am your worst fear, caballero; an unpredictable Mexican with a huge mustache, three chips on my shoulder and extra-hot sauce on my cobra tongue." I begin to bark. He finally breaks his silence:

"It's, it's a pleasure to meet you. My name is Mario López. I just came to fix the Xerox machine."

I go back to rehearsal feeling utterly embarrassed. That night I tell the story to my audience. They crack up. The hapless victim of my poetic chamber of tortures, Mr. López himself, is sitting right in the front row. I feel like killing myself. I truly do.

Deported to the North

(An earlier version of this text was published in my book New World Border *under the title "The Artist as Criminal." Though this version hasn't been significantly rewritten, I felt it was absolutely necessary to include it in this book, because of the new meanings it takes on in this context. The original version was translated by Christopher Winks.)*

I remember that cold afternoon in Buenos Aires vividly. It was mid-August 1993, and my colleague Coco Fusco and I were performing a version of our project, *The Guatinaui World Tour*, right on the corner of Callao and Corrientes, one of the busiest intersections in the city. As part of our performance projects subverting pseudo-ethnographic exhibitions of humans and the colonial format of the "living diorama," we spent three days inside a gilded cage displaying ourselves as "exotic primitives" from a fictitious island in the Gulf of Mexico. On the second day, suddenly, from within the crowd , a mysterious character in a black trenchcoat approached me, threw some kind of liquid at me, then vanished. Seconds later, I realized I had been the victim of a physical assault. My stomach and legs had been burned with acid.

One of the theories circulating in the Buenos Aires artistic community was that this attack involved a political misunderstanding. There was speculation that the assailant was an ex-military man who felt implicated by our performance, probably because he believed that our project was a direct commentary on Argentine military culture, which jailed thousands of youths before the alleged democratic transition of 1987. It makes sense.

For politicized artists experimenting with the tenuous and ever-fluctuating frontiers between art and life, real danger is always present, especially when the art event takes place outside the protected space of cultural institutions. It's one thing to carry out iconoclastic actions in a theater or museum for a public predisposed to tolerate radical behavior; it's quite another matter to bring the same work into the street, where it will be exposed to unpredictable social and political forces. In the street, the artist faces far greater risks. Some are obvious, such as the danger of confronting the intolerance of police, and in certain countries, extremist groups or the military. Others are more random, like a surprise encounter with a lunatic who happens to cross your path. Performance artists are well aware of these risks, but every now and then we don't accurately gauge the volatility generated by the combination of the context in which we choose to perform and the symbolic weight of our actions. Then, as we say in Mexico, "the devil shows up."

In mid-July 1994, I received a disturbing telephone call. The artist Hugo Sánchez (who shares his name with a Mexican soccer star), a native of Ciudad Obregón, Sonora, and long-time resident of Tijuana, had just been deported to – not from – the city of San Diego, California, for "desecrating the Mexican flag" in a performance. The newspapers, including the infamous Mexican tabloid *El Alarma*, published incendiary photos and headlines portraying the *norteño* artist as a psychopath.

The facts, hallucinatory as they may seem, are the following:

On July 11, Hugo Sánchez arrived in Tijuana to participate in the filming of "Fronterilandia," co-directed by Rubén Ortiz (from Mexico) and Jesse Lerner (from the US), and sponsored by the Fundación Cultural Mexicana (Mexican Cultural Foundation). The film-makers describe the work as "an experimental chronicle, half documentary and half poetic essay, of the mythical perceptions which both sides of the border have about each other."

The directors planned to shoot a performance by Sánchez, using the streets of Tijuana as a backdrop. The portion of the work to be filmed focused on the topic of migration. The hybrid persona played by Sánchez was an "undocu-mented Zapatista/*charro* (cowboy)," decked out in a mariachi sombrero à la "Tj curio-style," a ski-mask, a flag wrapped around his chest, with a cow's head, representing (in the artist's words) "the pain of the immigrants who cross the border daily, and who are sacrificed like animals by an inhuman work/police system."

Filming began early on July 12. The crew consisted only of a cameraman, a photographer, and a sound technician. The two opening scenes were filmed without mishap, the first in front of a strange edifice known as the "Wadah," in the shape of an Ionic column, and the second next to the Monument to the Freedom of Expression – a curious foreshadowing of what was to come. After these sequences were filmed, the group made its way over to the Monument to the Textbook (located in front of the Lázaro Cárdenas School). The crew prepared to shoot a scene in which Hugo was to insert nails into the cow's tongue (which came out of his mouth, appearing to be his own tongue) as a commentary on "the pain engendered by the linguistic misunderstandings between races and countries." Lights, camera, action. Suddenly, Ricardo Luna and Jorge Nava, two agents from the Municipal Police, appeared. The filmmakers showed them a letter from the Binational Foundation, one of the sponsors of the film, explaining that it was "a cultural project, not a political action." A long discussion ensued. The policemen lost their patience and their sense of humor, and decided to arrest Hugo Sánchez under suspicion of "disrespect for the flag." Numerous patrol cars arrived and all hell broke loose.

Since Hugo was being charged with a federal offense, he was immediately transferred to the office of the Federal Prosecutor (PGR). Tabloid photographers surrounded the "Zapatista cowboy" and captured his rage and confusion – flash, click, *Alarma* style. Eagerly, they took close-ups of the cow's head and of the sacrosanct "bloodstained" flag. Subsequently, the police transferred the performance artist to a clinic for drug addicts and people with psychological disorders. Fortunately, after a meticulous examination, the doctor declared that the artist was "neither a drug addict, nor mentally-ill." Upon being returned to the cells of the PGR, Hugo was subjected to a full-body search amidst the constant insults of the law-enforcement officers. As a protest, he decided to go on a hunger strike.

The deputies found a United States passport in the artist's clothes. Hugo explained that although he was born and had always lived on Mexican territory, his mother made him a nationalized North American when he was young, just like millions of other border Mexicans. The officials confiscated Hugo's passport, and decided he was Chicano (a US born Mexican), not a Mexican.

On July 13, through the desperate efforts of Hugo's friends, various organizations got wind of the situation. Representatives of the National Committee of Human Rights, the *Casa de la Cultura de Tijuana*, and the Tijuana Cultural Center began to pressure the PGR for Hugo's release. Also on that day, the artist had to present his version of events before legislator Socorro López. Hugo contended that he never had any intention of desecrating the flag, and that, paradoxically, the performance had been conceived as "a patriotic gesture of symbolic defense of the Mexican immigrants who daily risk their lives crossing the dangerous border." Ms. López burst out laughing.

The PGR authorities got in touch with agents from Mexican immigration, and together they decided that the artist (who has devoted much of his life to defending undocumented workers) was "illegally" dwelling in Mexico (his native land). Hugo's risks were multiplying. As he was considered a "foreigner," the insult to the flag would have more serious consequences for him than it would for someone recognized as a Mexican citizen. He was alerted to the real possibility of becoming "persona non grata" under Article 33 of the Mexican Constitution, which would forbid him from ever setting foot in Mexican territory again. He was transferred to the sinister prison known as "la ocho" (Number Eight), where they locked him up with other "foreigners." His deportation proceedings began.

On the morning of July 14, a (Hispanic) representative from the US Consulate visited Hugo Sánchez in his cell. Hugo was told not to worry, that soon he would return to his country. Hugo tried to explain that "his country" was Mexico, and it was there that he wished to remain. The consular envoy didn't get it.

On July 15, accompanied by an agent from Mexican immigration and a deputy, Hugo was transferred to the Customs Office of the City of Tijuana. There, he was required to pay a fine for being a foreigner and acting in a Mexican film without being in possession of the appropriate permits. Fortunately, a curator from the Tijuana Cultural Center telephoned the agents and convinced them not to fine the artist, arguing that "people don't make money doing this type of art (performance)."

Hours later, Hugo was finally handed over to the US Immigration and Naturalization Service authorities. "*Maestro*," Hugo told me, "for the first time in my life, the *migra* [the US border patrol] gave me a hero's welcome. They even gave me lunch money. It's like I just walked into a mirror where reality's turned upside-down."

Later, on the very day of his deportation, the exhausted and humiliated artist decided to return to Tijuana "illegally" and confront the Mexican authorities. He went to District Court No. 7 to inquire about his case and the whereabouts of his passport. He was told that the judge was on vacation. An employee who had read about the "case of the lunatic" in the newspaper, assured him that he would receive a summons to appear in court, and warned him that he should be prepared to receive, according to the judge's discretion, either four years in prison (in Mexico) or permanent deportation.

As befits the hair-raising paradox of this binational thriller, Hugo's first court appereence was set for September 18, two days after the celebration of the Mexican Declaration (*Grito*) of Independence. When September came, he was notified of a change of date; this time he was set to appear in court on October 11, one day before the alleged "discovery of America," which is known in Mexico as *Día de la Raza* (birth of the mestizo race). A few days later, Hugo's court date was postponed indefinitely. Desperate and penniless, Hugo decided to cross the border and await the new date in his (fictitious) country of origin. Mexico, his true country, had been transformed into a juridical nightmare out of a Chicano Secret Service *pochonovela*.

Hugo Sánchez's case is unique: a Mexican deported to the United States for doing a performance. Why? Perhaps it had to do with the politically charged context and time. It was indeed an extremely tense period in Tijuana: the recent assassinations of the ruling-party's presidential candidate, Luis Donaldo Colosio, and of Tijuana's Chief of Police Benítez had created a pervasive climate of melancholy, mistrust, and fear that affected everyone. Perhaps it was the timing of the incident, one month before the Mexican elections scheduled for August 21, which the opposition party had a real possibility of winning (Tijuana was in the hands of the right-wing opposition at that time). But other, inescapable, extra-contextual factors are also part of the picture. The intolerance of the police for alternative culture and the heavy restrictions on freedom of expression in Mexico definitely contributed to Sánchez's Kafkaesque nightmare. Sadly, in an authoritarian society (even one that so desperately wants to be seen as the eternal protagonist of a transition to democracy), the borders between art and illegality are becoming increasingly thin.

In a letter of support for the Mexican artist, the Chicano artist and writer Rubén Guevara wrote: "Hugo Sánchez's performance was as 'offensive' as the social conditions that inspired it. The artist is nothing if not a catalyst of social and cultural forces, and his work is a stylized reflection of reality . . . The shameful judgment passed on Sánchez is a test of the new government's (Zedillo's) democratic image . . . The test consists precisely in allowing *any* cultural gesture, however radical or strange it may seem, to be not just tolerated, but respected."

Thanks to media pressure (including publication of this essay in Mexico's national daily newspaper, *La Jornada*), the judge decided to dismiss Hugo's case in December. The passport disappeared mysteriously from the Mexicali archives. (Maybe now there is a third "Hugo Sánchez" wandering the streets of San Diego, Los Angeles, or San Francisco.)

The challenge for performer Hugo Sánchez now is to overcome his fear of using the street as a laboratory for artistic creation, and to recover his fragile and bruised Mexican identity. As for me, only a scar on my right leg remains as a sinister memory of the dangers involved in doing performance in the 1990s.

LOS ANGELES, 1994

"One Nude Woman, Thirteen Roaches and No Arrests"
Radio Chronicle

My dear friend Miya Masaoka is a terrific experimental composer and performance artist based in San Francisco. She blends Japanese traditions with Electro-acoustic music, computer art, and performance. As I describe what she does, I suddenly realize how hip and harmless it sounds. However, this Japanese American artist has had some serious run ins with the millennial guardians of morality and high art. The following incident took place at the University of Riverside, California on 11 April 1977:

The music department invited Miya to perform a multimedia piece in which she asked the audience, in her own words, " to reconsider pre-conceived notions of gender, eroticism and ethnicity." The performance featured Miya lying naked on a table with thirteen hissing Madagascar cockroaches crawling slowly over her motionless body. Through computer manipulation, the sound of the roaches was mixed with those of a dissonant koto, the traditional Japanese instrument, modified by Miya. A video projected on a large screen showed close-ups of the gigantic insects, which resembled pre-historic creatures. The piece was hypnotic and quite poetical.

The press releases went out describing the piece, and all hell broke loose. A barrage of angry phone calls and faxes protesting the performance began to pour in to the office of the music department. Daily letters of complaint were published by the local paper. Some protested the nudity, while others objected to the participation of the cockroaches. The common denominator was the word "immoral." One letter stated: "I was a physics professor at this university and am appalled that such an institution is inviting Miss Masaoka to perform with *her insects*. The cockroaches should not be allowed to perform!" Another letter remarked: "The university has gone too far. Have we no morals?" A letter to the editor in the *Press Enterprise* stated, "This is not acceptable education. This is sick, sick, sick!!"

As opening night got closer, the protesters became more defiant, and a group of "concerned citizens" threatened to picket the event. The troubled faculty notified Miya of the ever-growing scandal, but she insisted on going ahead with the project. After a long debate about the possible political or financial repercussions of the protest (most institutions in the 90s were afraid of losing funding because of scandals created by performance art), the brave faculty felt confident that they were within their legal rights to present the performance, and everything proceeded as planned.

On the night of the performance, several policemen were stationed outside the recital hall. Flyers posted on the entrance warned "those offended by nudity not to enter." Nonetheless, the protesters did enter the theater, and seated themselves in the front rows. The place was packed with people standing in the aisles. Everyone, including Miya, was expecting trouble. The performance began in an atmosphere of extreme tension. The protesters refused to clap during the first part of the program, in which Miya, still fully clothed, played the koto virtuously. Before the much-awaited fifteen minute-long "controversial" section, a faculty member walked on stage and instructed the audience to be "quiet, non-disruptive and respectful." The piece began. No one jumped on stage and tried to break the hypnotic trance with a spontaneous arrest. Coitus interruptus. To everyone's disappointment, the piece went on without a problem. As people were leaving, they had the option of either buying a CD of Miya's music for $12, or purchasing one of her collaborating hissing roaches for only $10.

The next day, on the front page of the *Press Enterprise* was the headline: "ONE NUDE WOMAN, 13 ROACHES AND NO ARRESTS." The article concluded, "The piece was neither shocking nor titillating." Sadly, incidents like Miya's unnecessary nightmare are becoming more frequent in the US. Why? Are Americans becoming more parochial and scared? Or are they simply bored and unable to find more pertinent issues to worry about? My theory is that "citizen action" in the 90s has become a weekend sport, a way to meet people and add some excitement to one's life. And performance artists are fair game.

On Censorship

(Different versions of this piece have been presented live, on radio and video.)

Dear reader/dear listener:

Imagine a US of A controlled by far right, Christian fundamentalists. They believe that "the liberal media" and experimental art have thoroughly destroyed our social fabric, our moral and family values, and they are determined to restore them at any cost. As part of their great project of "moral restoration," they have decided to scrutinize carefully everything that is broadcast on radio and TV or said in printed journalism, including this very ■■■. So, from ■■■ to sit coms, and from news ■■■ to ■■■ programming, they have digital censors which can detect key words that trigger ideological or cultural difference. Since it is practically impossible to monitor everything, they have devised a mechanism via which ■■■ the syntactic and conceptual coherence of a thought is ■■■, especially when dealing with conflicting opin■■■. So, when it comes to, say, sexuality, most explicit words have been ■■■. And I mean, just words, such as ■■■ or ■■■. In politics, things are not that different. In order to ensure that "ideologically tende■■■ information" does not pollute the minds of true American patriots like you, they have ■■■■■■ forbidding the use of terminology like ■■■ or co■■■ or even a term like ■■■. In a world such as this, content would be restricted to ■■■ and the possibility to make intelligent civic choices would limit our funda■■■ to ■■■■■■. Imagine what kind of a world this would be.

22 Benny, crippled in a gang fight, with Savage Nomads' Colors. Puerto Rican Diaspora
Documentary Project.

"I make art about the ongoing misunderstandings that take place in the border zone. But to me, the border is no longer located in a geopolitical site. I carry the border wherever I go. I also find new borders wherever I go. In fact, there is a border right now. Can you feel it?"

FROM THE FILM *BORDERSTASIS*, 1998

Communities in Despair
Border Pulp Stories

The Larger Context, in a Nutshell

In late 1997, using one of my most abrasive, activist voices, I wrote:

A war has been declared against US communities "of color," particularly Latinos. Since the "backlash era" began (1994), we have been portrayed by nativist politicians and the mainstream media as the primary source of America's current social ills and financial tribulations, and treated accordingly. The main strikes thus far have been camouflaged as "legislation." The social and psychological effects of California Propositions 187 and 209, and of the (anti) immigration law of last April 2nd (1997), have been devastating. Our parents, aunts, and uncles are losing their already insufficient and precarious medical benefits. Our friends are getting fired for speaking Spanish in the workplace. Newly arrived immigrants trying to escape the side effects of Mexico's dramatically increased militarization and the economic fallout of the sudden implementation of a free market economy are getting deported without any possibility of appeal.

The criminalization and further disempowerment of Latino youth appears to be a deliberate political maneuver played out on multiple fronts. Our young men have been (indirectly) armed by the very same government that subsequently incarcerates them; the US political class loves to blame and punish its own victims. Misplacing their anger,

Latino "gangs" continue killing each other. Cops and politicians witness this internal massacre with a complicitous delight. We are doing the job for them. We all are doing the job for them . . .

The drama unfolds in other territories as well. Latino students are having a much harder time entering and/or remaining in the univerisity system. In California, since the anti-affirmative action Proposition 209 came into effect, the population of Latino students has decreased by 40 per cent. Our communites are ferociously divided by class, race, gender, country of origin, age, and metier; this is true even among the intelligentsia. The relations between academicians, artists, and activists are marked by distrust and indifference. We all suffer from a serious lack of enlightened leadership, and if this weren't enough, our cultural institutions are sinking for lack of funding . . .

Now, the Untold Story

In the absence of political mechanisms and cultural platforms to articulate and cope with the unprecedented crisis threatening Latinos at the close of the millennium, our "ethnic" and "professional" communities end up internalizing these attacks and misplacing our rage. Our confusion and feelings of helplessness lead us to strike against our beloved ones, our own kind: other Latinos and other equally victimized groups, who in turn do exactly the same to us. This internal warfare ends up contributing to the further disenfranchisement and fragmentation of our respective communities, unraveling the bonds that ought to unite us. And no one is willing to talk about it. Why?

I can only speculate. There seems to be an acute crisis of communication in America. As a result of the bloody "cultural wars" (1987-1994), the terrain of public debate is riddled with landmines, and the language and terms of identity politics have come to be seen as dangerous, punishing weapons. As a result, we have lost our ability to discuss, rather than merely to declare, the nature of our conflicts. In other words, in the absence of a clear and generous language first to articulate and then publicly to discuss the myriad schisms, ruptures, wounds and misunderstandings afflicting our communites, institutions and families, we find ourselves in a stalemate, lost in an endless semantic labyrinth.

What I wish to do in the following stories is to begin articulating the unspeakable – that which never gets talked about openly, and only surfaces in bar conversations, gossip, and the closed-door conversations of private cabals. I have chosen to tackle the subject anecdotally to ensure that I can be as specific as possible. To avoid gossip, I will only describe incidents in which I or my immediate colleagues have been active participants, and events that I judge to be emblematic of larger issues. I will avoid naming the not-so-innocent individuals and institutions implicated in these narratives in order to focus attention on the complexities and true dimensions of the actual phenomena. This text does not offer any solutions; I am fully aware that possible solutions can only be actualized through collective effort, and that all affected communities must take part in this process.

Dear reader, breathe in . . . let's open the can of worms.

1 The Chicano Inquisition

Sunday, 4 pm, Chicano Studies Conference Room, University of Wisconsin – Madison. Roberto Sifuentes, Sara Shelton-Mann and I have postponed our trip back to California, as the students and faculty of the Chicano Studies department have invited us to a *tamalada* "to informally discuss some internal matters within *la comunidad.*" We've just finished an intense one-week residency that included a poetry reading; a town meeting; dinners and discussions with faculty, students and local activists; and two performances of a new project titled *BORDERscape 2000*, the second added at the last minute to accommodate the many Chicanos who didn't get tickets to the performance before it sold out.

My performance collaborators and I are a bit hung over and have had far too little sleep for longer than we'd like to remember. As we enter the conference room, our non-Chicano colleagues (Sara and our local producer, both of whom are Anglo-American) get stopped at the door by a self-identified "Chicano veteran" who informs them that only Chicanos are allowed to enter. Instead of the "informal" gathering we had been promised, Roberto and I suddenly find ourselves facing an academic Board of Inquisitors: a handful of sombre professors and thirty or forty nervous students who wait in tense silence. The tamales are missing. The coffee is cold. The interrogation begins:

"Gómez-Peña: You're Mexican, right? Why did you suddenly decide to make Chicano art? To get more grant money? Or because it's cool?"

I spill my cold coffee on the table. I do everything I can to keep my composure. "I am a Mexican in process of Chicanization," I reply, "and I make art and write about that very process. I've been doing it for almost twenty years."

Next question: "What do you vatos really do for la *comunidad*?"

Answer: "We tour the Southwest regularly and perform at least 50 per cent of the time in Latino/Chicano/Indigenous institutions. Many of these performances are fundraisers and benefits. We are doing our part, believe me . . . And you?" No response.

At first I think this is just an aggressive way of starting a juicy political conversation – after all US academics aren't exactly known for their tact or politeness. But the questions keep getting increasingly more vicious and personal.

A graduate student asks what we are doing working with a white woman, referring to our dear collaborator who was not allowed into the room. "Because Sara Shelton-Mann is one of the most amazing choreographers and performers we've ever seen. We've been working with her for almost three years. Our aesthetics are totally compatible. Besides, what's the big deal?"

"Don't you think that there are equally good Chicana artists out there?"

"True, we also work with many great Chicana artists in other projects. But the piece we are currently touring is in fact a collaboration with Sara."

Long silence. The next question comes out of left field: "How do you feel about black and Chicano male role models going out with white women, like O.J.?" In the spirit of the question, our answer is flippant and superficial: "Hey, love is blind, que no?"

We have clearly found ourselves in the middle of a battle that has nothing to do with us or with our work. At one point, I excuse myself to go to the bathroom, and swallow my rage at having to show my identity papers to provincial scholars who seriously need a sabbatical to go check out the world outside of their ivory towers.

Roberto is now alone facing the Grand Jury, and a Chicana scholar throws the mortal stone at him: "Roberto, you were seen leaving the dinner party we threw for you guys with...a gringa! In fact, you spent that whole dinner talking to her, and ignored all the Chicana sisters. We tried to kick her out of the party, but she refused to leave." Pause. "Did you sleep with her that night?" Pause. "What kind of role model are you?" I return to the conference room just at the moment that Roberto, visibly disturbed but desperately trying to keep his cool, is explaining to the sister that her question is completely out of line. He also reminds her that her own lover, whom we had met at the same party, is also a white woman. "That's different," she yells back. I try to lighten the air by joking: "Hey, the crux of interracial relations is desire, que no?" I only make things worse.

The essentialist lynching ritual goes on for two more hours. We actually have to re-schedule our flight a second time. During all of this, our "white" colleagues wait for us in the parking lot, unaware of what is happening. Roberto and I finally escape from the room, dragging our wounded psyches and bruised souls. When we finally meet up with our friends in the parking lot, two Chicanas still have the nerve to confront Sara. "You bitch, what business do you have working with *our* men?" one of them snaps at her. "Nothing personal, honey," the more conciliatory of the two women adds. "We're sure you're very nice, but there are plenty of Chicana choreographers out there." Sara is dumbfounded, completely unable to answer.

We fly back to San Francisco with daggers embedded in our chests, Sara crying discreetly. We had become an easy target for a dysfunctional and isolated academic community to vent its own interpersonal problems and recite its naive and reductive essentialist dogma. We were completely unprepared to deal with the virulent neo-nationalism of the 90s, which clearly thrives on certain university campuses where some of the "old guard" faculty – members of the first generation of Chicano/a scholars, who have either ignored or failed to comprehend the subtler nuances of post-colonial theories of identity – indoctrinate wide-eyed students.

A week later, a friend from Wisconsin phones to tell us that before we had even arrived at UW–Madison, a Chicano professor (one of the participants in the lynching) had tried to lead a boycott of our performance, but the students who attended our initial talks were turned on by the fact that our images and ideas spoke to them in a more direct way than the dated nationalist jargon they were getting from the professor. The success of the performance also engendered serious resentment from other faculty who felt we were challenging their academic notions of Chicanismo. We didn't even know who they were, or what were they teaching . . . It's so fucking sad.

2 The Take Over of the Santa Fe Museum of Art

Spring 1994, Santa Fe, New Mexico. Roberto and I are scheduled to perform "New World Border" at the Santa Fe Museum of Art in the majestic Saint Francis auditorium, which looks like a colonial church. Two weeks before our arrival, we begin to receive lots of faxes and UPS packages from an artist/activist we've never met (we'll call him "Wolf" in our story), who wants to make us aware of the extremely thin ice we're about to step on. According to Wolf, the place where we're getting ready to perform "only presents Classical European recitals and high art stuff," and we will be "the first Chicano/Latino performance artists ever to perform there," in a city with a strong Mexican and indigenous history, majority population, and "official" cultural identity. This was clearly a symptom of a much broader and more serious problem. Thousands of wealthy, burnt out Europeans and transplanted yuppies from the East and West Coasts were moving in, displacing the previous Mexican and indigenous residents, and turning Santa Fe into "Santa Fake," a theme park of Indian and New Mexican culture (without Indians or Mexicans, of course). The museum was perceived as complicitous in this process as a result of its Eurocentric curatorial choices and its history of presenting only "apolitical, high art [. . .] the cultural version of gentrification," according to Wolf.

From the moment Roberto and I get to town, we know that we've landed in a mine field. We ask the authorities of the museum whether they are aware of how certain sectors of the artistic community perceive them; they tell us not to pay attention to "the angry local artists" who are "just looking for trouble and unmerited visibility." During the first days of our visit and under the guidance of Wolf, Roberto and I meet secretly with local activists working on various fronts: land rights, housing, police brutality, and environmental racism. What they really want from us is to offer them a platform within our performance to talk back to a perceived power elite, and our reputation as "political artists" gives us no other option but to accept the challenge. Our dilemma is truly thorny: we sympathize with the plight of our new activist friends, but at the same time we don't want to cause problems for the independent producer who brought us to town (the museum is merely hosting the project). Besides, we worry that it would be arrogant for us as total outsiders to believe we have the right to intervene in local politics in such a dramatic way, especially since we won't be the ones around to deal with the fallout. After a long discussion, Roberto and I decide that all we can do is to take on the role of performance brokers and animateurs of debate.

We devise the following plan: first, our new activist friends should make sure that the various local activist communities of color will show up at our performance; we tell them that we'll try to get as many comps as possible for special guests who can't afford the admission. We decide that for our performance, we'll "segregate" the audience according to historical criteria and allow them into the theatre in groups: first the indigenous people, then the Mexicans, then the "hispanos" and finally all the "remaining others." Our intention is to whimsically invert the social hierarchy of the city and make the indigenous New Mexicans feel truly welcome. Once the performance was over, we decide that instead of our usual question and answer with the audience, we'll have an open mic so that community members would be able to give testimony on various issues. We know it's risky, but it feels like the right thing to do. And we decide not to tell the museum authorities anything about our plan.

Opening night arrives, and the lobby is packed with "people of color." The chief curator is happily nervous. "All these people we've never seen here! You guys must be popular." The segregation process proceeds as planned, and so does the performance. We comment on the ecclesiastic environment by staging our piece as a "border mass." At the end of the piece, we invite people to use the open mic. One by one, they step up to the microphone to present their testimony about the dark side of Santa Fe – elders and activists, Indian and Chicano artists, the mother of a child gunned down by the cops. We watch as the lid of Pandora's box springs open, and all the colonial ghosts start flying around in the auditorium. Everyone is succinct, respectful and direct. Some people cry. The impromptu town meeting goes on for about two hours.

The museum had arranged a reception for Roberto and me after the opening. We politely tell the museum staff that we want these venerable members of the community to attend, and that there's a great norteño (Northern Mexican) band willing to play at the reception. They reluctantly accept. We take over the whole second floor of the museum – a wonderful group of working-class Indians and Mexicans, most of whom have never set foot in the building before. The band plays farmworker corridos and Chicano oldies; everyone dances, including the museum staff. By midnight, the security guards throw everyone out. We continue the party at a local bookstore owned by a friend, then later in our hotel room, until the people at the front desk call to tell us that guests are complaining about the "rowdy Mexican fiesta" in room 332.

The next morning when Roberto and I go to the museum, we're sure that the staff is going to be furious at us. But they aren't. Instead, they seem a little confused and, we can tell in their faces, secretly excited. They had experienced for an evening what it means to be a true center for contemporary art. (Postscript, five years later: Those were the final golden days of multiculturalism, when we all still felt it was possible to create a more inclusive art world. Needless to say, Roberto and I were never invited back.)

3 The Spy Movie of US/Mexico Relations

Summer 1997, Denver, Colorado. I've been invited to curate a performance art festival as part of a larger "salute to Mexico" organized by the city of Denver in conjuction with the Cherry Creek Arts Festival, a three-day event attended by more than 100,000 people. Since I wholeheartedly believe that performance must engage with popular audiences rather than speaking only to a so-called cultural elite, I gladly accepted the challenge. Roberto and I arrive in the city with a wild *flota* of artists from Mexico City and California. Our intention in these performances is to portray a different Mexico, a nation in permanent crisis and flux, which does not stop at the US border; consequently, our working group makes no distinction between "Mexican" and "Chicano" artists.

The new Mexican consul in town, a not-so-diplomatic freetrader with little experience in the border wars, decides publicly to disassociate himself from our project. When interviewed by the *Denver Post*, he asserts that the Mexican consulate was never consulted about the choice of artists, and that we "by no means represent" Mexico's national character. It's no big deal. I'm used to this new generation of "neoliberal" diplomats, who are tactless and politically clumsy, unlike the intellectuals appointed as consuls and ambassadors by Mexican Presidents up to the time of Miguel de la Madrid. At a dinner party, the consul tells a friend of mine from the Arts Council that I am considered "persona non-grata," and that another participant in the festival (rockero Guillermo Briseño, a member of a citizen group brokering between the Zapatistas and the government) is a "terrorist sympathizer." My friend replies to the consul that these are serious accusations, attempting unsuccesfully to defend my reputation to the novice politician by reminding him that I have been awarded both a MacArthur Fellowship and an American Book Award. The diplomat is reportedly unimpressed.

The festival begins. My colleagues and I perform in open tents on the crowded streets of Cherry Creek for five hours each day. Our performance area is surrounded by crafts stalls, food and beer stands, games, and all manner of Southwestern regalia. The tents to some extent camouflage our respective performance areas, so that we'll better blend in with the carnivalesque spirit of the overall event. Despite the sensitive content of the material, the performances are fun and participatory, and the audience is enthusiastically responsive, with sometimes as many as 500 people at a time crammed in front of our small tents in the 95 degree heat. Roberto and I are at the entrance of a street featuring "international artists" – mainly painters and craftspeople, with a dozen performance artists. A fake Pre-Columbian arch with a banner that reads "AT&T Presents a Salute to Mexico" frames the entrance of the street, and a plaster replica of an Olmec head sits in the middle of an intersection right in front of our performance space. We couldn't possibly have designed a more appropriate (or more ironic) set.

On the second day of our performance, right in the middle of the piece, a distinguished-looking Mexican man in his late forties approaches Roberto, screaming at him with a typical Mexico City accent: "Baboso! Imbecile! You are not even Mexican, hijo de la chingada!! Your performance is ludicrous!" He then walks toward me, but I welcome him with a pseudo-shamanic scream in fake Nahuatl. He walks away, scared, which I regard as a small performance victory. The audience applauds as if the conflict was staged. One hour later, Roberto and I, still performing, are suddenly surrounded by cops and security agents from the festival. Since we are in performace mode, we can't stop to ask what's happening. After the show we tell the festival staff about the incident with the angry man. They seem unsurprised. Only much later do we find out that soon after the incident, a death threat was phoned in to the organizers of the festival, who decided to call the cops for our protection. They chose not to tell us anything about the phone call, nor do they say anything when more threats are received later that night.

On the final morning of the festival, we begin our performance surrounded by a semi-circle of Denver policemen in full riot gear. They seem to be there to protect us from something or someone. Their presence adds drama to the event, and makes for a deliciously ironic backdrop to the performance, intensifying the paradoxical relation of performance and social reality. As the policemen look behind them to see what exactly it is they're protecting, they discover Roberto as CyberVato beating himself in slow-motion with a police baton, while I, El Mexterminator, point a fake uzi at the crowd. We can read in the faces of the cops their ambivalence at having to protect a "holy gang member" and a "jalapeño pusher."

Later on at the hotel cafeteria, while exchanging performance anecdotes with the other artists over coffee, we realize that we are being carefully observed by a gentleman sitting on a nearby table, a consulate "spy" in a shiny polyester suit who awkwardly pretends to be reading the paper. To confirm our suspicion that we're being watched, we migrate to the bar; the B-movie spy follows us and sits at the table closest to ours. We loudly make fun of "the clumsiness of the consulate." The spy moves to a more discreet distance.

On the day of our departure, we phone the consul to (politely) convey our opinion of his poor diplomatic skills. The secretary tells us that el señor consul is unavailable. We ask her to convey the message that we are thankful for the consul's support, that the festival was a total success, and that we got a kick out of the sleazy and obvious spy tactics. (Postscript, two years later: Those were the crazy days framed by NAFTA, Zapatismo, binational narco-politics and US Mexiphobia, the dangerous days when the PRI, the Mexican ruling party, was beginning to lose control of its image outside of Mexico.)

4 Chicano Freetraders in the Danger Zone

In February of 1995, cultural organizers Josephine Ramirez (LA), Lorena Wolffer (Mexico City) and I organized a binational performance project called "Terreno Peligroso/Danger Zone," which brought together Chicano and Mexican performance artists to deal with border issues and identity politics. The first two weeks of the event took place in LA, hosted by the University of California–Los Angeles, Highways Performance Space, and Plaza de la Raza. The second half of the project took place in Mexico City at X-Teresa Arte Alternativo, a seventeenth-century convent converted into a museum of experimental art. The event turned out to be a huge success, not only in terms of attendance and media coverage, but also for the dialogue it sparked regarding the tensions and possibilities for rapprochement between Chicanos and Mexicanos.

Mexico City, May 1995. A flamboyant Mexico City curator accosts me as I attend the opening of another art event at X-Teresa some months later. She tells me that she considers it a "blessing" that the Terreno Peligroso project has finally come to an end, and that she had never seen so much publicity and attention devoted to "US minority art" in Mexico.

I inquire whether she means *Chicano* art, and she confirms that she does, then goes on to ask how we managed to get funding and public attention for the project. "Are you guys part of the whole NAFTA package, o que?" Since I'm sure she's aware that Chicanos have been extremely critical of NAFTA, it's obvious that her comments are intended to irritate me. My intellectual glands begin to produce venom, but I try to keep my cool. "We are part of 'the other Nafta,'" I reply, "the untranslatable 'Tratando de Libre Comerse, or Cojerse.'"

She laughs artificially, and continues venting her resentment and contempt, characterizing Chicano art as "a new international fad," and Chicanos as "the new colonizers of Mexico." I can no longer restrain my cobra tongue. "Sure," I tell her. "In a couple of months, all *chilangos* [Mexico City natives] will be speaking Spanglish, wearing cholo fashions, and rapping like Kid Frost or Cypress Hill. So, *watchala, esa*!!" She responds by saying that unfortunately this is already the case. "Oh truly?" I reply. "I guess I'm behind." My saliva becomes extra-caustic as I assume the positionality of my Chicano colleagues: "*We* can't even keep up with the impact of our own colonizing powers!"

The curator stalks off with theatricalized anger, fully aware of how successful she had been in provoking me. After twenty years of painful dialogue and cultural exchange across the border, the members of the socially privileged Mexican intelligentsia are still unwilling to engage with Chicano art and border culture. They continue to regard our artistic work as *chafa* – "subcultural," peripheral, picturesque at best. Paradoxically, due to the extreme popularity of Chicano/Latino pop culture, which is regularly imported to Mexico from South of the Border, we are perceived as having genuine cultural and political power in the US. This (unfortunately fictional) "power" leads members of the Mexican cultural elite to perceive Chicanos as a threat to their attempts to establish "unmediated dialogue" with a so-called "international" (read Eurocentric) art world, yet another sinking ship in the troubled binational waters of neoliberalism. Rather than navigating responsibly the dangerous minefield of Chicano/Mexican relations, these privileged artists and intellectuals prefer to cross the border by plane, so to speak, traveling directly to Anglo cultural centers and appealing to monocultural institutions.

5 Embittered "Colleagues"

October 1996, Washington DC. Roberto and I are setting up our performance/installation, *Temple of Confessions*, at the Corcoran Gallery in Washington DC, just a few blocks away from the White House. We've been sleepless for a couple of nights, anxiously waiting to hear the results of a grant application we had submitted. We desperately hoped that the request for funding would be approved, since we were in the final stages of preparing for a project and would have to max out our personal credit cards to pay for the completion of the project if we didn't receive support.

Crossfade: A high-powered foundation grant review board meeting, somewhere in Mexamerica. The debate about funding our proposal has dragged on for two days. Final results: three in favor, two opposed. The panelists who vote against supporting the project (we are later informed) are a Central American professor who lives in New York but hasn't seen my performance work for at least eight years, and a Caribbean curator who has never been to any of our live performances – a fact which (as we are also told) they neglected to mention to their colleagues on the review board. They relentlessly argued against supporting our work on the basis that our "irresponsible use of Mexican stereotypes" contributed to the deterioration of US/Latino–Mexicano relations, and that our work and ideas were "divisive" and further aggravated existing conflicts between Mexicans and Chicanos. Luckily, other members of the review board were better informed about the substance and content of our work (some of them had actually *seen* our performances) and defended the application with equal vehemence.

When I first learn of the discussion, I am initially unfazed, as it seems typical of the cut-throat dynamics of the art world. As a veteran of many such battles, I know better than to take things personally (or at least, I tell myself, I ought to know better). After all, we got the grant. And there's something both ridiculous and perversely flattering about the fact that people could imagine that two brown performance artists (Roberto and myself) were in a position to have an impact on US/Mexican relations. But the more I thought about the subtext of these arguments, the more angry I became. It seemed that Roberto and I had become the object of unspoken schisms and resentments between academics and artists, between Mexicans and other US Latinos, and among the various Latino cultural cartels.

It's somewhat ironic that the allegedly "divisive" performance we were presenting in Washington DC (one of our most ambitious collaborative projects to date) involved three Mexicans, one Colombian, two Chicanos, a Chinese-American, a Puerto Rican/Scots-Irish hybrid, and five Anglo-American collaborators all working in different capacities. It really wasn't a grant recipe; it's just the way we normally work.

6 The Church of Indigenous Fundamentalism

Spring 1997, somewhere in Washington State. As part of our political praxis, Roberto and I work closely with Native American artists and cultural institutions. So when a Native American cultural organizer (for purposes of this narrative, let's call her Ana) invited us to perform the *Mexterminator* project at a "Longhouse" Community Center in the Pacific Northwest, we gladly accepted. Little did we know that we were about to have a *tête à tête* with a bizarre brand of moral fundamentalism.

The night we arrive in town, our producer invites us to dinner at her home, where we meet her lovely kid and monosyllabic husband. She spends the entire evening complaining bitterly about everything and everybody: Anglo students at the local university who want to "go Native," acculturated Indians, and Native youth strung out on "the drugs and booze of the white man." Her tone is maniacal, and her gaze messianic. She tells us about her activist work "back at the rez," where she has been trying to shut down the one and only bar, which she views as the primary source of crime and hopelessness in her community. She complains that few people on the reservation support her, which she interprets as a symptom of internalized colonialism. Roberto and I humbly suggest that perhaps things are more complex than she wants to admit, and that maybe the bar isn't really the main source of the problem. Besides, we argue, if she were to succeed in closing the bar, all people would need to do if they wanted to drink would be to drive a few miles outside of the reservation to get liquor. Ana is offended by our line of argument. We leave her house a bit perplexed.

The next day, we begin the activities of the residency with a slide and video presentation at the local university campus that talks about our interactive diorama work, in which we turn racist notions of ethnicity and Mexican identity inside out and upside down by posing as "artificial savages" and "ethno-cyborgs." The students seem really into it, but Ana seems troubled by our presentation. One of her colleagues takes us aside and scolds us for promoting "images of gratuitous decadence and self-indulgence." We're a little startled by the attack, but try to explain that our job as artists is to articulate crisis and contradiction, not to promote them. She doesn't buy a word of it, continuing in her moralistic speech about the dangers of "following the white man's path." We listen, trying hard not to react. That night, some local artists invite Roberto and me to a bar, where we exchange ideas and anecdotes. Opting for discretion, we decide not to ask our new friends about Ana's self-righteous campaign to purify indigenous culture by reinstating Prohibition on the rez . . . and in Chicano performance art.

The next morning we are scheduled to begin setting up the performance, but the Longhouse is closed and Ana is nowhere to be found. Abandoned by our producer, we don't quite know how to go about dealing with setting up the space for the performance. Later that day, Roberto and I give a spoken word performance; still no sign of Ana. That night, we wait for someone to open the Longhouse. Finally, Ana's assistant shows up and tells us that her boss is furious. She had heard about our "disgusting party at the bar," drinking and smoking and doing God knows what else with other Indian and Mexican artists. Ana had told her assistant that she was disappointed in us, and that we were definitely not what she had expected, promoting the "white man's legacy" of sex, alcohol, and violence, both in our work and in our personal lives, and that she wanted to dissociate herself from the project. The assistant explains that Ana is painfully aware that the performance has to take place, since posters have already been distributed and calls for tickets are piling up on the answering machine, but because the Longhouse is a holy place, there are some rules that Ana insists we follow: no live or dead chickens, no alcohol, no weapons, and (most especially) no images of overt violence or sexuality.

We can't believe our ears. Ana and her Puritan micro-cartel are behaving like right-wing evangelists, but speaking in jargon that's hardcore indigenist, separatist, and anti-white – fundamentalist dogma and conservative moralism derived precisely from the white culture they reject and claim is destroying Native communities. It's a surreal, upside down image on the mirror of race relations: an indigenous woman messianically committed to a peculiar campaign of "decolonization," but completely unaware of the extent to which her own behavior and strategies reveal how profoundly she herself has been colonized, to the point of adopting the rhetoric and moralism of conservative Anglo-Protestant culture.

Roberto and I explain to the troubled assistant that the weapons used in our performance are actually toys (cheesy silver-colored plastic sci-fi pistols), that the bottle of tequila is a mere prop filled with water, that the chickens are practically a trademark element in our work, and the content – I mean, the content is *definitely non-negotiable*. We also remind her that all the props used in the show were listed in the techwriter faxed to Ana months before we arrived, and that it's a little too late for her to decide that she objects to the content of our performance. The assistant apologetically states that she's only relaying messages, and that none of these things are for her to decide.

After talking to people in town who know Ana, we discover several things we wish we had found out earlier: she's a member of a hyper-traditionalist wing of the Indian church, with a strong missionary agenda. She was raised by abusive, alcoholic parents. According to a local artist, she booked us solely on the basis of a video she had seen of *Border Brujo*, a solo piece in which I perform the role of a shaman, and evidently took it at face value. In other words, she truly believed I was some kind of spiritual leader ready to use my mystical powers to help her realize her evangelist/nationalist agenda. She obviously never bothered to read any of my "decadent" writings.

Understanding the root causes of the situation, of course, does nothing to solve our immediate problems. The performance still needs to go on, with or without a producer, and there's no way we're going to water down the piece so as not to offend her Puritan sensibilities. We call everyone we've met in town, and ask for their help in creating an ersatz tech crew. People respond right away. With the assistance of ten volunteers, we spend the whole night and all of the next day hanging lights, installing the sound system and setting up platforms. An art student even goes to buy chickens and secretly kills them for us. We finish setting up the performance space just as the audience begins gathering in the lobby.

The Longhouse is jam-packed with young people, both Anglo and Native. With the help of performance "docents," we encourage audience members to interact with the living specimens (Roberto and I as CyberVato and Mexterminator) in a number of ways. They are allowed to feed us, take us for walks on a leash, alter our identity by changing our make up and costumes, or replace us for a short period of time to experience what it feels to be exocitized. The audience is extremely playful, and at times a bit racist in their behavior – but that's part of the symbolic contract we establish with them, allowed by the rules of our performance "game." Ana shows up for a few minutes, but leaves, horrified, as soon as she gets a good look at what's going on in the performance. The next morning, she phones our agent, Nola Mariano, to complain about our homo-erotic imagery, our alcoholism (one of my performance personas is a drunk shaman) and our willingness to become sexual toys for a racist audience. (Post-script, two years later: in retrospect, I don't regret this experience. Often the work of performance artists becomes a blank screen for people to project their own agendas, personal struggles, and tribulations, especially when it opens infected wounds. That may be where the power of performance lies. What has become clear to us now, however, is that if we wish to continue doing "community work", we need to be better prepared to respond constructively to situations in which polarities and oppositions are not drawn according to lines of race or gender.)

Epilogue

What to make of all these incidents? What to do when you inadvertently step through the looking-glass of intercultural relations to find yourself on the opposite side from people with whom you are supposed to agree, or at least to sympathize with? What to do when sectors of your own communities reveal themselves as formidable enemies? Or when your work becomes a *tabula rasa* onto which divisive factions and dogmatic micro-cartels project their unresolved conflicts and neo-fundamentalist views? Are the stories related above truly paradigmatic, or are the experiences of conflict they record an aberration? Should my colleagues and I regard such incidents as intrinsic to the work we do, an inevitable response to our efforts to open the wounds of cultural misunderstanding?

In 1994, I wrote (in one of my most conciliatory and optimistic voices):

> I truly believe that artists and cultural organizations can perform a crucial role in the healing of our communities in despair. Artists can function as community brokers, citizen diplomats, ombudsmen and border translators. And our art spaces and cultural organizations can perform the multiple roles of sanctuaries, demilitarized zones, centers for activism against xenophobia, and informal think tanks for intercultural and transnational dialogue. These spaces can provide us with the conditions for the creation of collaborative projects among artists from different communities and nationalities. These projects can send a strong message to both our communities and to the larger society: "Yes, we can talk to one another. We can get along, despite our differences, our fear, and our rage."

As I re-read these words, five years later, I am biting my lips and thinking seriously of getting a new tattoo, this time on the right side of my chest: an image of a crucified mariachi, with lettering underneath reading "El Vato Kamikaze." Right now, my lips are bleeding (the most inconsequential of many wounds) and my patience has grown quite thin.

I ask the reader to excuse my many contradictions and my open display of anger and fragility. I am just trying to figure things out.

SAN FRANCISCO, SEPTEMBER 1998

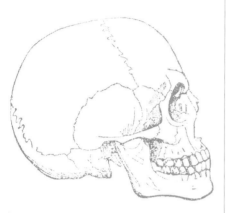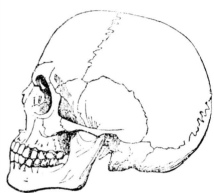

CONVERSATIONS ACROSS THE BORDER FENCE

PART 3

23 Sara Shelton-Mann as a crucified mariachi. Atlantic Center for the Arts, Florida.

"Symbols, aesthetic gestures and metaphors are contextual. And when they cross a cultural border they either crack open or metamorphosize into something entirely different. Artists operating in a multiracial and culturally pluralistic context must be fully aware of this phenomenon. In contemporary America it would be naive to expect that our performance work can be presented exactly the same way, say: in an alternative space or a mainstream theatre; in a Catholic Latino community center or within a protestant Anglo milieu. A symbol can mean contestation in one context and affirmation in another. Humor not always translates to other communities. Radicalism is also contextual. What is perceived as a transgressive gesture in Mexico, is not necessarily radical in the US and vice versa. In this sense, any performance artist who wishes to cross borders must be a cultural relativist and a border semiotician. He/she must also be prepared to constantly face cultural misunderstanding."

FROM GÓMEZ-PEÑA'S PERFORMANCE DIARIES, 1994

Away From the Surveillance Cameras of the Art World: Strategies for Collaboration and Community Activism

A conversation between Guillermo Gómez-Peña, Roberto Sifuentes, and Lisa Wolford

(The text published below is part of the fourth in an ongoing series of conversations with members of Pocha Nostra [Guillermo Gómez-Peña, Roberto Sifuentes, Sara Shelton-Mann, and a fluctuating group of additional collaborators that includes Juan Ybarra and Rona Michele] that I recorded beginning in October 1998. This particular meeting took place over a long meal at a "pan-Caribbean" restaurant in Ann Arbor, Michigan, decorated with murals of exotic birds and jungle foliage – true midwestern tropicalia. L.W.)

Lisa Wolford: During one of the rehearsals for *BORDERscape 2000,* you talked about being "hunters of images." I'm wondering if both of you could talk about that process.

Guillermo Gómez-Peña: In this oversaturated culture, it has become increasingly difficult to find original images that speak for the times. Most metaphors and symbols seem overused, hollow, or broken. I think that one of the many jobs of an artist is to look for new, fresh metaphors and symbols to help us understand our everchanging realities and fragmented cultures. We go about doing this in many ways. Sometimes we find images in everyday life, in the streets, and we capture them with our photographic eye and then re-enact them in more complex ways on stage. At other times, we create composite images by departing from a highly charged, traditional icon such as the crucifixion, the captured primitive, the political monster, the mariachi performing for outsiders and tourists, the witch doctor . . . Then we begin to do nasty things to these images. We begin to layer them as a kind of palimpsest. We add layers of contradiction or complexity, or we begin inserting details and features from other sources until these "traditional" images implode. The result is like genetically engineered Mexicabilia. The ultimate goal is to look for images that will create a disturbing sediment in the consciousness of the spectator, images that the audience cannot easily escape from, that will haunt them in dreams, in conversations, in memories.

Roberto Sifuentes: It's very important for us that the complex images we use in performance be open to multiple interpretations that we may never have imagined ourselves. It's always interesting for us to hear the varied readings of our diverse audiences. For example, the image of the hanging chickens in our performances: on one level, there's our intention behind using this charged metaphor, which is that it recalls the fact that Mexican migrant workers were hung by the Texas Rangers.

Gómez-Peña: Even nowadays, migrant workers are derogatorily referred to as *pollos*. But we don't necessarily expect our audiences to know this. We welcome other readings of the hanging chickens. Every image we use is a polysemantic image. It changes meaning with the context . . .

Sifuentes: Bringing this image out of its culturally specific context and presenting the work in the deep South brought out a completely different reading, which had to do with the fact that African-American slaves were hung for stealing chickens. In the Caribbean, after hearing about the image, people thought we might be into some kind of Santeria or "Mexican Voodoo" rituals . . .

Wolford: Are there ever moments when this process of interpretation becomes too elliptical, too open-ended? When audience members read something into an image that you didn't intend to communicate at all, or when a very specific message isn't recognized by the spectator? Like this idea that you're practicing Santeria . . .

Sifuentes: Yes, sometimes the interpretations of our images are really surprising. We were performing at at small college outside Kansas City, where the audience was described to us as right-wing Christian extremists who had, just a couple of weeks before, attacked a queer performance artist colleague of ours. So imagine how surprised we were to find out that these fundamentalists took an image on the publicity posters, that showed Guillermo in his mariachi suit, completely at face value. So these five hundred Republicans showed up to our performance with drums and maracas, ready to party, because they thought they were coming to "Mariachi Karaoke" night. And imagine how surprised they were when they saw our particular brand of Mariachi night!

Gómez-Peña: I used to fear being misunderstood, five or six years ago. Since intercultural misunderstanding is often the source of racism, I used to think that for the performance to be understood was very important. Now I think that whether the audience feels they understand us or not is completely irrelevant. In fact, I now distrust people who come up to me right after a show and tell me "I understood everything and I am with you." I answer: "Are you sure you are with me?" If you see a narrative film or a theater play, you immediately assume an ethical or emotional positionality. Whether you like it or not, you align yourself with certain characters, with certain notions of good, justice, freedom, rebellion, etc. You walk out of the theater and you say I got it, I liked it or I didn't.

Wolford: With some kinds of theater, not all.

Gómez-Peña: But with performance art, it's different. You walk out of a performance feeling troubled and perplexed. The performance triggers a process of reflexivity that continues through days and sometimes weeks, creating sediments in the consciousness of people. People slowly begin to come to terms with the images and make up their minds about what they saw, but it takes them weeks, even months. Sometimes people think they are offended because they don't want to face certain realities or certain scary feelings they harbor, and it's very easy to say "I'm offended," as opposed to trying to understand what wound was opened.

Wolford: Guillermo, I think that really interesting, important theater can have that effect as well. But that's another conversation. In terms of the images, why do you think some people get offended? I don't mean something like the use of the chickens *per se* – I know that animal rights groups have been very vocal about objecting to that, but their reasons are fairly straightforward. I'm thinking about people who manifest strong reactions to some of the more poetical images, such as the crucifixion imagery, or the gang member's stigmata . . .

Sifuentes: Most of the time, the audience is completely comfortable with images like a Chicano "gang member" being beaten by the police, or dragged out of his home in front of his family by the LAPD. They see it on syndicated TV every night, on shows like "COPS" and "LAPD: Life in the Streets." What our spectators find disturbing is witnessing these images of violence recontextualized in high art institutions by two Mexicans who talk back to them. I remember that during one performance we did, the melancholic image of Guillermo as a mariachi in a straightjacket confessing his intercultural desires so disturbed one upper-class Latina that she came onstage and whipped Guillermo so hard across the face and genitals that he crumbled to the ground and was unable to continue the piece for a few minutes. She ran out of the theater and was stopped by our agent and asked why. She only responded that this was offensive, and didn't represent her as a Latina. And this happened in the first five minutes of the piece.

Gómez-Peña: There's a very disturbing tendency in America to take things literally. Since our work is highly symbolic and metaphorical, it appears to be very much out of context in the current culture. We're living in a time in which confessional narrative is the primary means of communication, and we don't engage in confessional narratives of authenticity. Neither do we engage in psychological or social realism. The work is really not about "us" . . .

Sifuentes: It's not autobiographical. We're not performing our authenticity as Chicanos; what we're doing is performing the multiplicity of mythologies and perceptions of Mexicans and Chicanos in the US. Unfortunately, some audiences don't think of Chicanos as "cultural thinkers" or "conceptual arists," so when I first began to portray the "Vato" (street hipster) covered in tattoos, wearing baggie clothes, and manipulating weapons, many audience members and even some journalists thought I was a Latino gang member brought to town and put on display by Gómez-Peña.

Wolford: So the fact that you're both coming out of an experimental performance tradition already contradicts the ways in which people may tend to want to label your work. Also the incorporation of different media, the extent to which your performances reference theory and critical discourse, etc.

Gómez-Peña: Roberto and I are first and foremost conceptual artists. We always depart from a theoretical proposal, an idea which first becomes a blueprint for action, and eventually becomes a performance piece, a video, or a radio piece. But some of our collaborators come from very different traditions, especially when we work with actors, singers and dancers. Sara [Shelton-Mann] comes from the apocalypse dance theater movement that uses a lot of contact improvisation and physical movement to create original imagery and visceral rituals, and then the collaborating artists conceptualize around the imagery they have developed in the rehearsal room – that's basically the opposite of the way we work. Roberto and I don't spend that much time in the rehearsal room. What we do instead is write, brainstorm, debate with other artists and activists, and every now and then we rehearse. We usually only rehearse physically the month before launching a new project. But we are learning tremendously from Sara. We are beginning to shyly incorporate some of her methodologies into our work.

Sifuentes: And Sara is begining to incorporate our methodologies. She now thinks of Doc's Clock (our local bar in the Mission) and La Boheme Cafe as viable rehearsal spaces.

Gómez-Peña: Imagine Roberto and I doing contact dance and Ch'i Kung. It sounds ridiculous, que no?

Wolford: Hey, I've seen it – it works. I really don't think you could have gotten to what you're doing now in terms of the physical images on stage without it.

24 Performance jamming session at Theater Arnaud. (Gómez-Peña, Margaret Leonard, Roberto Sifuentes, Sara Shelton-Mann and Nao Bustamante).

"*The hidden civic goal in our collaborative projects is to create an ephemeral community of artists, technicians and activists in which my texts become a mere blueprint for action. This collaborative work is consensual by nature. It gets made in constant dialogue with others . . . In my solo work, I get to be more 'personal,' as personal as a Mexican can get.*"

FROM GÓMEZ-PEÑA'S PERFORMANCE DIARIES, 1995

Gómez-Peña: We are hoping to develop a kind of dialectic in which these two processes, the conceptual and the visceral, go together. When we brainstorm with our collaborators about how to incorporate a new vignette, we inevitably talk about politics, about other issues. Our discussions during the creative process are not just about the work itself. We talk about what we saw on TV the night before, about a new book we are reading, about cinema, computers, sex, anthropology, you name it . . . We share an experience we had the week before. We describe a rare prop we just found in a roadside museum on our last trip somewhere. And then, out of these eclectic discussions, where language and ideas are like personas in a conceptual mini-proscenium, the stage of the dinner table or the bar table, a new image or a new text begins to emerge. Then we try it out informally in front of friends. When we are in San Francisco, we have performance salons at least once a month. There we try out all the new material and invite other performers to try out fresh material.

Sifuentes: A text can begin in a salon, evolve into a radio commentary and then become the basis for a major section in a proscenium piece, or else the radio piece gets worked into the soundtrack for a diorama performance. But really, the performance personas, their actions, the texts, and juxtapositions of images, never get finalized. They are always in process of development. We test them in front of an audience and that's the moment when they begin to blossom, to really take form.

Wolford: When you stage a new piece, I know you often have a very short rehearsal period. Obviously, before you begin mounting a performance, you work conceptually, or you work with the text if it's a scripted piece. You work in your apartment, or in transit, but when you come into a venue with a script to mount a performance, normally you've got about a week to get it up on stage –

Gómez-Peña: At best.

Wolford: Often even less if it's an installation piece. And during the short time you're actually working in a performance space, you end up putting a lot of attention to the technical aspects of the piece, which can be very elaborate.

Sifuentes: Not to mention the shortness of the run. We've never performed more than three weekends in one city. Most of the time it's one show, two shows, a weekend at most . . . When we produce ourselves, we manage to squeeze out three weeks in a venue, but we don't normally have the luxury of presenting the work for the time that it really needs to evolve. As artists of color in the US, we aren't given the space, time, and funding to be able to sit and create a piece of work. Yes, we create on the road, in airplanes and hotel rooms, in cafes. No matter how visible we are, Chicanos don't have the infrastructure or financial support that would allow us to sit and create in peace, to spend half of the year in artist retreats.

Gómez-Peña: Let's face it, rehearsing all the time is a privilege that most Chicanos don't have. Besides, we have community responsibilities, and our community reminds us all the time of our civic duties, which include benefits for grassroots organizations, workshops in community centers, fundraisers for particular social causes, impromptu appearances at civic events or on Public Access TV – you name it. And you cannot say no. You have to give back. It's a basic ethical issue. Besides, the work we do in the civic realm feeds the other work. It gives strength and weight to our work in and around the art world. We constantly cross the border back and forth between the civic realm and the art realm, and this is much more important to us than rehearsing all the time. In a sense, our grassroots activities are part of our rehearsal time.

Sifuentes: Traveling and performing is our sole means of economic survival. But at the same time, that's also our means of production. We have turned the necessity of working all the time into our creative process. We travel to the most unlikely places where our audience has never encountered Chicanos – which means that often our performance begins the moment we step off the plane. We become, in a sense, field workers conducting "reverse anthropological" research. I am also not about to begin complaining about the amount of touring we have, because that's something we've fought tooth and nail to achieve. It never gets any easier, even though because of our visibility, some people might get a false sense that we have the corner on the Latino performance art market. The fact of the matter is that we are constantly pushing, struggling, trying to find our niche, in order to make the work happen in the places where it needs to happen. We travel all the time, working in many different contexts from community centers to high art museums, from major urban centers to rural communities, from the US-Mexico border to New York and beyond . . .

Wolford: Could I ask you to talk a little bit about the structure of Pocha Nostra, your performance company? In the past, Guillermo, I know that you've collaborated with people whose primary professional identity wasn't as performers – theorists, cultural critics, visual artists. But in your more recent work, the two of you have been integrating a number of dancers and experimental theater artists.

Gómez-Peña: The way we work is that we have a core group of performance collaborators; for a long time, it was basically Roberto and myself, and more recently Sara. We also have another group of collaborators who are specialists in other areas. People like Mexican filmmaker Gustavo Vazquez, soundscape composer Rona Michele, or digital media advisor Suzanne Stefanac. Incredible performance artists from Mexico city like Juan Ybarra, Violet Luna and Yoshigiro Maeshiro. Chicana performance artists like Norma Medina and Isis Rodriguez. And all of these wonderful *locos y locas* bring something very special to the performances. Their individual creative output finds a new context and a new syntax within the frame of our installations and proscenium performances. Then we have a much bigger, outside circle of collaborators. Some of them are performance artists based in other countries or other cities, and we collaborate with them for specific projects, usually when we're doing a residency or presenting a performance in the areas where they live.

Sifuentes: Suomi violinists in "traditional" costume sitting on stuffed reindeer in Helsinki, English singers interpreting traditional Welsh songs while doing erotic things with opera singers, gringo rasta tattoo artists tattooing performers onstage, neo-primitives naked on a platform displaying their bodies as art . . .

Gómez-Peña: Given what has happened to arts funding in the 90s, it's financially impossible for artists like us – politicized, experimental performance artists – to maintain any kind of big group. But we still have the desire to bring other people into the work, so the strategy we've developed is to create ephemeral communities that come together around a specific project, and once the project is over, they go back to their homes, to their own practice. Very often, we develop ongoing relationships with artists during our travels. For example, we've done several projects with our Crow friends from Montana, Susan and Tyler Medicine horse, and we have plans to work with them again in the future. We are a tribe of nomads and misfits.

In some of our projects, we also like to collaborate with people who don't have specialized performance training. Along these lines, we have been working with all kinds of wonderful people: politicized strippers, activists with very theatrical personalities, hip hop poets, extremely articulate transsexuals who are willing to deconstruct their performance personas on stage, mariachis and other civic artists who have chosen to transgress their own tradition . . . We love to work with eccentrics who have performative personalities and important things to say. Whenever we collaborate with people who don't have formal performance experience, our work has been to contribute to shaping their material so that it gets presented in the best possible way.

Sifuentes: Then it can be incorporated into the larger context of the work that we are doing.

Gómez-Peña: Exactly. And they always get to have the last word about their own material and their representation. Our role is to coordinate, design, and stage the larger event, not necessarily to direct it. Our goal is to attempt a model that is not colonial, in which we don't manipulate these wonderful "involuntary performance artists," and in which they get to have editorial say. We help them shape the material (I don't even want to use the word help, because it's condescending), but we work with them to structure their material because we have certain skills and experience that we have developed throughout the years.

Wolford: I want to shift back to the discussion of audience reception of the work, if that's okay. In the diorama performances, there is no spoken text – the text that exists is part of the soundscape. Because you work with multivalent, polysemantic images, and because irony is such a central aspect of your performance strategy, some of the journalistic responses to the diorama performances suggest that without spoken text it's impossible for the work to deliver a clear political critique.

Gómez-Peña: Who can deliver a clear political critique nowadays? When all the philosophical and political systems are bankrupt, who can possibly claim that they have found a political positionality that is not susceptible to being challenged? I cannot assume a clear positionality vis-à-vis any progressive movement, even those closest to my heart. All the ideological systems that used to be sanctuaries of progressive thought are undergoing a permanent process of renegotiation. We now know that obvious ethical or ideological borders are mere illusions, that the enemy is everywhere, even inside of us – especially inside of us. I think that in these senses, we cannot possibly assume one clear political position in the performance.

Sifuentes: Also, part of the point is that we want to see where people position themselves. The responses of our live audience in performance and the written intercultural fantasies, fears, and desires we've collected through the *Temple* and the website become a barometer for America's intolerance towards other cultures. In the 90s, handing the microphone to our audience, so to speak, has been a very effective performance strategy for dealing with sensitive issues.

Gómez-Peña: I think that what we are trying to do is to open up spaces of ambiguity where there are contradictory voices and contradictory ideas clashing in front of the audience – spaces of ambiguity in which audience members can undergo multiple emotional and intellectual journeys that lead to different responses and different political positionalities within the performance, especially if the performance lasts, say, five to six hours over a three-day period. Also, our own positionality is contextual.

Wolford: In what sense?

Gómez-Peña: When we're in Mexico we end up behaving a bit like Chicano nationalists, because Mexicans can be quite insensitive and ethnocentric toward Chicanos. But when we perform for primarily Chicano audiences, we question this type of nationalism. When we perform solely for Anglos, we tend to assume a pan-Latino or pan-subaltern space, but when we are performing for traditional or essentialist Latino audiences, we often defend cultural kleptomania, transvestism, and hybridity as a response to neo-essentialism in our own communities. Performance art allows us to shift these positionalities. We are constantly crossing invisible borders, reframing our voices, reinventing our identities.

Sifuentes: We tailor-make our performances to be specific to the context, regardless of where we are. When we go further away from the US/Mexican border, we adapt the work a little bit so as to ground the piece in different experience, say, to find the connections between the Chicano experience and the local subaltern or immigrant group. Performance art is all about contextualization, about doing site-specific pieces that speak to the moment and the context for which they are created.

Wolford: What are some of the aspects of your performance strategies that remain consistent even when you move among extremely different contexts?

Gómez-Peña: What we're attempting to do is to articulate unspoken complexities of race and gender relations in such a way that people don't close down. Discussions around sensitive issues of race and gender have reached a stalemate in contemporary America, and in order to get out of this stasis, we need to become almost like flashers. If people don't want to see something, we show it to them when they least expect it, and in a way that they actually accept it, even enjoy it. If they don't want to talk about a certain issue, we scream at them, but we make them laugh. If they just want us to whisper it, we say it louder and force them to confront the issues they don't want to talk about, but in such a way that they don't realize right away that we are forcing them to confront these issues. Performance art utilizes a very complex set of communication strategies.

Humor is a good way to deal with heavy issues so we don't get shot, because it takes people by surprise and disarms them for a little while. They bring their guard down a little, and that's exactly when we hit them with the tough question or with the bold image. It's a subversive strategy in our work. We often get criticized for being too humorous.

Wolford: What do you mean?

Gómez-Peña: In a Eurocentric tradition of conceptual art, humor is often equated with lack of seriousness and sophistication. There's an unwillingness in the US and European art world to understand that highly sophisticated conceptual constructions can coexist with very bald humor, so often when people from certain artistic milieus see our work, they just don't know what to think. These apparently sophisticated post-posty post-colonial Mexicans who travel all over are also capable of being crass, direct, sexually outrageous, and making people laugh. It just doesn't jive. There is also a kind of sacred irreverence in our work, a spirituality paired with satire, and that also takes people by surprise, because spirituality in the US is supposed to be a serious and solemn matter, and so are hardcore political subject matters, like racism, sexism, police brutality, etc.

Sifuentes: So when people see Sara crucified as an androgynous mariachi with a strap-on dildo, or when Guillermo as a "holistic techno shaman" in a mechanical wheelchair baptizes the audience by spitting bad tequila on them, or when Tyler Medicinehorse sells audience members "real" Indian names in the Crow language that translate to absurd things like "itchy butt," reactions vary from utter repulsion to raucous laughter.

Gómez-Peña: Irreverent humor, merciless, uncompromising humor, has been at the core of Mexican and Chicano art, and it has always been one of our most effective political strategies. This humor has always taken many shapes, from social parody to self-parody to exaggerating a racist stereotype until it explodes or implodes. I would go so far as to say that humor is a quintessential feature of Mexican and Chicano art and activism. From the Royal Chicano Airforce to Superbarrio and Marcos, we've used humor to help fight our battles. But people forget this. Paradoxically, certain nationalist and essentialist sectors, mainly humorless activists and academicians, have become guardians of solemnity. They have forgotten that humor is profoundly political. They seem not to notice that Chicano and indigenous communities are actively engaged in humor as a mechanism of survival, as a means to generate attention to sensitive issues, as a way to elicit public dialogue. If you are funny, you can get away with murder, and you can appeal to a much larger audience. I'm not saying that all irreverence is subversive by any means – there is insensitive humor, and there are racist forms of irreverence – but our communities let us know how far we can go.

Sifuentes: Mexicano/Chicano audiences never let us take ourselves too seriously because they themselves are irreverent. They get it, they get a kick out of the humor, they laugh a lot. Maybe what makes some intellectuals uptight about our work is that they're afriad we're making fun of them, or that they'll do or say "the wrong thing" in one of our interactive performances and end up getting laughed at by our "less informed" Chicano audiences.

I do with the Chief of Police of Mexico City, even if he's Mexican. Or as a Chicano, Roberto probably has more in common with a Jewish performance artist than he has with a Chicano border patrol officer. Our political coalitions and our artistic work have to do with more than just our ethnic and cultural backgrounds. But what I was talking about before was really specifically about the "guardians," the self-proclaimed Anglo gatekeepers who believe they have the right to decide, from the outside, whose work gets canonized, included or excluded, who does or doesn't count as a member of a particular community.

Wolford: You're right, that's a very different issue, and an incredibly complicated one, with all sorts of problematic implications in terms of ways that white institutions, curators, or theorists try to maintain a position of privilege over artists of color.

Gómez-Peña: With all humility, I think that Roberto and I have paid our dues, and I'm getting a little pissed about theoreticians who say that we aren't involved in grassroots activism, that we've become mere darlings and pets of the "liberal" art world.

Wolford: So there's more of a wound there than you were admitting before about your relationship with cerain sectors of the Latino community?

Gómez-Peña: What can I say, the wound does open every now and then. We've been involved in political struggles for many years, and these struggles take place in the outside world, not in university department meetings. We've been working on the front lines, so to speak. We've been touring the Southwest and the Chicano communities of the US for many, many years, and we have very good relations with them.

Wolford: That's certainly true here in Ohio. You have very strong ties with Baldemar Velasquez and the Farm Labor Organizing Committee [FLOC], which is based here in Toledo.

Sifuentes: It makes perfect sense that a visionary like Baldemar has asked us to present our spoken word pieces and experimental work at the forefront of an ongoing farmworkers' movement. And Baldemar and all the campesinos

25　Roberto Sifuentes as CyberVato tortures himself with a police baton. Museo del Barrio, NYC.

"In my performance country, there are no rules; or better said, there exist only the rules that my colleagues and I agree to establish temporarily. Even these rules can be broken at any moment. In this sense, the worst enemies of performance are formulas, fixed structures, norms and traditional narrative forms."

FROM GÓMEZ-PEÑA'S PERFORMANCE DIARIES, 1989

have been responding very positively to the work. They see its value in the community centers, that it can speak very directly to the farmworker experience. That for me is a very encouraging affirmation of the work, because so often people want to believe that only muralism can speak to these communities, only campesino theater can speak to the campesinos, and that has not been our experience at all.

Gómez-Peña: Next weekend, it's possible that FLOC is going to bring a couple of vans with migrant workers to see the *Mexterminator* performance at the Detroit Institute of the Arts, just like they did last year when we did a public lecture in Bowling Green [Ohio]. That's not atypical of our work; it happens all the time. When we were in Kansas City a couple of years ago, there was a bus completely full of migrant workers who drove three hours in order to see the performance. This idea that we are speaking only to white "liberal" audiences is really a misperception. It's completely misinformed. I don't want to suggest that there's anything heroic about what we're doing, because many of our Chicano/Latino performance colleagues have similar experiences. But it's paternalistic to pretend that the farmworkers or the young homeboys in the barrio won't understand our work because it's too heavy, too dark, or too theoretically sophisticated.

For the last year and a half, we have been engaging in a dialogue with FLOC, and we have just formalized our association with them by having been declared honorary members, with very serious ethical responsibilities that go along with accepting this position. After our performances, when we engage in public discussions with the audience, we've committed to promote their boycott of corporations that are oppressing and mistreating migrant workers in North Carolina, and to teach audiences how they can effectively participate in this national boycott. I think that this is a very important part of our performance work, and we really don't care if this is lauded or not; whether it is visible to the art world or to academia is absolutely meaningless to us. We are simply trying to figure out ways to be useful to Latino communities in despair and in need, and we feel that we cannot shy away from direct activism. Perhaps one of the reasons why I was more careful about entering into direct activism in the past was because of my condition as a "resident alien," because I'm not supposed to be affiliated with political organizations. That's part of the condition of receiving the resident card. If you are directly affiliated with a political organization considered to be a troublemaker, you risk being deported. But I'm hoping to acquire dual citizenship very soon, so that would no longer be a problem.

Sifuentes: You can begin to finally exercise your civic rights.

Gómez-Peña: Half of the work we do is in the civic realm rather than in the art world, but it goes unnoticed by the surveillance cameras of the art world. Wherever we go we have a double agenda. We work with a mainstream cultural institution that pays the bill and helps us to present a piece of work in the best possible way, and we also engage in a number of "parallel" activities. Those are often the most significant part of our work, but they go unnoticed. We're now on our way to Florida to do a residency at the Atlantic Center for the Arts, and also to do a number of presentations for farmworker communities; it's very likely that those presentations will never be documented, and that the piece at the Atlantic Center for the Arts will be covered in some way. There is no way out of this predicament. The art world is simply not interested in these other activities. And it's good that the art world is not interested, because that grants us special freedoms. They can see what we're doing with the right hand, but they never see what we're doing with the left hand.

Wolford: You're right that a spoken word performance at the Sofia Quintero Cultural Arts Center in Toledo probably isn't going to get written up in *Artforum*, but I certainly understand why it's important to do that work. Could I ask you to talk a bit more about some of the other facets of your work in the civic realm?

Gómez-Peña: We have been designing what we term "experimental town meetings" in different cities across the US. The biggest up to now took place in Washington, DC. The premise was as follows: the performance artists designed the stage and structured the event carefully, as if a performance art piece was to take place, with lights, video projections, sound, etc. Inside this performance space, we placed a table with activists and radical scholars from the Latino, Indigenous and African-American communities. The performance artists, in character and in costume, with our voices processed by an SPX machine, would get to ask these panelists questions about lack of leadership, about the state of affairs in our communities, about intra-Latino conflicts, about inter-ethnic conflicts, and so on. There was a mediator, radical psychiatrist Leticia Nieto, who would broker between the panelists and the audience. So there were many things taking place simultaneously on different levels and fronts, and any time the conversation would drag or become uninteresting, the performance artists were allowed to "intervene" with a skit or a spoken word text. At the main table where the panelists were seated, food was being served by performance artists dressed as waiters, and every now and then the waiters would go into performance mode. It was a very complicated script to write and put together, a sort of hyper-textual script with lots of open ends. Initially there was some anxiety, especially from the activists. Of course they didn't want to make fools out of themselves. We had very prominent people working with us. Susan Harjo was there, and Baldemar Velasquez, among other people. Abel Lopez, the national director of NALAC at the time, he was there. One of the top immigration lawyers in Washington was there. Of course, some of these people were apprehensive in the beginning about what it meant for them as political activists, as lawyers and union organizers, to put themselves into this situation, which was framed in a very per-formative way. Susan was not, because she herself is a performance artist extraordinaire; she's one of the co-founders of Spiderwoman Theater and also a poet, along with being one of the most important Native American politicians we have in the country. She was also very familiar with our work, as was Baldemar. He was absolutely not apprehensive, as he himself is an involuntary performance artist, one of the most charismatic and compelling speakers I have ever met. But the others were. So it took a lot of talking to persuade them that we were not going to make fun of them. The event took place and it was a huge success, a strange hybrid of a hardcore political town meeting and an epic performance performance art piece. I wish all the performance art curators had been there, *esa*. A few days ago, for the closing ceremony of the Latino MacArthur Fellows visit to Toledo, we tried another version, smaller scale. The Latino MacArturos confronted the local political elite, and Roberto and I were asked by Baldemar to design the town meeting and to be the performance animateurs. We are very interested in continuing these experiments and fine-tuning this model, this new genre, utilizing performance art as a means to design, animate, layer, and reframe very tough political debates.

Sifuentes: It's important that we find a new forum to discuss these issues, because so often political panels or discussions around Latino issues and intra-community conflicts get stuck. People have gotten locked into particular ways of discussing identity and race relations. The discussion gets glazed over and audiences become completely uninterested, or else the debates wander into incredibly petty or inflammatory discourse, which is absolutely unproductive. In the context of these experimental town meetings, the performative interventions help us to break through these dynamics. Because the panelists have agreed to be part of this performance context where they can sense the energy of what's going on in the performance space, they tend to be much more concise, energetic and dynamic themselves in what they have to say. But if there are moments when the conversation starts to lag or go in an unproductive direction, the performative interventions are a good way to bring the discussion back around to the main issues we're trying to talk about, and also to diffuse the heaviness and the solemnity that often accompany political discussions. As performers, part of what we're trying to do in this context is to bring back the irreverence to these discussions, so that we don't take ourselves so seriously. That's the model that we're going for – looking for ways to keep the discussions dynamic so that people can encounter these issues in new ways.

Chihuahuas, Rockeros, and Zoot Suits: Notes on Multiculturalism without People of Color

A Conversation between Guillermo Gómez-Peña and Josh Kun[1]

Introduction

I first met Guillermo Gómez-Peña in 1997, when I interviewed him for an article I was writing for the *San Francisco Bay Guardian*. At the time, what interested me most about Gómez-Peña's work was his use of Mexican rock, the connections and allegiances he was drawing between performance art and rock art, between the literal masks that he wears (Marcos masks, luche libre masks, calaveras) and the aesthetic masks that rockeros/as have been taking off and putting on as part of rock en español's countercultural strategy since the early 60s.

Flip through Gómez-Peña's back catalogue and he's jumping rope to La Cuca (I imagine the song to be "Son del Dolor," their metal re-fry of a traditional Mexican song); putting the "grunge rockeros" at the center of his vision of a

1 Josh Kun is a music and cultural critic whose writing has appeared in *The Village Voice*, *SPIN*, *Salon*, *Color Lines* and *The Boston Phoenix*. His column "Frequencies" appears bi-weekly in the *San Francisco Bay Guardian*, where he has been a regular contributing writer since 1994. He is Assistant Professor of English at the University of California, Riverside and is currently completing his forthcoming manuscript, *Strangers Among Sounds: Listening, Difference and the Unmaking of Americans*.

"borderless future;" and as he does in *BORDERscape 2000*, slipping La Lupita's take on Los Tigres del Norte's norteño staple "Camelia La Trejana" into a sound collage that includes Yma Sumac and Gómez-Peña himself singing The Eagles' "Hotel California" as a demonic mariachi while Roberto Sifuentes beats dead a chicken with a police stick.

Most date the Mexican rock/performance art relationship to the 1985 Mexico City earthquake, when the shaking of the city birthed a new generation of chroniclers, or cronistas, desperate for new ways of documenting the world of rubble and devastation surrounding them. Post-quake art had to grapple with social reality, and rockers and performance artists were just some of the torch-bearers – along with cartoonists and other engaged cultural workers – who were committed to bringing the voices of Mexico's urban margins into the country's unsettled public sphere (a sphere made even more unsettled and even more artistically fertile nearly a decade later by the 1994 double-blow of NAFTA and Chiapas). Since then, the elaborate theatricality of bands like La Castaneda, guacarock pioneers and charro rocanroleros Botellita de Jerez and solo artists like Sergio Arau have brought performance art into the rock club, making the line between the two genres more and more difficult to draw.

In Gómez-Peña's case, rock en español's cross-border cultural migrations and its position in a transitional NAFTA economy make it a perfect partner in art crime. His "high-tech Aztec" fusions are indebted to the way rock bands take music from abroad and transform it with music from home (which Mexico City can mean anything from huapango and mariachi to ska, mambo and Afro-pop). His "new world border" utopia – complete with "micro-republics" and "mysterious underground railroads" – is actualized in the way rock en español continues to serve, as the great Jaime Lopez once put, as "un canto fronterizo" (a borderlands song) that connects rockeros in the D.F. with Chicano/a and immigrant rockeros/as in places as disparate as San Jose, Chicago and New York.

The conversation that follows[2], which took place in October 1998 in Amherst Massachusetts and which flows everywhere from Taco Bell to cyberspace, may not be limited to this terrain of transfrontera sounding, but it's where its heart lies.

---

2   A truncated version of this interview appeared in *Aztlán: A Journal of Chicano Studies* 24/1 (spring 1999), 187–99, © 1999 by Regents of the Unversity of California.

Josh Kun: I wanted to start this whole conversation off by asking you to talk about your intellectual relationship to Subcomandante Marcos, the lead strategist and mysterious, ski-masked political philosopher of the EZLN (Zapatista National Liberation Army), who launched their revolutionary struggle for dignity and social justice from the Lacandón jungle in Chiapas, Mexico, in 1994. I remember you recently telling me that you considered yourself an unofficial disciple of Marcos. Why would Marcos matter to a performance artist?

Guillermo Gómez-Peña: I've always regarded Marcos as a performance artist extraordinaire. I think that perhaps Marcos's genius lies precisely in his ability to understand the symbolic power of performative actions; the symbolic power of props and costuming. He also understands the importance of new technologies as a means to enhance his voice; the importance of staging press conferences-as-performance, and of course, the strategic use of poetics in a time in which political language is completely hollow and bankrupt. He understands the power of language to help us constantly reinvent ourselves, and that to me is the essence of performance art. Performance artists are interested in exactly the same things. Roberto (Sifuentes, Gómez-Peña's current collaborator) and I see clear parallelisms in our methodologies. Of course, we are operating on a much smaller scale and without the consensus of hundreds of thousands of people.

JK: You also seem to have begun to echo Marcos in your approach to technology and your commitments to developing new technological strategies of representation and activism. In the last few years, your work has become increasingly invested in mining the symbolic and communicative power of the web and exposing the cultural politics of Internet technologies and cyberculture. Marcos is one of the supreme examples of the subaltern, the ex-third worlder, harnessing what are positioned as first world technologies and using them to launch a counter-strike on first world institutions and systems of domination.

GGP: His is one of the most efficient activist uses of new technologies. It's unbelievable. Once the ceasefire occurred, his revolution became first and foremost a cyber revolution, a revolution that took place in virtual space. The Net has been his main means of communication with the outside world and the way to keep his mythology alive and the presence and aura of Zapatismo alive in the world imagination. And he did it so successfully at a time in which the debates on new technologies (1994–96) were completely apolitical –

JK: – and top down

GGP: And top down. For years, people were wondering how the hell he managed overnight to send his communiqués and the discussions of the commandancia Zapatista straight from La Realidad (where his headquarters are located) – at a time when La Realidad didn't have electric lights – all the way into the highly designed Zapatista web sites. It was a total mystery. Now people know how he's doing it, but it took everybody by surprise, that this group of insurrectionists living in pre-industrial conditions in the Mexican jungle would so successfully broadcast their plight through the Internet in a more sophisticated way than city intellectuals were doing it at the time.

JK: Absolutely. But what's also interesting about his use of technology in combination with the way he and the Zapatistas manipulate their media images, is that they are also tapping into how the Internet has become a site of performative activism. That is, so much of Marcos's agenda has been centered on the way he performs himself as an insurrectionist – the masks, the hidden identity, dropping out of sight for months at a time, showing up at soccer games – in ways not terribly far from the strategies of say, El Santo and Superbarrio, other masked heroes of the people. And the Internet has, among so many other things, become a site of everyday performance – its very structure, its anonymities, its disconnections from physical visible bodies, have opened it up into a kind of everyday theater of self re-actuation that is perfectly suited for Marcos's campaign.

The Internet has become about creating fictional identities, inviting and in a sense, requiring, its users to take on alternate selves, virtual selves. I'd be curious to know if this quasi-normalization of performance has affected the parameters of performance art. Has it changed the way you work, the way you think about what constitutes performance art and performative action in the age of the Internet?

GGP: The performance art world is merciless. Since it defines itself always in opposition to its immediate past and it's always inevitably and acritically looking

26 "Mex-Porn" Signore magazine, Mexico City.

27 Sara Shelton-Mann as a transgender mariachi cyborg.

at the future, you are forced to redefine yourself constantly if you want to remain seated at the table of debates in the field. Otherwise you are out . . . gone. The speed at which the field changes is vertiginous, unlike any other field, and a performance artist nowadays has a very hard task, which is that of constantly reinventing him or herself and developing new and surprising strategies in order to remain alive and current.

And the performance field is constantly shifting: what is performance today won't be performance in two or three years and what was performance five years ago is no longer performance. Performance deals in the realm of the immediate, in the here and the now, and there is a sense of urgency and immediacy that in many ways makes it closer to journalism than to theater.

JK: The difference (one of them anyway) is that journalists rarely realize that what they're doing is a performance, that their bylines signal their own role-playing, their articles their own fashionings of rearrangements and in many cases, extreme misrepresentations of the world they chronicle. Your work, though – especially recent pieces like *Temple of Confessions*, *El Mexterminator*, and *Friendly Cannibals* – has overtly responded to the ubiquity of Internet culture –

GGP: One is constantly re-evaluating one's methodologies. By 1994 my accomplices and I found ourselves faced with a dilemma. The art world had declared multiculturalism dead, very conveniently. The backlash against multiculturalism started to spread into academia, mass media, pop culture, mainstream politics and suddenly matters of race and gender were seen as passé. And we found ourselves in a serious dilemma. We needed to redefine all of our strategies. Suddenly, there was no longer a place for the angry black man or for the rabid Latino revolutionary or the angry feminist sister talking back. Liberal audiences began to experience "compassion fatigue" and they were no longer willing to tolerate strident, in your face, kinds of messages.

At the same time, the art world began to celebrate the arrival of new technologies in a very acritical way, especially in California. The utopian discourse about new technologies coming out of the Bay Area was completely ludicrous. *Wired* magazine, and some of the theorists of technology to remain nameless –

JK: – the Internet as some new digital manifestation of egalitarian democracy.

GGP: Sure carnal. People were saying that virtual space was a truly demo-cratic space, that everybody regardless of race, culture, class, or gender could participate equally, could "belong" at a time when no one was feeling a sense of belonging to any community. So because of this new conceptual configuration we had to crash the new digital art world yet one more time or we would be left behind. And believe me, there were no Chicanos in virtual space at that time.

JK: Or at least anyone identifying themselves as such –

GGP: Yeah. So we began to not shyly venture into cyberspace as web-backs, as cyber-immigrants, fully aware that we were going to face the cyber-migra eventually. Then there is this other issue. Being "transgressive," "alternative," or "rebellious," are notions that have become very hollow in the 90s because the mainstream has realized that they can profit from the more thorny margins, the more poisonous margins. Now you can witness extreme performative behavior on cheesy talk shows, HBO programs, and Hollywood films that surpasses the outrageous behavior of performance artists. You are then forced to re-evaluate your position as a social provocateur. If Jerry Springer or Howard Stern are capable of engaging in more "transgressive" social or sexual behavior than your colleagues, what does it mean to be "transgressive"? Or what does it mean to be kinky when in the trailer parks of rural America or in the halls of the White House there is more kink, raw kink, than in the most sophisticated vampire Goth clubs of New York City? It's disorienting ese.

JK: Which is precisely why the question that, for a brief moment, plagued reception of the Jerry Springer Show was: are your shows real? or is it all staged? Talk shows always walk this line between the "actual" and the "performed," and it's a line that millions of TV watchers are fascinated by. Performance is made everyday in this way. We are getting more and more accustomed to seeing "real life" as staged, more and more accustomed to assuming that what is being offered up as real TV, real life, reality programming, is a product of elaborate performances.

GGP: Performance art is national daily spectacle. There is no question about it.

JK: This issue you raise of marketing transgression makes me think of these new GAP ads for khaki pants. Have you seen them? They feature multi-racial skaters, rave kids, swing kids, punks, and b-boys all performing their subcultural difference in the same brand of pants. The first one was swing, then hip hop, now they have "Khakis Soul" and "Khakis Country," and you realize just how good mass culture has gotten at harnessing and containing difference while letting people think they are still being different – perform your difference by wearing our pants. Be marginal, be transgressive, just do it wearing the same pants.

GGP: Illusions of difference can be easily commodified. Retro-lounge culture and swing are like multiculturalism without people of color. That's what they are. Martini bars in San Francisco or Manhattan – choose the theme. Polynesian? Afro-Mambo? Miami Galore? Tex-Mex? You choose the subject matter. In these clubs there are no people of color. The impresarios of this new hype managed to somehow create a sexy "multicultural" scene without having to suffer the anger of being confronted by people of color and being accused of appropriation or bad dancing. They have successfully managed to erase the political text of difference. It's brilliant. They always outsmart us.

JK: Let me try to redirect us back to the role of the Internet. What I find interesting in relation to your use of it – especially if we can talk reductively about your work as moving from a site-specific approach to the border to a more elaborated, extended, or symbolic approach to it – is that one place you always hear about "erasing borders" or "going borderless" is in Internet discourse. According to the boosters, the Internet is the ultimate borderless zone. And of course there are any number of ways to critique this: borderless as long as you post in English, borderless as long as you can afford a computer with ample memory and the passport software required to enter this zone, and on and on. But in your work you deal with the Internet on the one hand as a space of possibility in terms of cross-cultural circuitry and transgressive identity enactment, but on the other as a place that is still policed.

GGP: I think that by 1995–6, the tone of the debates began to change because cyberspace was crashed by feminist theoreticians, by anarchists, by hackers, by pirates, by people of color, by third world intellectuals, by postcolonial theoreticians who learned the new lingo in a few years. And suddenly it became highly politicized and all these white guys who felt they had found a safe place of escape away from the complexities of the times, were once again scared of the cyber streets – there went the cyber-neighborhood, so to speak.

JK: So would we be willing to say that there's a relationship between the erosion of radical multiculturalism as a cohesive, viable discourse on the left, i.e. before multiculturalism became the discourse of the right, and the birth of the Internet as an alternate sphere of possibility? There's an interesting connection between the decrease of public sphere multiculturalist intervention and the potential gain of the Internet as a space of radical intervention.

GGP: Yes and no. The two main organizations, at least in the art world, dealing with new technologies – CyberConf and ISEA (International Society of Electronic Art) – have found a seasonal place for Roberto, myself and a handful of other politicized Chicano/Latino colleagues. But just like in the early days of multiculturalism, we're the unwanted, necessary guests at the party; the temporary insiders; the mariachis with a big mouth; the savages who unexpectedly fart. We are given the microphone for a couple of hours, and we use it fully knowing that we may not be invited again. But as we keep crashing those conferences year after year we don't see more representation coming. In fact in the last couple of years, what we see is the emergence of a "friendly backlash" type discourse . . ." Oh, we already dealt with this or that issue two conferences ago."

To give you an example. Roberto and I proposed to ISEA a huge international town meeting with techno disc jockeys in cyberspace coordinating multiple activities happening in so-called marginal communities and third world countries simultaneously for a span of two days, where performance artists, theoreticians, and activists were going to participate in a very exciting unmediated dialogue that would be the centerpiece of this year's (1988) international ISEA gathering. Then two months before it was about to happen, they canceled on us alleging they couldn't fundraise all the necessary money to make it happen. I truly believe they suddenly realized how complicated and potentially dangerous it was going to be.

Because of incidents like this one, I am much more realistic than I was during the multicultural era, much more pragmatic. I know Chicanos and Latin Americans will always be temporary insiders or insider/outsiders, and that is in fact a condition we will bear until we die. And I don't mind it because it grants us a special kind of freedom. I don't want to be an official cyber artist by any means. I remember when I became the official border artist and believe me it was a pain in the ass. The fact is that the art world only knows what we do with our right hand but they never know what we do with our left. Half of our activities, often the most interesting ones, go unnoticed. The art world is only interested when we hit the Corcoran gallery, the Walker Art Center or the Brooklyn Academy of Music.

JK: But not when you're meeting with farmworkers in Ohio –

GGP: – or with troubled teens in San Antonio or Native Americans on reservations in Canada and the US, nobody pays attention. None of our work taking place in extra-artistic contexts over the past five years has been covered by the art world and it's definitely the most interesting work we've done so far. So this condition of being insider/outsider is in fact a very convenient one – it keeps us from being entirely co-opted. I don't know if this is clear.

JK: It is and it also doubles back on something we were discussing the other day, when you asked me if I thought it was possible to successfully be a public intellectual in the US. Perhaps it's this insider/outsider position, never fully being one or the other, that is the condition necessary for the emergence of a public or "organic" intellectual. Because you're not fully inside the art world or academia, it forces you to inhabit the gap between them and that's where community enters. I'm really interested in your anxiety about your own status as a public intellectual. I was surprised to hear you say that. I was surprised to hear you say that you're looking for models.

GGP: In the US, because we don't have a tradition of organic, public intellectuals, and my generation is just in a process of trial and error, trying to develop models, because of this we never quite know what our real impact is. For example, my role as only one of two Latinos who ever get to speak on All Things Considered (National Public Radio) – does that mean that I truly have a national voice or not? I am not sure. I know that there is a potential audience of five million people for my radio essays and that the programs in many cities get to be re-broadcast twice in a day so there might even be a potential audience of ten million, and that makes me feel very good. I mean with one of my radio commentaries I get to reach more people that I ever will with all of my live performances put together. It's wild. So I put as much time into my three- or seven-minute radio pieces as I put into a very elaborate performance piece, because I know that to go on the air is a real political victory for a politicized performance artist. But then I never know if the fact that if I have to craft my voice to fit the All Things Considered format means that I'm taking the chile and the spices out of my food.

I mean, I try to push the envelope but in public radio, the envelope is quite stiff. Sometimes, when I do a piece that truly challenges radio tolerance, I inevitably receive a call from my editor, "Guillermo, can you . . . How can I put it? Make your ideas more understandable?" Or if the piece slips through the cracks and gets recorded exactly as I wanted it, then suddenly the tape disappears mysteriously from the shelves or its broadcast gets postponed indefinitely. It's fine with me. It's like a little game, each side trying to reposition the borders of permissiveness.

JK: It's the same with my music writing, though on a much smaller scale. Whether it's for alternative weeklies or national musical magazines, I'm always faced with trying to put something out to a potential audience – making a political point, introducing a new artist, raising issues that I feel other writers ignore – while making sure not to alienate that audience. Because I do see each piece as a rare window of opportunity to actually make an intervention in a public way.

GGP: It's also a great challenge of simulacrum, a great exercise in expropriation of the form. It would be ludicrous if you attempted to be as experimental as you can when you write for the *Guardian* or if I were to use my most transgressive performance techniques when I do a radio commentary for NPR. It would be politically kamikaze.

JK: And thoroughly counter-effective.

GGP: The point is to expropriate the format and push it one more degree and find an outer limit within the format. That is the challenge. And it is not an individual task, it must be a communal task, a task that a whole generation of thinkers, artists, activists, politicized journalists, must undertake.

JK: Sure, because if not, then the one person suffers from burdens of collective representation and suddenly you find yourself as not just NPR's leading Latino but as standing in and speaking for the Latino community as a whole, which as you know, is incredibly problematic to say the least, for everyone involved.

GGP: Very problematic.

JK: And you become the token brown voice –

GGP: – the Andrei Cordescou of Tijuana (*laughs*), or the Joseph Beuys of the grassroots (*laughs more*) –

JK: You laugh, but that kind of qualification, that kind of recontextualization, happens all the time when I try to get editors at national English-language magazines to approve story ideas involving rock en español bands, punkeros, Latino pop artists, Mexican rapero crews, etc. Usually the only way I can get them to say yes is to couch the artists in the context of the world the editors privilege. Speaking of Cafe Tacuba as an avant-pop band from Mexico City who transform traditional Mexican and Latin American musics means nothing, but calling them the "REM of Mexico" or something equally ridiculous perks an editor's ears.

When US publicity for the Monterrey-based hip hop/lounge/electronica duo Plastilina Mosh started rolling out, they were the "Beck of Mexico" or the "Mexican Beastie Boys." That kind of comparison may serve some degree of purpose in terms of cross-cultural translation, but it also works to elide the very real and important fact that in Latin America the kind of pastiche and recycling that both the Beastie Boys and Beck practice have been fundamental aesthetic strategies for centuries, if not from the very moment of colonization itself. So suddenly all that history is erased and Plastilina Mosh is just some Mexican copy of a first world original. It's frustrating and deeply problematic. There's never a way to talk about it that upsets the balance of cultural power. It keeps them exotic, foreign, and marginal and always reinstates colonialist hierarchies of representation. And when they do get written about, it's only one band every few months; running more than one review or article on a Latino/a or Latin American band in the same issue is a complete impossibility.

For example, a recent issue of *Details*, their "music issue," was themed as a sort of "world music" issue and was supposed to focus on artists across the planet. I was assigned a piece on the Venezuelan group Los Amigos Invisibles, but because there was also a piece on narco-corridos at the border, my article got killed. The exact words of my editor were, "Because of space, we couldn't have two articles on Spanish music." Spanish music! It wasn't even the old case of lumping together acts as nationally and stylistically distinct as a Venezuelan disco-funk band and Sonora corridistas into the vague "Latin music" generalization. It was seeing them only in terms of either their shared language – which would emphasize the extent to which so much of this comes down to an English-only language politics – or their shared colonial links to Spain.

Regardless, it always comes down to this attitude of patronizing and paternalistic inclusion, of being generous enough and taking enough of a perceived demographic risk with advertisers, to allow one of these groups in. It's the old "bringing the margins to the center" saw – never realizing that the center is marginalized, never realizing that Rolling Stone's white male demographic of Fleetwood Mac and Pearl Jam fans is rapidly becoming an imaginary one that the magazine is working overtime to re-create and keep alive.

GGP: We always make fun of that. When I was part of the so-called performance monologue movement in the late 80s, I used to call myself "Spalding Wet" in reference to Spalding Gray and like espalda mojada – wet back – and I had a performance called "Swimming to Tijuana." I always like to joke about the fact that we are always being referenced through the filter of US and European art and pop culture and never seen on our own terms – like Roberto and I being called the Cheech and Chong of the art world.

JK: Maybe this is a good juncture to get back to this question of being a public intellectual. As an artist who inhabits the US and Mexico simultaneously as a state of mind –

GGP: – and as a conceptual cartography –

JK: – do you think that being a public intellectual in Mexico works differently? I ask this because a term like "public intellectual" is always nationally moored. Your work and your performance itinerary, the map you are always moving across, is transnational in its scope, and this transnationalism, be it geopolitical

28 Mexican and Chicano Rock & Roll are a direct aesthetic influence in the Mexterminator Project. CyberVato gets ready to "shoot-up".

or cultural or performative, I think poses a challenge to how we generally characterize public intellectual work. So how does it work for you being in both Mexico and the US? Is it easier to play that role there?

GGP: It was up to the early 90s. Since Mexico wholeheartedly jumped into the troubled waters of neo-liberalism and globalization, my beloved native country has gone from being a partially industrialized society to an information-based, advanced capitalist society in a matter of say eight years without ever enjoying the goods of capitalism or information; without ever completing its industrialization phase. So we have engaged in the most dysfunctional form of capitalism and media culture, but nevertheless Mexico has thoroughly become a virtual nation that only exists in the cultural-scape of Televisa, the mega-media conglomerate. More and more, Mexico is experiencing the malaise of a post-industrial information-based society and as a result of this the intellectuals are becoming less and less national players and more and more media celebrities and only those who know how to play the media have made that leap. The great majority haven't. They are still writing for newspapers and only a small educated portion of the population reads the paper. And there's nothing wrong with this, but there was a time when in Mexico intellectuals could be heard regularly on radio, seen on television, could write for the national papers, could engage in debates with the political class, where everybody knew them in the country, much more so than in the US. And this is no longer the case.

Probably the best example as a marker is Octavio Paz's relationship with Televisa. When suddenly Paz was adopted as the official intellectual of Televisa about ten or twelve years ago, a new type of intellectual was inaugurated in Mexico, the official media intellectual. So now intellectuals in Mexico are experiencing the same marginality that US intellectuals experience. Here (in the US) it is perhaps a little worse because the only real space an intellectual has to survive in is academia and academia is not exactly connected to media or pop culture or community praxis. It's self-contained and self-referential, like a reservoir of intelligence, and only a handful of intellectuals existing in academia are really allowed to broadcast their views in national media, and we know they are not the most critical voices. If the US was a healthy and truly democratic society, we would see Naom Chomsky and Mike Davis and Michelle Wallace and Susan Harjo and Ed Said, we would see them regularly on television talking about politics and culture. Instead we get obscure social scientists and lawyers, lots of lawyers, and idiots like Bill Maher (on Politically Incorrect) explaining society to us.

JK: Part of the reason I brought this up again was because the more musicians I speak with and write about in Mexico, the more instances I find of musicians as intellectuals, or intellectuals as musicians – musicians who in Mexico truly are cultural workers. Musicians who double as journalists, columnists, community leaders, video makers, writers. There's much less of that in the US. Someone like Pacho in the Mexico City rock fusion band Maldita Vecindad. He uses his music to address cultural and political issues and in a sense, either rehearses those ideas or extends them, in his columns for the *Reforma* newspaper. It's rare to see entertainment and political dialogue coexist and inform each other in the public sphere in the US – being a rockero and a critic, a drummer and a cronista.

GGP: No, you're right. There's still some instances of this – Felipe Ehrenberg, the performance artist, and Roger Bartra the social anthropologist. They write in daily papers for example – but there's less and less of it. Besides, people like Felipe, Roger, and Pacho should have their own TV shows. Can you imagine que locura? Another factor that contributes to intellectuals and artists becoming increasingly less visible is the fact that it is practically impossible for them to live strictly from their work. So they are forced to engage in double or triple production and wear many hats and masks in order to survive.

JK: But isn't part of it also that in the US, in the case of rock music, there's a very different mythography and a very different culture attached to rock than the one in Mexico? In Mexico, if you're a rockero, you're not just performing as a musician, you are, whether you like it or not because of the politicized history of rock in Mexico, enacting a certain kind of resistant, subcultural identity. This was of course especially true in the 70s and 80s, from Avandaro until after the Mexico City earthquake, before Televisa decided to support rock and introduce it into the federally sanctioned national media culture.

GGP: True. There was a time when the rockeros were the great alternative chroniclers of "la reconstrución" of the city after the earthquake –

JK: Exactly. There's more of a slippage between these two spheres – cultural expression and politics – in Mexico than in the States, or at least the two have been more frequently brought together out of necessity, as a survival strategy.

GGP: But NAFTA has made it harder, neo-liberalism has made it harder, globalization has made it harder. Mexico is looking and behaving more and more like the US, and soon, in five or ten years, there won't be visible cultural differences across borders in this continent – both ways.

JK: So what do you do with that? How is this different from what you yourself have written of as 'the new world border,' an artistic transcontinental border zone?

GGP: In my performance work and writings I have attempted to articulate this "other cartography," a transborder culture not imposed from above but organically emerging from within –

JK: An anti-NAFTA transborder zone?

GGP: Exactly. At times, it looks similar at a far distance but when you get closer you realize they are fundamentally different. On the one hand you have the CNN or Discovery Channel type of continental or "global culture," the Benetton worldview, the pseudo-internationalism of world beat and the Internet, and on the other hand you have this more proletarian or grassroots "transworld culture" that is emerging organically from within, from street level up so to speak, in which chavos banda (rock kids) from Sao Paulo or Mexico City are not behaving that differently from youth in the Bronx or Oakland. The rockeros in the outskirts of Buenos Aires are dealing with similar issues as –

JK: – as North Africans in Paris –

GGP: – or Chicanos in East LA or Pakistanis in London –

JK: Something like a subaltern transnationalism.

GGP: An ex-centris kind of internationalism, a new internationalism that has nothing to do with Fifth Avenue tycoons or Parisian ethno-music impresarios. I mean, this internationalism escapes the CNN cameras.

JK: In a talk I gave once, I proposed rock en español as a good example of how this happens, how as a movement and now a genre, it has created a series of aesthetic and political transnational bridges between Mexicanos/as and Chicanos/as. And someone responded by saying that he couldn't think about transnationalism apart from imperialism. My point was precisely the opposite, that thinking in that way is a trap, thinking that way blinds you to the workings of cultural expression that works within the very channels of economic imperialism. Rock en español has been a force of reconnection between rockeros in Mexico City and rockeros in say, Chicago or San Jose. Jaime Lopez called it "un canto fronterizo" for good reason. We have to remember that there can be transnational resistance within economic transnationalism.

GGP: That's a very good way to put it. When you see a Lacandon Indian wearing a t-shirt of Ozzy Ozborne ten years later in the Yucatan jungle, that doesn't mean that he has been colonized. He has, in fact, co-opted it and turned it into a symbol of resistance, in this particular case against the government sponsored folkloric culture that Indians are supposed to wear and represent. So even though at times, corporate transnationalism and grassroots transnationalism can look very similar, one has to be very careful to distinguish them.

And also, at the end of the century, in this era of rabid globalization, alliances of political affiliation are of a different order; they're very eccentric and don't necessarily respond to ideological patterns.

JK: So take a band like Molotov, who mix Chicano-inflected hip hop with metal, who are from Mexico City, and who are signed to Universal. Their politics are supposedly progressive. They're anti-Zedillo, anti-PRI, anti-Televisa; they rap about political corruption and media hypocrisy, about economic injustice and call for redistributions of power. And yet, they are fully misogynist and homophobic and supposedly come out at one point as big supporters of the PAN [the right-wing opposition party]. Yet people have been writing about their music as radical and revolutionary. They've gotten support from leftist intellectuals like Carlos Monsivais. But is this musical leftism? Is this progressive? How do we talk about this kind of production that frustrates existing political alliances and allegiances?

GGP: I'm not sure. A culture that is used to suppressing anger in the public sphere, maybe it allows the commodification of anger. But on the other hand, groups like Plastilina Mosh and Molotov are more about the performance of anger than the content behind that anger. It is this sexy performative anger that appeals to people more than the political ideals behind it. It is the possibility of saying "chingada" in a song –

JK: – or in Molotov's case, "puto" [fagot] and then "dame todo el poder" [give me all the power] –

GGP: – and not the content of what these words actually translate into. I think this is very much a 90s phenomenon. We are already living in a society beyond content, in a world without theory, without ideology, where style is what matters, the form is what matters, the total experience is what matters. Complex ideas seem to be dated. It's really scary.

JK: My favorite thing about Molotov is that the gringo from New Orleans in the group, the drummer, landed in Mexico City because his father moved the family there when he was working for the DEA.

GGP: That's a perfect example! It makes total pinche sense! That's the thing. We have to be cautious when we assume an easy binary position because it simply doesn't work anymore. All the progressive conceptual territories that used to be sanctuaries of freedom and tolerance and contestation are now undergoing a process of redefinition and reconfiguration. So we cannot be blindly Zapatistas or entirely Chicanos. It doesn't work anymore. Our alliances are shifting with the shifting topography of the end of the century. Excuse my metaphors but we are in the middle of the earthquake. All the buildings and bridges are falling around us. And what is progressive in one context is not necessarily progressive in another. And this might change tomorrow.

JK: Which complicates the way rock and hip hop have started bringing Chicanos and Mexicanos together, the way that so many Mexican musicians are sounding more and more Chicano.

GGP: The Mexicanos who haven't had an immigrant experience in the US have a much harder time accepting this fact than the Chicanos and other US Latinos. The process of Chicanization in reverse that Mexican culture in all territories – in pop culture, in the arts, in fashion – has experienced in the last five to seven years is profound and irreversible and the Mexicanos are having a very hard time accepting it, especially the privileged intellectual and political elites.

JK: Rubén Martínez wrote a great piece about – and I'm greatly summarizing here – how gang names in Neza [Mexico City] are borrowed from gang names in East LA and South Central when none of these kids have ever been to LA. But they have seen *American Me* and *Mi Vida Loca*. So with this coupled with the way, say, Mexican raperos like Control Machete, Plastilina Mosh, Molotov, El Gran Silencio, are emulating cholo style and language – for the first time in a long time, Mexicanos aren't looking at Chicanos through Octavio Paz's eyes as cultural *huérfanos* [orphans], as empty of identity and culture, as Mexican sellouts. They're looking at Chicanos, especially Chicano youth culture, as models for new identity. But this gets complicated by what you've said, because what would be a progressive Chicano politics in 1999 might meet with resistance on the streets of Monterrey or Tijuana or Mexico City.

GGP: In the early days of rock en español, when the rockeros started syncretizing rock with traditional Mexican music, they were so invested in being perceived as original. So when they were confronted with the fact that Chicanos were already doing that in Los Angeles and San Antonio, they didn't like it and didn't want to acknowledge any overt influence. That was ludicrous. I remember engaging in very tough conversations with post-earthquake rockeros Mexicanistas in 1987-8 and saying, "You guys are sounding more and more Chicano and that's really cool," and them getting really pissed. This also happened in the performance art world with many of my colleagues as well as in literature and cinema. The diaspora always ends up influencing the homeland. But artists in Mexico are so insecure vis-à-vis the US and Europe and so ethnocentric regarding Chicanos that they have this desperate impulse to always be perceived on their own terms, as original, and innovative.

Luckily things are changing and I'd like to venture a theory. Before Zapatismo erupted, Mexicans thought that Mexico had already overcome its identity crisis since the Mexican revolution. And that it was those Chicanos, those ex-Mexicans living on the other side of the border, who were afflicted by a permanent identity crisis. In those days, the notion of identity was closely linked to language and territory. If you spoke Spanish and lived in Mexico, you were Mexican. And if you crossed the border you *ipso-facto* became a renegade, a traitor, a pocho. That was a complete fallacy based on a very old-fashioned binary model of identity. The Zapatistas came to prove this model wrong. When their revolution exploded in 1994, the country realized there was not just one

Mexico; there were many. And many of which had been forgotten and had never been part of the national life of the country. There were certainly a number of indigenous Mexicos that had nothing to do with the hegemonic views of national identity, and who were finally demanding recognition. So suddenly Mexicans became aware of their acute crisis of identity and they realized their crisis was at least as grave as that of the Chicanos on the other side. The potential for a new alliance, a new reconciliation began to emerge. On both sides of the border we are children of crises and orphans of two dysfunctional nation-states.

JK: One of the biggest effects of neo-Zapatismo on the rock en español scene, on both sides of the border, has been the increase of support for the Zapatistas. And it's happened to such an extent that voicing support for Marcos or playing a Zapatista benefit show has almost become de rigeur to the point of ideological emptiness, like wearing a red AIDS ribbon in the States. In the beginning, only a handful of bands, Maldita Vecindad, Tijuana NO, Santa Sabina, were doing benefits for the Zapatistas, pledging public support, using images of Zapatistas on record covers, using Marcos speeches on their albums, then it became a more widespread political gesture. And by 1998 or so, the Zapatistas had become a central part of what we were talking about, the commercialization of rebellion, with Marcos as just another revolutionary on a t-shirt.

GGP: But it's also true that without the support of the rockers, of the Internet, and without the sponsors of international hype, without ethno-sexual tourism – the myriad Europeans who arrive in Chiapas in search of an Indian maiden – without the support of all these bizarre things, the Zapatistas would have been wiped out by the Mexican government.

JK: This happens in the US all the time as well, the way subcultural performance and expression often relies on its very co-optation for survival.

GGP: Look at the lucha libre [Mexican wrestling] phenomenon in San Francisco, all these "Mexican wrestlers" who are in fact post-punk white kids performing a fictional identity. But as much as we criticize these new bohemian yuppies who are hardcore consumers of S&M, of fringe performance art, and world foods, tattoos, piercings, they are half of our audience in the 90s. Therefore we have to mimic the very objects of desire of these new audiences in order to appeal to

29 Ceding control to the audience. Audience member holds Gómez-Peña on a leash.

them and turn them around. It is a very interesting predicament for us. We don't want to shy away from those audiences, so we are very interested in mimicking a certain aesthetic that from a distance appeals to them because it explores the fringe desires and extreme aesthetics they are into. But once we have them, we turn it around them.

JK: How do you explain this shift in your audience's desires?

GGP: In the past years, performance art audiences have experienced an acute case of compassion fatigue. They have grown increasingly more intolerant of intellectually challenging and politically overt work, and at the same time much more willing to participate acritically in performance art events which allow them to engage in what they perceive as "radical behavior." As a response to this, my colleagues and I have been experimenting with new performance formats which can effectively speak to them, and catch them by surprise with their guards down so to speak.

JK: Can you give me some examples?

GGP: We are designing political raves and peep shows in which audience members get to become cultural transvestites and voyeurs at the same time. We are also working on interactive TV programs and designing a conceptual web page in which audience members assume some of our performance personas, are given tasks by us, then go and carry them out in public and then reconvene at a live performance event. We are hoping to be able to crossover with dignity into the pop cultural terrain and stage large populist spectacles without losing our souls, our political clarity, our thorns and edges. The new goal is to accept the Faustian deal, but hopefully to outsmart the devil. I still don't know if this is possible. It is still too early to gauge the success of these experiments.

JK: You have to be paradoxical in order to make your point. And it seems to me this is a very particular paradox that belongs to a very particular moment in the history of multiculturalism. One of the ways you've chosen to deal with and, in a sense, embrace this paradox is to highlight the extent to which so-called multiculturalism in the nineties has really become less about transformative politics and more about cultural confessions and collective racial therapy sessions.

In *Temple of Confessions* you entered this very territory, the connection between multiculturalism and cultural confession. I'm interested in how multiculturalism has become just another form of confession, of confessing our sins. And especially how this mode of confession has shifted agency and voice away from people of color and toward Euro-Americans, how multiculturalism is now very centrally about white folks confessing their multicultural sins, desires, guilt, phobias – a lot of guilt and phobia. The key then is to recognize how deeply confession has saturated multiculturalist discourse and then to regain control of it by controlling the mode of confession itself. *Temple of Confessions* attempted to do this, I think. You took the confessions. You manipulated the confessions.

GGP: Earlier, we were talking about the similarities and differences between journalism and performance art. Another difference is that performance art deals with the invisible forces of social phenomena, with what I term "the geology of social and cultural phenomena." It also deals with subtle, hidden or indirect psychological and spiritual forces. In other words, performance deals with the subtextual more than the textual; with the forbidden, and the unspoken. Because of this, as a performance artist, I am particularly interested in revealing the hidden texts of multiculturalism, those that were never part of the public debate. For instance, in early 1994 when Roberto and I began our confessional experiments, I was particularly interested in tapping into the collective subconscious of my audience in order to articulate all the unspoken relationships between the South and the North, between Mexico and the US, between Anglos and Latinos. And this meant dealing head-on with issues of fear and desire; interracial sex, and all the sensitive stuff that academicians and the mass media rarely talk about. Mexico and the US have always had a very complicated relationship of intertwined fear and desire. Anglos and Latinos are both scared and seduced by one another. The marines in San Diego who are trained to go and kill Central Americans, they all have Mexican wives or go to Tijuana on the weekends in search of a "señorita." Meanwhile, Mexican nationalists listen to US rock and roll, watch American movies, wear puro US fashion and if they can, they fall in love with blonde foreigners. I mean, our fears contradict and complement our desires. It's inevitable.

JK: Ralph Ellison once wrote about a group of white kids harassing black kids while listening to a Stevie Wonder record.

GGP: That's the territory we are interested in, the forbidden texts. There are many undercurrents beneath the US–Mexico border and that's what I want to get at. For example, I want to understand the connection between racism and sexual attraction; or the connection between racism and the exoticization of the other. A lot of people in this country, many of whom are racists, fantasize about wanting to be of another race, about wanting to escape their own race and ethnicity. I mean, a great majority of Americans. Whites wanting to be black, Latino or Indian; Latinos wanting to be blonde or Spanish, Blacks wanting to be white, everyone wanting to be Indian. To want to become an Indian is a quintessential American desire. Those who spout racist statements against Indians, they're completely seduced by an alleged indigenous spirituality and mysticism.

As much as they hate "real" Indians in the big city, they'd love to be Indian warriors or shamans. Same with Mexico.

One of the things we are doing lately – it's so dangerous we have only been able to perform it three or four times under very careful circumstances – we call them "identity make-over booths." We invite the audience into spaces where they go through different stages of "ethnic transformation." First, they check out a catalog where they get to choose their favorite cultural Other. It can be a mythic cultural other, say a mysterious Arab terrorist, a macho Mexican revolutionary or an angry Afrocentric activist or they can create their favorite composite identity, incorporating elements of the various identities in the menu. Then they go to the next room where special effects make-up artists begin to transform their faces and the color of their skin. Then they go to another room where professional costume artists give them the right clothes and then, once they are finished with the transformation, they finally get to perform their fictional identities in a diorama for ten minutes. At times, they get to choose their poses, and believe me what they come up with is extremely revealing. Other times, we as performance artists get to direct those poses, and we turn them into "human paper cut-out dolls," which is the exact opposite of what we do in the Mexterminator, where we become the passive cut-out dolls for our audiences. We reverse the experiment.

So you have these audience members at the end of the performance who are fully transformed into their favorite cultural others and we often encourage them to go into the streets with their new identity; to go into a bar or a restaurant and experience how it feels to occupy these identities. And it's only in the morning after, when they wake up with a horrible cultural hangover, that they realize the implications of the experiment. Then, they feel angry, pissed or betrayed. It's a very delicate experiment.

JK: It may be delicate because it exposes the extent to which that kind of outfitting, that kind of organized racial transvestitism, happens everyday in a very mundane, unremarkable, organic way. Wearing the identity of an Other is common practice within American culture, particularly of course among whites – blackface, cowboys and Indians, white Negroes. Contemporary white youth cultures, for example, are built upon racial fantasy, appropriation, and cross-dressing. I just went to a hip-hop show in Western Massachusetts a month ago and virtually the entire audience was white, with very few black kids around.

the Mayans and went native all the way. He was technically the first hippy of the Americas. At the end, Aguilar actually fought on the side of the Mayans against Cortez and lost his life at the hands of other Spaniards. Cabeza de Vaca the Spanish explorer became an apprentice of an Indian shaman and almost lost his mind in the process. There are hundreds of examples. This type of cultural transvestitism is at the core of continental American culture, and all we can do as artists is try to understand it.

One of the things we have done in the past years is to collaborate very openly and very textually with white women, in defiance of Chicano and Chicana nationalists. They have been extremely critical of the fact that some of our main collaborators in the last couple years like Sara Shelton-Mann and Rona Michelle have been Anglo women – not all, because we also work with wonderful Chicana, Latina colleagues. Besides the fact that we respect their work, Roberto and I collaborate with these women because they are unapologetic about their cultural kleptomania and transvestitism. And to articulate these processes on stage is extremely important to us. We try to do it critically of course. But our critique is not a morally righteous one. We are not condemning them for appropriation. We are again bringing to the surface the unspoken texts of multiculturalism and trying to do it in a very creative way.

JK: You're making me think again that we can no longer afford to keep discussions of multiculturalism separate from corporate culture, because this is the very convergence that makes the everyday transvestitism possible. In the 20s, for example, if you were a white singer interested in black music, you went to a bar or a nightclub to watch black singers and musicians. If you were say Al Jolson or George Gershwin, you went uptown to Harlem, watched and listened, and then went back downtown and re-created what you saw and heard in your own language and musical grammar. The difference now is that you don't have to go uptown. You watch it on cable, on BET. You pay for it each month. You sit in your bedroom in suburban Ohio or Iowa or wherever and watch Wu-Tang or Master P videos and there is no sense of what's at stake. Because it's on cable, on your TV, in your private bedroom, it in a sense becomes yours and you claim ownership of it and appropriate it without having to deal in any way with the physical realities that once had to be negotiated. And then you go to your local mall, buy the record, and not think twice about taking that identity on.

GGP: Exactly. The Northern (Anglo) multicultural model as opposed to the Southern (Latino) multicultural model is a Danteian model. You leave the self-proclaimed center, and from the center you either descend to the nine circles of hell or you venture towards the margins. And in the process of "descending" you find enlightenment. Then you come back to the center and speak about it. Or you "discover" an exciting type of otherness which later on you will sponsor, emulate, or be a ventriloquist of.

JK: How would you say the Latin American "multicultural" model differs?

GGP: At its best, the Latin American model is about ascending the social scale and taking the power away from those who have it or moving from the margins we've been forced to inhabit to the center and occupying the center, de-centering it. This is what the revolutionary projects have been about: ascending, taking power, and de-centering. But since US multiculturalists are engaged in the opposite process and venturing in the opposite direction – from the center to the margins – what happens is that we merely bypass one another. The result is mutual misunderstanding. Anglos don't seem to understand why Latinos and blacks in this country are so obsessed with going towards the center. And it's so obvious. If you have been marginalized for five hundred years, the margins are no longer romantic or desirable to you. Once the Chicano and African-American rappers are able to leave the "ghetto" or "barrio," and stop wearing those clothes, they will do it. For them, it is no longer romantic. But for the Anglo kids who have been raised in the suburbs, to look like "gangster" rappers is definitely a romantic proposition.

JK: I guess what I'm trying to get at is that, as you said in the context of the Irish dandies "going native," now to go native you don't actually have to go anywhere and you don't need any actual natives.

GGP: You have Burning Man –

JK: Sure, but you don't even have to go there. You order a CD off the web, you watch BET, you watch MTV. The sampling debate has touched on this too. In the days of anthropological field recordings, ethnomusicologists traveled to indigenous communities to record ritual songs, ceremonial chants, work songs, whatever. Now you can buy a digital version of those recordings in a record store in London or New York, sample and loop it on a digital sampler, put some high-speed breakbeats beneath it and release your own twelve-inch. Sampling is traveling without the travel. When Loop Guru, two white British DJs and producers, or Deep Forest, two white French studio engineers, sample pygmy music or North Indian ragas, they're going native without having to leave the space of their recording studio.

GGP: This is happening in a different way with border culture. Since the early 90s, border culture has been fully commodified. Mainstream culture has stripped border culture of any of its political content and has turned it into an object of desire. Border cantinas became chic in New York in 1993 and Macy's had a border fashion shop. Border imagery can be seen on the pages of *Colors* magazine, and on the album covers of LA rock bands. MTV is filled with hip images of the border, Fridamania, Guadeloupabilia, bleeding hearts, Mexican altars, wrestler masks, Chicano gothic tattoo art, you name it. So what do you do with that, with the border no longer being a zone of danger and contestation but a hip conceptual mall? You then have to reposition the border. That is what is so fascinating about border culture. The border has to be redefined over and over again.

JK: Because for better or worse, the border has always been a site of image control – how the government portrays it, how Hollywood portrays it. So as a consequence, there always has to be this shift in image control, among artists and cultural workers and activists, to redirect how the border gets envisioned and talked about. The border also becomes a set of condensed floating images, disconnected commodity objects like the Taco Bell chihuahua. That dog doesn't represent the border as such but it –

GGP: It's the most famous Mexican in the US!

JK: – conjures up older archives of cultural stereotyping.

GGP: This friend of mine, Michelle Ceballos, the Colombian performance artist living in Phoenix, has always been talking about the invisibility of Latinas in the US. She recently told me something hilarious, she said that she had finally discovered how to solve the problem of Latina invisibility: just buy a chihuahua dog. "I got myself a chihuahua and I have become visible in America. No matter where I am people talk to me."

This is just one aspect of how the border becomes re-centralized. It went from being a site of contestation, the source of a binational project of decentralization to a site of re-centralization by transnational cultural institutions. So, for example, look at how border art has gone from being a subaltern cultural movement to becoming a world expo . . . InSite (Tijuana/San Diego), a huge binational art expo sponsored by mainstream museums and the PRI with a decreasing number of local border artists. It's border art tourism at its best. Curators, fashionable artists, and jet-setters get to go hang out at the border. They get to do the border safari, see real life migrant workers be chased by the border patrol, see real life lowriders. They get to go to the border fence, to Tijuana sex clubs. Then they go back to the art openings and exchange anecdotes and border trivia. It's kind of sick. It's official multiculturalism gone wrong.

The job of artists and theoreticians, then, is to move away from hipness once hipness has become institutionalized and to go where the cultural energy goes. Our job is to follow that energy and do everything we can to articulate it.

IN SEARCH OF A
NEW
TOPOGRAPHY

PART 4

"The only way to avoid becoming an exotic anti-hero is to constantly reinvent oneself; to disappear every now and then, and then to come back with a new set of strategies, metaphors, voices, costumes and weapons."

FROM GÓMEZ-PEÑA'S PERFORMANCE DIARIES, 1996

"Our great challenge is to continue creating new languages which can perform the role of 'bridges' with the social realm. For the moment we know what not to do, and that is to repeat ourselves . . . The future of zapatism is language."

MARCOS INTERVIEWED BY ARGENTINE POET JUAN GELLMAN

The "Subcomandante" of Performance

(An earlier version of this text was originally published in a book titled "First World, ha-ha-ha," City Lights, 1994. Though this version has been re-written, I caution the reader to bear in mind the vertiginous speed with which contemporary political and media landscapes change. By the time this book gets published, the fate of Marcos and the Zapatistas will very probably have changed drastically, along with their performance strategies.)

➤ I

The sleepy colonial city of San Cristobal de las Casas (Chiapas) was chilly. It was about 12 noon, October 12, 1992, and the San Cristobaleños were getting ready for the official festivities of the "Discovery of America." Suddenly over 5000 indigenous people crashed the party. They marched into town costumed as "Hollywood Indians" with *taparrabos* (generic tribal underwear) and home-made spears. They went straight for the statue of psychotic conquistador Don Diego de Manizales, "the founding father of San Cristobal," and trashed it. One man dressed as an "Indian king" delivered an impassioned anti-quincentennial speech in Spanish and an Indian language, and when the spoken-word intervention was over, the vernacular performance troupe disappeared from town. This epic perfomance, perhaps one of the largest political performance pieces ever, was in fact the first public intervention of an obscure guerrilla movement bubbling away in the *chiapaneca* jungle. The press reported the incident as a mere curiosity.

➤ ‖

Mexico City was hung over. Early in the morning of January 1st, 1994, its inhabitants were recuperating from the epic New Year's Eve celebrations. Turning on my television, I was suddenly confronted with images of *guerrilleros* which resembled the Sandinista upheaval of the late 70s and the Salvadoran civil war. At first, I thought it was a documentary about Central America. Then, an excited reporter announced that "an armed group calling itself the Zapatista National Liberation Army has taken over the city of San Cristóbal de las Casas, and several small villages in the jungle of Chiapas . . . They have declared war on the Mexican army" and the "illegitimate government of Salinas de Gortari." My heart began to pound rapidly. I phoned some of my friends. I woke them up. They thought I was kidding.

What made the Zapatista insurrection different from any other recent Latin American guerrilla movement was its self-conscious, highly theatrical and sophisticated use of the media. From the outset, the EZLN was fully aware of the symbolic impact of their largely conceptual military actions. They strategically chose to begin the war precisely on the same day that NAFTA went into effect. Since the second day of the conflict, they have placed as much importance on staging press conferences and theatrical photos as on their military strategy. The war has been carried on as if it were performance. Most of the Zapatistas, indigenous men, women, and children, wore *pasamontañas* [black ski masks] "in order to reveal their true identities" as forgotten and generic Others. Some even utilized wooden rifles as mere props. One of the leaders, Subcomandante Marcos, turned out to be a consummate *performancero*. He was undoubtedly the latest pop hero in a noble tradition of performance activists which includes the now legendary Superbarrio, Fray Tormenta (the wrestler priest who used to wrestle professionally in order to support an orphanage), Super-Ecologista, and Super-Animal, all self-styled "social wrestlers" who have utilized performance, media strategies and a good dose of humor to crash the rowdy political "wrestling arena" of contemporary Mexico.

➤➤ III

Since his first appearances in the media, Marcos, otherwise known as *"el Sup,"* has appealed to the most diverse and unlikely sectors of society. Why? In the confusing era of "the end of ideology," his utopian political visions of a multiracial, multigendered, multiparticipatory Mexico – presented in simple, non-ideological, and poetic language – went straight to the jaded hearts and minds of students, activists, intellectuals, artists, nihilistic teens, and even apolitical middle-class professionals. In an era of ferocious neo-nationalisms, he made sure to avoid separatist jargon and dogmas. His combination of political clarity, bravado, and humility seduced progressive politicians and activists throughout the world. His eclectic discourse, spiced with irreverent humor and an array of surprising references to pop culture, contemporary writers and topical world news, revealed a sophisticated internationalism. Despite all this, he remained humble, or effectively performed the role of humility. (He defined himself as a mere *"sup,"* diminutive for subcommander, a kind of secretary of public relations, a humble "interpreter" to the outside world.) His serious but nonchalant demeanor (the *rockero*), adorned with a pipe (the intellectual), and a Zapata-style bandolera (the rebel) with huge bullets that didn't match the model of his weapon (the actor), made him extremely photogenic. His persona was a carefully crafted collage of twentieth-century revolutionary symbols, costumes, and props borrowed from Zapata, Sandino, Che Guevara, Arafat and the IRA, as well as from celluloid heroes such as Zorro and Mexico's movie wrestler, "El Santo." Because of all this, the *New York Times* christened him "the first postmodern guerrilla leader," and newspapers and magazines throughout the world made it a priority to obtain an interview with him. The cult of Marcos was born, and unlike pop stars or sports heroes, no Televisa or Fifth Avenue tycoon was involved in the making of the myth.

El Sup planned his relationship with the media very carefully. The international press was a priority, of course. *Le Monde, Der Spiegel, Le Figaro*, the *New York Times*, the *San Francisco Chronicle, NACLA*, and *Vanity Fair* were immediately welcomed into the jungle. With regard to the Mexican press, he was a bit more cautious. He favored two independent dailies, *La Jornada* and *El Financiero*, and developed a direct line of communication with them. He also put a lot of emphasis on radio, since for most of the indigenous communities of Chiapas and throughout rural Mexico, it is still the main source of information. The pro-government media conglomerate, Televisa, was banned from press conferences and peace talks. This, of course, was an act of defiance that Televisa couldn't resist. Their reporters did everything they could to get close to the hero. They tried to sneak in as members of other TV networks, and when they couldn't, they bought footage from European television.

Someone gave Marcos his first lap-top, and he immediately ventured into cyberlandia. He began to engage in ongoing communication with the "outside world" through web sites sponsored and designed by US and Canadian radical scholars. (It is still a mystery to me how his communiqués arrive literally over-night from his headquarters in the jungle village of "La Realidad" in Northern Chiapas – which still has no electricity – to his web pages.)

The results of the mega-publicity campaign orchestrated by Marcos and Compañía were epiphenomenological (excuse the big word). In a matter of weeks, Marcos became a household name around the world. An industry of Zapatista and Marcos-inspired souvenirs flourished overnight. T-shirts, ski-mask condoms, key chains, posters, and Indian dolls with tiny ski masks and wooden rifles were favorites among political tourists. Besides, it was common to see masked teens attending rock concerts in support of Zapatism, and not just in Mexico. I attended a concert of French fusion rock band Mano Negra in the Vasque Country and more than half of the audience was wearing Zapatista masks. At one point it became hard to draw the line between radical politics and pop culture, between solidarity and revolutionary consumerism.

Eroticism was a crucial ingredient in Marcos' hype. His soft and sincere voice, and "beautiful hazel eyes" framed by the black mask, turned him into a sex symbol, an icon of forbidden sexuality. Many lonesome housewives and starry-eyed students projected their sexual fantasies onto him, writing passionate love letters that were regularly published in national newspapers. Marcos answered each and every one of them. One of his most famous letters, addressed to writer Elena Poniatowska, began with the following line: "Señora, I am prostrate at your feet." In one letter I read in *La Jornada*, an upper-class woman described her irresistible desire "to get lost in the jungle with Marcos for good."

The bizarre phenomenon of eroticization/exoticization of Marcos and the Zapatistas inspired many artists. In a cabaret theater piece by Jesusa Rodríguez, a suave Marcos did an incomplete "mask striptease" to the beat of a cumbia. In San Francisco, Chicana performance artist Isis Rodriguez developed a "Zapatista stripper" act to raise consciousness about the rights of sex workers. My own performance work was inevitably influenced by this phenomenon: in *Borderama*

(1994-5), various nude Zapatistas, masked men and women, mopped the stage in slow motion to the melancholic sounds of an aria, while an S&M "Zapatista super-model" holding a rifle showcased "the latest revolutionary wear" and "activist lingerie." The romantic iconography provided by Zapatismo filtered through the semiotic and visual codes of most contemporary Mexican and Chicano artists, cartoonists, filmmakers, performance artists and rockers. Even the most apolitical artists participated in auctions or benefit concerts to raise funds in order to send supplies and medicines to the indigenous peoples of Chiapas.

➻ IV

Though Marcos became the most famous Mexican celebrity in the world, no one knew who he really was. Obsessive discussions about his "real identity" dominated the conversation in homes, at the workplace, and in cafés. Magazines and newspapers exhausted theories and speculations. Although deep inside no one wished to unmask him, every Mexican had a colorful theory about his identity. In one of the most popular early theories, he was thought to be a foreign intellectual (he speaks fluent English, French, and a few indigenous languages), but soon his Mexico City accent spiced with *norteñismos* (slang from Northern Mexico) caused most to discard that rumor. Many detected traces of liberation theology in the mystical tone of his communiqués, parables, and interviews, and concluded that he was a radical Jesuit priest, but the Catholic Church vehemently denied this hypothesis. Others perceived him as an ex-leader of the 1968 student movement, but a journalist who spent time with *el Sup* revealed that he was only 38 years old at the time of the Zapatista insurrection, which meant that in 1968 he would have been 13. Other theories described him as a puppet of a dissident faction within the PRI sponsored by a megalomaniac ex-president, a frustrated writer enacting the book he was unable to write, a bisexual playboy, and a mystic propelled by ancient forces and fulfilling Mayan prophecies written in the Popul Vuh and the *Chilam Balam*. Real-life events often helped to nurture the image of Marcos as messiah. During the *Convención Nacional Democrática* [Democratic National Convention] which took place in August of 1994 in the Chiapaneca village of Aguascalientes, at the precise moment when Marcos spoke the final words of his speech, the giant canopy built to protect the 6,000 visitors from the rain suddenly collapsed on top of them.

30 Chicana performance artist Isis Rodriguez as a Zapatista stripper.

most popular souvenirs was a rubber figurine of ex-president Salinas, by then in exile in Ireland, with vampire wings, looking like a nerdy cousin of Batman.

One night, my friends and I were hanging out in a Mexico City barrio, when suddenly we heard a megaphone coming from a nearby fair, announcing "the exhibit of the one and only Chupacabras." We ran to it like kids. We found a decrepit bus decorated with rótulo-style paintings of Mexican folk monsters. Inside, we could see "the last living Aztec dog," a midget turkey, a two-headed snake, a five-legged calf, and assorted stuffed animals, including a gigantic rat (clearly an embalmed puma with a taxidermic facelift). At the end of this bizarre traveling dime-museum was a red velvet curtain and a tiny child impresario dressed in a tuxedo, demanding extra money "to witness the superstar vampire himself." When the curtain opened, this is what we saw: a stuffed eagle with the moving head of a goat, bearing three huge glued-on horns, and a child's voice coming from behind. "I am the Chupacabras," he said. "Don't you dare to look at me! Don't you know that if you look at me I will cease to exist?" And then the curtains closed.

I believe El Chupacabras does exist . . . in the collective imagination of working-class Mexicans. He is undoubtedly the incarnation of every Mexican's fears. Someone or something, is sucking our blood, our civic spirit, our savings, our sense of reality. He seems to represent the blood-sucking political class, and more concretely, the neoliberal political cartel headed by Mr. Salinas, which is responsible for the worst inflation in modern history, and for many unresolved political crimes. But I also believe that at one point, politicians themselves found it expedient to promote the fame of El Chupacabras in order to distract us. What they didn't foresee was that people have the capability to expropriate official myths, turning them into political satire and irreverent pop art.

➤➤ll Nafta Witchcraft (1997)

The Spanish word "brujería" conjures a much wider range of images and meanings than, say, "witchcraft" or "magic." It speaks of an ancient indigenous belief system that connects its eccentric practitioners to higher or parallel worlds where time, space, "reality," and ethics have entirely different meanings. And the Indian noun "chamanismo" means not only Indian medicine; it also implies ritual performance, proletarian psychiatry, and in some cases, political activism.

Throughout the years, my friends and I have become regular clientele (or, more specifically, audience members) of such brujos or shamans. Being performance artists ourselves, we view them as colleagues. Their job, like ours, is to create, with the use of chant poetry, surprising gestures and ritualized actions, highly charged props and elaborate costumes, a coherent symbolic system that helps patients (or in our case audience members) understand themselves, their existential malaise and their socio-cultural circumstances a little better.

We've met many amazing brujos. At center stage of my memory stands Don Feyo, "the black Christ" from the Mexican state of Morelos, a huge man with a goatee and slow and purposeful movements who practices surgery with the help of "invisible doctors." According to Mauro, one of Don Feyo's loyal apprentices, he is involved in a mysterious political campaign: to fight corrupt politicos though brujería. Mauro is convinced that el maestro and his secret colleagues are responsible for putting in jail many PRI politicians who have fallen from the party's grace. "La India" is another eccentric bruja who has a double life, along with her husband Gus. At the popular Sonora market in Mexico City, they aid working-class people suffering from black magic curses with their *sui generis* blend of Cuban santería and Mexican brujería. They first "read" the caracoles to make a diagnosis on the source and nature of a person's condition, then offer a one-day limpia ritual at a river on the outskirts of the city. The mystical duo claims that once a month they get flown to Los Angeles by wealthy New Agers to perform limpias in Santa Monica beach houses, and exorcise the bad luck out of newly opened nightclubs and restaurants. And when they tell you this, you somehow believe them. Many brujos are binational practitioners and members of intricate multinational networks. Doña Erminia from La Mision in San Francisco is the spiritual madrina (godmother) of many Chicano artists, including myself. She is a traditional altar maker, a drummer, a songwriter, a chef, and a humble bruja. During weekdays, she cleans houses and cooks for people who don't have the slightest idea who she really is. On the weekends, she hangs out at art events and organizes "reuniones espiritistas" with other Latina immigrant women. They invoke the spirit of their deceased loved ones to help them cope with the labor hardships of immigrant life.

"El Shanik" is the only brujo in San Juan Chamula, Chiapas, who welcomes "ladinos" (white outsiders). The misspelled wooden sign outside his tiny shack reads in Spanish, English and French: "Traditional witch doctor." He claims he once met "el señor (George) Bush" in 1992 and cured him of seven different mysterious illnesses. And he's got a photo of him and Bush in the Oval Office movement operating out of fear of modernity and change. The Virgin was certainly not aware of the way her powerful image as "The Mother of all Mexicans" and "The Queen of the Americas" was being used by zealots. She didn't know, and still doesn't know, that in her name, many people in Mexico have been forced into social submission, political passivity and fear – fear of religious and cultural difference, fear of sex, "sin", and eternal punishment, fear of contradicting the majority, of being an inadequate Mexican. And ultimately, fear of metaphysical orphanhood, of not belonging to the great (and mythical) Mexican family.

Mexico's ruling party, the PRI, has always been keenly aware of the importance of nurturing a mythology capable of unifying an extremely diverse society. In the official Olympus of la mexicanidad,[2] "La Reina" Guadalupe stands proud next to Aztec martyrs Moctezuma and Cuauhtemoc, Independence *caudillo* Father Hidalgo, Indian president Benito Juárez, revolutionary leader Emiliano Zapata and a few other mighty Mexicans. And together, from the clouds of the volcanos which surround Mexico City, they guard our identity, our national character, and our sovereignty. Again, La Vírgen doesn't know this.

In the late 1970s, I realized that although I was a strong critic of institutionalized Catholicism, I was culturally and ethnically a Catholic, whether I liked it or not. My (ex-Catholic) agnosticism was merely the other side of the same coin. In other words, five hundred years of Mexican Catholicism couldn't simply be erased with political awareness. When I began to write poetry and practice performance art, Catholic images and ritual ceremonies inadvertently began to emerge in my work, right next to my contestatary politics, my pagan (and eclectic) spirituality, and my sexual explorations. Despite a conscious rejection of formalized religion, my sensibility and symbolic languages were soaked in the pathos, high drama, and excessive aesthetics of Mexican Catholicism[3]. And this, of course, got me into serious trouble.

In late 1983, I was abruptly made aware of the dangers of re-contextualizing Catholic imagery, especially that of Guadalupe. My performance troupe, Poyesis

2   An inventory of static idiosyncratic characteristics which supposedly constitute Mexican identity as defined by Mexican writers in the twentieth century from Samuel Ramos to Octavio Paz.

3   Mexican Catholicism is a syncretic blend of the form and content of the Spanish Catholic church with a myriad indigenous traditions. The result is much more baroque, and "pagan" in the best sense of the term.

Genetica,[4] and I were rehearsing a piece titled *Ocnoceni* (a Nahuatl term used to describe geographical otherness) at the Casa de la Cultura in Tijuana. In one scene, a slide of the Virgin of Guadalupe was projected onto the white habit of a gigantic nun, performed on stilts by dancer Sara-Jo Berman. The nun suddenly broke into a sweaty tropical cumbia and began doing a full striptease to the delight of a horny Latin American general exiled somewhere in Southern California, performed by myself. The night before the opening, during dress rehearsal, a group of conservative-looking women in their fifties with elaborate hairdos showed up and sat quietly in the back row of the theater. We didn't pay much attention to them. They stayed for about an hour and left. The next morning when my colleagues and I went back to the theater, we were told by a nervous security guard what had happened: a group of militant Guadalupanos, tipped off by the women who witnessed the rehearsal, had broken into the theater at night and trashed the set and the costumes. They took a gallon of theater blood and painted religious slogans all over the floor and back wall. The message was clear: you simply don't mess around with the Great Mother of Mexico. We cleaned up the mess in silence, our hearts trembling with an alien sentiment of sin. Despite the chilling effect this incident had on us, we had to open the show and perform it for four consecutive nights.

In 1987, a Guatemalan artist named De la Rosa had a scarier experience. He opened a show at the Museo de Arte Moderno in Mexico City that included collages in which he superimposed pop cultural images onto Catholic iconography. One of the pieces was a Virgin of Guadalupe with the face of Marilyn Monroe. Another presented an image of Christ preceding the Last Supper with the face of legendary Mexican actor and ranchero singer Pedro Infante. Soon after the opening, a crowd of fierce Guadalupanos stormed into the Museum and demanded the resignation of the director. It was election time, and in order to appease the conservative opposition, the Mexican government complied and fired the troubled Museum director. De la Rosa had to go into hiding for several months. It was a sad day in the history of Mexican freedom of speech.

Effectively, La Guadalupe is an untouchable icon. If we research the myriad *chistes* (irreverent jokes) involving Catholic characters, we can find Jesus

---

4   Poyesis Genetica is discussed in my first book, *Warrior for Gringostroika*, Greywolf Press, 1993.

Christ, Mary Magdalena, the apostles, and even the Pope engaging in outrageous behavior, even in overt sexual actions, but La Vírgen is conspicuously absent.

➤ ❙❙

When I moved to California in 1978, my relationship with what I saw as official Mexican iconography began to change. Suddenly the political and religious images that I used to question as icons of authority and artificial generators of *mexicanidad* began to transform themselves into symbols of resistance against the dominant Anglo-Protestant culture. I also discovered that my new Chicano colleagues had a very different connection to Guadalupan imagery. Responding to a dramatically different cultural environment, they had expropriated it and turned it into a symbol of active resistance, something that Mexicans in Mexico have never been able to fully understand. They have failed to comprehend that symbols, aesthetic gestures, and metaphors are contextual, and when they cross a cultural border they either crack open, or metamorphosize into something else. Because of this, Mexicans without an extensive immigrant experience tend to perceive Chicanos as naive Guadalupanos.

In the Chicano movement, La Vírgen was no longer the contemplative mestiza mother of all Mexicans, but a warrior goddess who blessed the cultural and political weapons of activists and artists. She became politicized. She was against racism, the border patrol, bigoted cops, and white supremacist politicians. And in the Chicana feminist Olympus, La Guadalupana stood defiant and compassionate as a symbol of ancient female strength, right next to La Malinche (Cortez's misunderstood Indian lover), Frida Kahlo, Sor Juana Inés de la Cruz (the seventeenth-century nun/poet) and more recently, Tex Mex diva Selena. She no longer just stood motionless with praying hands and an aloof gaze. She could sit down and take a break, abandon

31 One of the classical 1970s performance photographs of Chicana artist Yolanda López posing as a jogging virgin of Guadalupe.

temporarily her holy diorama and go jogging, or let a working-class woman temporarily take her place, as in the artwork of San Francisco-based artist Yolanda López. She showed up in demonstrations and strikes, and generously lent her image to be used in barrio murals, lowrider cars, album covers, t-shirts and political posters. At times, she also dared to replace the Statue of Liberty and became the Vírgen of la Liberty, as in the work of Denver-based visual artist Fresquez. Clearly Chicanos and Mexican immigrants were able to reinvent and activate the icon of La Guadalupe in a way that would have been unthinkable in Mexico at the time. This became apparent when the brave Mexico City feminist magazine *Fem* decided to publish on its cover an image of a jogging Guadalupe by Yolanda López. The staff received several bomb threats and was forced to pull back. It wasn't until the mid- to late 1980s artists in Mexico – mainly the so-called "pintores neo-mexicanistas" – began to use images of Guadalupe in their art work. But even then, she was a decorative and somewhat neutral folk icon – a playful yet de-politicized symbol of rural or working-class *mexicanidad*. It wasn't a coincidence that some of these young painters were heavily promoted by the Mexican government as part of its diplomatic cultural agenda.

➺ III

For years, I felt that the mythology of la Guadalupe was an exclusive domain of Chicana artists and writers. (In the US, special interest groups and ethnic- or gender-based communities tend to presume total control over certain conceptual territories.) Ana Castillo tried to dispel my anxiety: "Precisely because of this, I want you to write about it. There is very little writing on La Vírgen done by Mexican men."

Now that I have accepted her challenge, I am slowly disentangling my contradictory feelings about Guadalupe as I write this text. Despite my continuous critique of the way her image has been used by conservative movements, both my house in Mexico City and my studio in San Francisco are filled with Guadalupanobilia bearing her image. Throughout the years, I have collected 3-D portraits, velvet paintings, bakery calendars, and electric figurines that light up. I also have key chains, mugs, bolo ties, belts, T-shirts, decals, pillows, and a baseball cap. And every year, on December 11 at midnight (December 12 is Guadalupe's fiesta), I "religiously" go to the Basílica de Guadalupe with friends to spend the night and witness the arrival of the largest pilgrimage in the

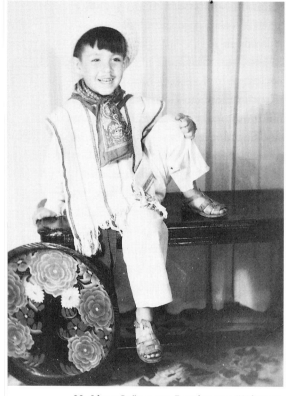

32 Gómez-Peña at age 5 posing as a "Chinaco". Mexico City, 1960.

33 Guillermo Emiliano at age 9 posing as a "Mexican Charro". Mexico City, 1998.

streets of Coronado Island on our way back from the beach, when the cops finally found us. They pointed their guns at us, and if it wasn't for my art press ID card (an intrinsic part of my Mexican survival kit), the incident could have had a much more dramatic ending. When my son, holding my leg tightly, asked what was happening, all I could say was, "Don't worry. It's just a bad movie. These guys are merely following a script."

In the summer of '95 another sad incident occurred, this time at the San Diego airport. While returning from Mexico City, Guillermito and I were abruptly separated by a border patrolman. When searching my luggage they had found twenty video cassettes containing the raw footage of an art film I was making, and concluded that I was a child pornographer traveling with my most recent subject matter. Again, a Latino male with a thick mustache holding the hand of an innocent-looking blond kid was in itself suspicious. We waited two hours for a group of INS officers to review every video. Finally, frustrated at not having found the confirmation of their racist fears, they told us to leave without an apology.

When Proposition 187 was voted in,[2] race relations in San Diego became more polarized than ever. At Guillermito's all-Mexican school in the Chicano barrio, suddenly a group of tough kids decided to start picking on him 'cause he "didn't look Mexican." Every time he chose to fight back, the teachers sided with the other kids, the "truly" Mexican-looking ones. One night he phoned me, crying, to ask why it was that if he spoke better Spanish and spent more time in Mexico than the bullies, they were calling him "gringo" and beating him up. One day in the media lab, he finally found a way to fight back. He waited for everyone to leave, went into cyberspace, and erased a website project made by the kids who were harassing him. The next day when the teacher asked who had done it, he stood up, trembling and accepted responsibility for his action, but was clearly unable to explain his motivation. He was only 7-years-old at the time. The teacher called the school's security guard, brought Guillermito to the front of the classroom, and labeled him a computer hacker and a cyber-criminal. The whole class booed him, and he went back home in tears. It took his mom a couple of days to persuade him to return to school. However, it should be noted that the bullies never bothered him again. Eventually his mom made the decision to

---

2   California Prop. 187 denied immigrants who coudn't provide proof of residence or citizenship access to medical services and education.

writer living and working between two countries and multiple communities, but also because the text attempts to describe fast-changing realities and fluctuating cultural attitudes that will probably seem dated in a very short time. As of now, I am still not sure of the best format to articulate these ideas: a "personal" chronicle as in the first section of the text, a theoretical essay capable of containing contradictory voices (anathema in traditional academic writing) as in sections 2 and 3, or an activist manifesto, as in the final part.

Throughout the text, I constantly shift from "I" to "we.", The "we" at different times refers to "my main collaborator Roberto Sifuentes and I," "my (techno-art) colleagues and I," "all Chicanos on the net," or "all outsiders/insiders on the net." This "we" is shifting, temporary, and contextual. I am fully aware of the risks of using such a collective pronoun, but I cannot escape the following predicament : " We" all criticize the problems of a "master narrative" in the 90's, and yet "we" all express a desire to belong to a community larger than our immediate tribe of collaborators. How to resolve this, I still don't know).

Fighting my Endemic "Tecnofobia"

I venture into the terra ignota of cyberlandia without documents, a map or an invitation at hand. In doing so, I become a sort of virus, the cyber-version of the Mexican fly: irritating, inescapable, and hopefully highly contagious.

My "lowrider" laptop is decorated with a 3-D decal of the Virgin of Guadalupe, the spiritual queen of Spanish-speaking America. It's like a traveling altar, an office and a literary bank all in one. Since I spend 70 per cent of the year on the road, my computer is second only to my phone card as a primary means of keeping in touch with my agent, editors, and performance collaborators spread throughout the US, Mexico and Europe. The month before a major performance project, most of the technical preparations, last minute negotiations and calendar changes take place in the mysterious territory of cyberspace. Unwillingly, I have become a techno-artist and an information superhighway bandido.

I use the term "unwillingly" because like most Mexican artists, my relationship with digital technology is characterized by paradox and contradictions. I don't quite understand them, yet I am seduced by them. I don't want to know how they work; but I love how they look and what they do. I criticize my techno-savvy colleagues who are acritically immersed in *las nuevas tecnologías*, yet I silently envy them; I resent the fact that I am constantly told that as a "Latino,"

34 One of the many conceptual billboards distributed throughout Houston to advertise the Ethno-Cyber-Punk Trading Post and Curio Shop Project, 1995.

I am supposedly "culturally handicapped" or somehow unfit to handle high technology. Once I have the apparatus in front of me, however, I am uncontrollably compelled to work against it – to question it, expose it, subvert it, and/or imbue it with humor, radical politics, and *linguas polutas* such as Spanglish, Franglais and cyberñol.

Contradiction prevails. Two years ago, my collaborator CyberVato (Roberto Sifuentes) and I bullied ourselves into the hegemonic space of the net. Once we were generously adopted by various communities (Arts Wire, Chicle and Latino net, among others), we suddenly started to lose interest in maintaining ongoing conversations with phantasmagoric beings we had never met in person (I must confess to a Mexican cultural prejudice: if I don't know you in person, I don't really care to converse with you). Then we started sending a series of poetic/activist "techno-placas"[1] in Spanglish. In these short communiqués, we raised tough questions regarding access, identity politics, and language. Since the responses were sporadic and unfocused (at the time we didn't quite know where to post them in order to get maximum visibility), our interest began to dim. It was

---

1   A placa is a Chicano tag, a kind of territorial signature.

only through the gracious persistence of our techno-colleagues that we decided to remain seated at the virtual table.

Today, despite the fact that Roberto and I spend a lot of time in front of our laptops conceptualizing performance projects that incorporate new technologies or redesigning our web site, every time we are invited to participate in a public discussion around art and technology, we tend to emphasize its shortcomings and overstate our skepticism. Why? I can only speak for myself. Perhaps I have some computer traumas, or suffer from endemic digital fibrosis.

Confieso: I've been utilizing computers since 1988; however, during the first 5 years, I used my old Mac as a glorified typewriter. During those years I accidentally deleted 300 pages of original texts which I hadn't backed up on disks and thus was forced to reconstruct from memory. The thick and confusing "user friendly" manuals fell many times from my impatient hands. As a result, I spent desperate nights cursing the mischievous gods of cyber-space, and dialing promising "hot lines" that were rarely answered, or if they were, provided me with complicated instructions in a computer Esperanto I was unable to follow.

My bittersweet relationship to technology dates back to my formative years in the highly politicized ambience of Mexico City in the 1970s. As a young, self-proclaimed "radical artist," I was full of ideological dogmas: in my perception, high technology was intrinsically dehumanizing (*enajenante* in Spanish) and was mostly used as a means to control "us" (little techno-illiterate people) politically. My critique of technology overlapped with my critique of capitalism. To me, "capitalists" were rootless (and faceless) corporate men who utilized mass media to advertise their useless electronic gadgets. They sold us unnecessary devices that kept us eternally in debt (as a country and as individuals), and conveniently distracted us from "the truly important matters of life." Of course, these "important matters" included sex, music, spirituality and "revolution" California-style (meaning, *en abstracto y bien* fashionable). As a child of contradiction, although I considered myself a rabid "anti-technology artist," I owned a little Datsun, and listened to my favorite US and British rock groups on my Panasonic *importado*, often while meditating or making love as a means to "liberate myself" from capitalist socialization. My favorite clothes, books, posters and albums had all been made by "capitalists" with the help of technology, but for some obscure reason, I was oblivious to the contradiction between my ideological stance and my affection for these devices.

Luckily, my family never lost their magical thinking and sense of humor about technology. My parents were easily seduced by refurbished and slightly dated American and Japanese electronic goods. We bought them as *fayuca* (contraband) in Tepito neighborhood, and they occupied an important place in the decoration of our "modern" middle-class home. Our huge color TV set, for example, was decorated to perform the double function of entertainment unit and involuntary postmodern altar, with nostalgic photos of relatives, paper flowers, and assorted figurines all around it. So was the humongous *equipo de sonido* next to it, with an amplifier, eight-track tape machine, two record players and at least fifteen speakers that constantly played a syncretic array of music, including Mexican composer Agustin Lara, Los Panchos (with Edie Gorme), Sinatra, Esquivel, and Eartha Kitt. Cumbia followed Italian operas, and rock and roll alternated with racheras. (In this sense, my father was my first involuntary instructor of postmodern thought.) Though I was sure that with the scary arrival of the first microwave oven to our traditional kitchen, our delicious daily meals were going to be replaced overnight by sleazy fast food, my mother soon realized that *el microondas* was only good to reheat cold coffee and soup. The point was to own it, and to display it prominently as yet another sign of *modernidad*. (At the time, modernity in Mexico was perceived as synonymous with US technology and pop culture.) When I moved north to California (and therefore into the future), I would often buy cheesy electronic trinkets for my family (I didn't regard them as "cheesy" at the time). During vacations, going back to visit my family in Mexico City such presents *ipso facto* turned me into an emissary of both prosperity and modernity. Once I bought an electric *ionizador* for grandma. She put it in the middle of her bedroom altar, and kept it there (unplugged, of course) for months. When I next saw her, she told me: "Mijito, since you gave me that thing, I can breathe much better." She never plugged it in, but she probably did. Things like televisions, short wave radios, microwave ovens, and later ionizers, walkman radios, crappie *calculadoras*, digital watches and video cameras were seen by my family and friends as *alta tecnologia*, and their function was at least as much social, ritual, sentimental, symbolic and aesthetic as it was pragmatic.

It is no coincidence that in my early performance work (1979-90), *chafa* (cheap or low) technology performed ritual and aesthetic functions as well. Verbigratia: for years, I used TV monitors as centerpieces for my "video-altars" on stage, and several "ghetto blasters" placed in different parts of the gallery or theatre as sound environments for my performances, each with a different tape and volume. Fog machines, strobe lights, gobos, megaphones and voice filters have remained trademark elements in my performances. By 1990, I sarcastically baptized my aesthetic practice, "Aztec high-tech art." When I teamed with "CyberVato" Sifuentes (1991), we decided that what we were doing was "techno-rascuache art." In a Glossary of Borderismos that dates back to 1994, we defined it as "a new aesthetic that fuses performance art, epic rap poetry, interactive television, experimental radio and computer art, but with a Chicanocentric perspective and an sleazoide bent." As of today, my relationship with high technology remains unresolved. I am able to theorize about its aesthetic possibilities and political implications, but I am incapable of implementing any of my theories "hands on." Luckily, thanks to Roberto and other cyber-accomplices, at times I can pass for a "techno-performance artist."

Mythical Differences

The mythology goes like this. Mexicans (and by extension other Latinos) can't handle high technology. Caught between a pre-industrial past and an imposed modernity, we continue to be identified as manual beings – *Homo Fabers* per excellence, imaginative artisans (not technicians), our understanding of the world strictly political, poetical or at best metaphysical, but certainly not scientific or technological. Furthermore, we are perceived as sentimental, passionate creatures (meaning irrational), and when we decide to step out of our "primitive" realm and utilize high technology in our art (most of the time we are not even interested), we are meant to naively repeat what others, primarily Anglos and Europeans, have already done much better.

We Latinos often feed this mythology by overstating our "romantic nature" and "humanistic" orientation, and/or by assuming the role of "colonial victims" of technology. We are always ready to point out that social and interpersonal relations in the US (the strange land of the future) are totally mediated, filtered, distorted, or managed by faxes, phones, computers, and other sophisticated technologies we are not even aware of, and that the over-abundance of information technology in everyday life is directly responsible for the social handicaps, sexual neuroses and ethical crises of US citizens.

Is it precisely our lack of access to these goods that makes us overstate our differences? "We," on the contrary, socialize profusely, absorb information ritually and sensually; and remain in touch with our (allegedly still intact) primeval selves. The mythology continues to unfold: since our families and

35 Gómez-Peña as one of the many Mexterminator "ethno-cyborgs" created by thousands of anonymous Internet users.

communities are not exposed to the "daily dehumanizing effects of high technology," we are somehow unaffected by philosophical "illnesses" such as despair, fragmentation, and nihilism, so characteristic of the postmodern condition in advanced capitalist societies. "Our" problems are mainly political, not personal or psychological, and so on and so forth . . . This simplistic and extremely problematic binary world view portrays Mexico and Mexicans as technologically underdeveloped yet culturally and spiritually superior to their northern neighbor.

Reality is much more complicated. The average Anglo-American does not understand new technologies either. People of color and women in the US don't have equal access to cyberspace, despite the egalitarian myths promoted by devotees of high technology. Furthermore, American culture has always led the most radical (and often childish) movements against its own technological development, naively trying to "get back to nature." (In the 90s, American Luddites tend to be much more puritanical and intolerant than their Mexican counterparts). Meanwhile, the average urban Mexican (more than 70 per cent of all Mexicans live in large cities), exposed to world transculture on a daily basis, is already afflicted to varying degrees with the same types of "First World" existential malaise allegedly produced by high technology and advanced capitalism. In fact, the new generation of Mexicans, including my hip generación-Mex nephews and my 8-year-old, fully bicultural son, are completely immersed in and defined by MTV, personal computers, super-Nintendo, video games and virtual reality (even if they don't own a computer). In fact, I would go as far as to say that in contemporary Mexico, generational borders can already be determined by cyberliteracy and the degree of familiarity with high technology. Far from being the rrrroomantic pre-industrial paradise of the American imagination, the Mexico of the 90s is already a virtual nation whose fluctuating boundaries are largely defined by transnational pop culture, television, tourism, free market economics (a dysfunctional version, of course), and yes, whether we like it or not . . . the Internet.

But life in the ranchero global village is riddled with epic contradictions. Very few people south of the border are on line, and those who are "wired," tend to belong to the upper and upper-middle classes, and are mostly professionals or corporate employees. The Zapatista phenomenon is a famous exception to this norm. Since 1995, Subcomandante Marcos, techno-performance artist extraordinaire, has been communicating with the "outside world" through the extremely popular Zapatista web sites sponsored and designed by US and Canadian radical scholars and activists. These pages are more familiar to those outside of Mexico for a simple reason: Telmex, the Mexican Telephone company, makes it practically impossible for anyone living outside of the main Mexican cities to gain internet access, arguing that "there are simply not enough lines to handle both telephone and Internet users."

Every time my colleagues and I have attempted to create some kind of binational dialogue via digital technologies (i.e. to link Los Angeles to Mexico City through satellite video-telephone), we are faced with myriad complications and assymetries. In Mexico, with few exceptions, the handful of artists who have regular access to high technologies and who are interested in this kind of transnational techno-dialogue tend to be socially privileged, politically uninformed, and aesthetically uninteresting. And the funding sources willing to support this type of project are clearly interested in controlling who is part of the experiment.

"Rebecca [Solnit] thinks America Online is like K-Mart, and keeps getting lost in the aisles somewhere between press-on-nails and flash sessions. This morning AOL fell asleep while I was forwarding your text to my brother (the Anglo-Sandinista one) and it disappeared. Maybe it's like a combination of K-Mart and the Argentinean military, what with all this disappearing, loco?"

EXCERPT FROM AN E-MAIL

Cyber-migras and "Webbacks"

Roberto and I arrived late to the technological debate, along with a dozen other Chicano experimental artists. At the time, we were shocked by the unexamined ethnocentrism permeating the discussions around art and digital technology, especially in California. The master narrative was couched either in the utopian, dated language of Western democratic values or as a bizarre form of New Age anti-corporate/corporate jargon; the unquestioned *lingua franca* was of course English, "the official language of science, information and international communications";[2] and the theoretical vocabulary utilized by both the critics and

2   Why then, several colleagues (including Meyer and Pisani) asked me, did I choose to write this text in English? First, because I only know two languages, and Spanish-speaking net-users are still a micro-minority. How else could a Mexican communicate with an African, an Indian and a German? How else would you, whoever you are, be reading this text right now? Secondly, I chose to write this text in English because in order to fight a hegemonic model I believe we need to know and speak the language of hegemonic control.

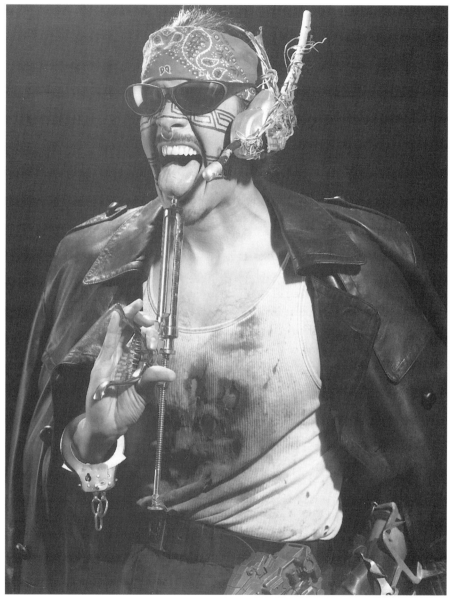

36 Sifuentes as an ethno-cyborg shooting up directly into his tongue with a horse-syringe, a cultural fantasy suggested by Internet users.

apologists of cyberspace was depoliticized (postcolonial theory and the border paradigm were conveniently overlooked) and hyper-, I mean *hyper*-specialized – a combination of esperantic "software" talk, revamped post-structuralist theory, and nouvelle psychoanalysis. If Chicanos, Mexicans and other "people of color" didn't participate in the net, it was presumed to be solely due to lack of interest, not money or access. The unspoken assumption was that our true interests were "grassroots" (which is to say, limited to our ethnic-based community institutions and the streets of our barrios), and our modes of expression oral, folkloric and pretechnological. In other words, we were to continue painting murals, plotting revolutions in rowdy cafes, reciting poetry, and dancing salsa or quebradita. Some colleagues consider the fact that Roberto and I, along with a handful of other Chicanos, are now temporarily welcome in the cyber "community" to be an enormous political victory. Others, more cynical, suspect that we're invited to the "great rave of techno-consciousness" to bring some Tex-Mex glamor and tequila to an otherwise monochromatic and fairly puritan fiesta.

When Roberto and I began to dialogue with US artists working with new technologies, we were perplexed by the fact that when referring to "cyberspace" or "the net," they spoke of a politically neutral, raceless, genderless, classless and allegedly egalitarian "territory" that would provide everyone with unlimited opportunities for participation, interaction and belonging – most especially "belonging," a seductive notion at a time when no one feels that they "belong" anywhere). There was no mention of the physical and social isolation or fear of the "real world" that propels so many people to get on line, invest huge amounts of time and energy there, and convince themselves that they are having profound experiences of communication, belonging, or discovery (three peculiarly American obsessions). To many, the thought of exchanging identities on the net and impersonating people of other genders, races, or ages, without risking any social or physical consequences was seen as liberating, rather than superficial or escapist.[3]

The utopian rhetoric around digital technologies reminded me of a sanitized version of the pioneer and frontier mentalities of the Old West, and also of early twentieth- century futurism. Given the extent to which the US had already begun to suffer from compassion fatigue regarding delicate issues of race, gender,

---

3   Many of my feminist colleagues have expressed the belief that exchanging genders in virtual space can be both liberating and transgressive for women.

and cultural equity, it was difficult not to see this cult of technology as an attractive means of escape from the social and racial crises afflicting the nation in non-virtual reality.

Like the pre-multi-culti art world of the early 80s, the new, technified art world assumed an unquestionable "center" and drew an impermeable digital border. Those condemned to live "on the other side" included all techno-illiterate artists, most women, Chicanos, Afro-Americans and Native Americans in the US and Canada, along with the populations of so-called "Third World" countries. Given the nature of this hegemonic cartography, those of us living south of the digital border were once again forced to assume the unpleasant but necessary roles of web-backs, cyber-aliens, techno-pirates, and virtual *coyotes* (smugglers).

"In the barrios of resistance, contemporary versions of the old kilombos, every block has a secret community center. There, the runaway youths called Robo-Raza II or 'floating greasers' publish anarchist laser-Xeroxed magazines, edit experimental home videos about police brutality (yes, police brutality still exists), and broadcast pirate radio and TV interventions like this one over the most popular programs.

These clandestine centers are constantly raided, but Robo-Raza II just moves the action to the garage next door. Those who get "white-listed" can no longer get jobs in the 'Mall of Oblivion.' And those who get caught in flagrante are sent to rehabilitation clinics, where they are subjected to instant socialization through em-pedagogic videos (from the Spanish verb empedar, meaning to force someone to drink, and the Mayan noun agogic, o sea, a man without a self, like many of you)."

FROM "THE NEW WORD BORDER", CITY LIGHTS, 1996

First Draft of a Manifesto: Remapping Cyberspace

In the past years, many theoreticians of color, feminists and activist artists have finally succeeded in crossing the digital border without documents. Luckily, this recent diasporic migration has made the debates more complex and interesting. But since "we" don't wish to reproduce the unpleasant mistakes of the "cultural wars"(1987–94) nor to harass the brokers, impresarios and curators of cyberspace in such a way as to elicit a backlash, our new strategies and priorities are quite different. "We" are no longer trying to persuade anyone that we are worthy of

37 Gómez-Peña as a terrorist intellectual reads a manifesto.

inclusion; we now know very well that we are, and will always be, either temporary insiders, or insiders/outsiders. For the moment, what "we" (newly arrived
cyber-immigrants) desire is to:

- **re-map the hegemonic cartography of cyberspace**
- **politicize the conception of cyberspace**
- **develop a multicentric, theoretical understanding of the cultural,
  political, and aesthetic potential of new technologies**
- **exchange different sorts of information – mythopoetic, activist,
  performative, imagistic**
- **hopefully accomplish all this with humor, inventiveness and
  intelligence**

Chicano artists in particular want to "brownify" virtual space; to "spang-
lishize" the net, and "infect" the *linguas francas*.

These concerns seem to have echoes throughout Latin America, Asia,

Africa and many so-called "Third World" populations within the illusory space formerly known as the "First World."

With the increasing availability of new technologies in "our" communities, definitions of "community art" and "politicized art" are changing dramatically. The goal of activist artists and theoreticians is to find innovative, grassroots applications for new technologies (i.e., to induce Latinos and other youth of color to exchange their weapons for computers and video cameras), and to link community centers, artistic collectives, and human rights organizations by means of the Internet. CD-roms and web sites that reflect community concerns can perform a vital educational function as cultural "memory banks" ("encyclopedias chicanicas," so to speak), spaces for encounter, dialogue, and exchange.

To attain all this, the many (predominantly white) virtual communities are going to have to get used to a new cultural presence (the Web-back, el nuevo virus virtual), a new sensibility, and a variety of languages employed in cyberspace. As for myself, hopefully one day I won't have to write in English in order to have a voice in the new centers of international power.

SAN FRANCISCO, CALIFAS JULY OF 1997

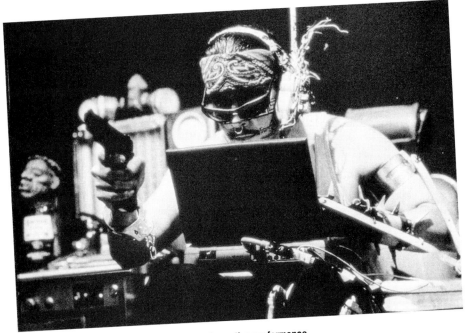

38 CyberVato sends cyber-communiqués during a live performance.

Letter to an Unknown Thief

Dear Thief:

I am the melancholic man who left his laptop computer on seat 8A of United flight #17, coming from JFK into LAX, on June 14, 1998, remember? It was the end of a two-month long tour. I had just completed two huge art projects: a performance/installation in Manhattan, and a "Spanglish Lowrider Opera" in LA (which, by the way, opened that very day), and I was exhausted, jodido. I hadn't slept for at least three days, so after the plane landed, I walked out like a zombie and went straight to baggage claim. Minutes later, I realized that my precious laptop was missing. I ran back to the plane like an (ex-zombie) madman, but the computer was gone, and never delivered to the lost and found desk. I don't know if you were a passenger who left after me, or a member of the cleaning crew. And I really don't care. In fact, I don't ever expect to regain my neo-Aztec high-tech control center. I just want to make you aware of what you unknowingly did to my sense of self and identity; to my past and to my ideas.

Ladrón. You stole my digital memory, ese, years of literary work. At least five years of work — poems, performance texts, film and radio scripts, essays, personal letters, and several chapters of my next book.[1] You don't have the least idea of what this means to a Chicano intellectual who has been fighting the erasure of collective and personal memory. You may not even know what memory is. Luckily, many of the older texts in my personal digital archive had already been published in books, magazines, and newspapers, but the recent stuff, auch!! Those are floating somewhere in virtual space, and only you or whoever you sold my machine to, have access to them.

Yes, cabrón. You stole my parallel mind and memory. Well, not entirely. I have found earlier versions of many documents, and I have spent the last two months on a Proustian project of reconstructing fragments of my already

---

1   In fact, the first draft of the manuscript of this book was stored on the hard drive of the stolen computer, and I didn't have backup disks or printed copies. Though I was able to reconstruct most texts from earlier versions, which I updated by memory, three texts specifically written for this book (two performance chronicles and one essay) were lost for good. After a series of clumsy attempts at reconstructing them from memory, I had a fit and decided to let them go.

fractured memory, using old computer discs, printed manuscripts, handwritten diaries, even napkins and envelopes with bits of text. And let me tell you, it's a pain, ese, but nonetheless a true Chicano Buddhist endeavor. Maybe I will emerge from this nightmare a better writer with a stronger sense of self, just like Mexico did after the burning of the Aztec and Mayan codexes by the brutal conquistadores. Excuse my epic tone, but I am understandably pissed.

By the way, how much did you get for my four-year-old laptop? Five hundred bucks? Did you feel any guilt? Did you at least have the curiosity to investigate the mindscape of your victim, and read my love poems and political essays? The breakdown of my taxes, perhaps? My most intimate secrets, the ones I never even intended to publish? Did you access my e-mail, enter my cyber-heart, and peek through hundreds of personal letters from friends, lovers and family? Or did you throw everything in the virtual trash before you sold the machine?

You know, pinche thief, as I write this letter I am realizing I don't really hate you. In fact, I am beginning to feel strangely thankful, for you have forced me into many harsh realizations. First, that my LIFE cannot be trusted to high-technology. That airports are not less dangerous than, for example, South Central Los Angeles. And that I must always, ALWAYS be prepared to reconstruct the humongous puzzle of my already fractured self, and to edit out entire chapters of my life without fearing that the whole structure will collapse. So . . . gracias ladrón.

But this philosophical realization won't exonerate you from divine justice. The crucial question still is, what will your punishment be? If you believe in karma, you are in deep trouble. For doing what you did, you might end up reincarnated as a stone or an oyster in your next life. Don't think you'll get off if you're agnostic, since in that case your punishment will be even worse. One day in the immediate future (remember that the future nowadays is always immediate), some nerd in Silicon Valley will invent a tiny device or a program to track down lost computers. And I will buy one immediately. I will then show up at your doorstep with my homeboys, costumed as one of my scariest performance personas: "El Mexterminator," the superhero defender of migrant workers' rights, and archenemy of racist politicians . . . and now, of computer thieves. We'll rough you up, believe me.

LOS ANGELES, AUGUST 1998

Keynote "Provocation"

An earlier version of the following text was delivered as a keynote speech during the Performance Studies International Conference, "Here Be Dragons," Aberystwyth, Wales, April 1999. Since the organizers of the event asked me the day before the conference began to come up with a "keynote provocation," I didn't have time to properly sharpen my ideas and the questions I wanted to pose to scholars in the field. The original text was written in a couple of hours in dialogue with Lisa Wolford. Because it was drafted so quickly, it contained a number of rethorical contradictions, generalizations and imprecisions. Besides, my use of "we" (usually meaning artists), "you"(usually referring to the theoreticians attending the conference), and "they" is adversarial and vague at times. Though this version is a bit more polished than the original, I chose to maintain its abrasive, polemical style, since it reflects the way my voice and thoughts tend to be at times. In early June of 1999, as I finish revising the final manuscript, I still stand behind 90 per cent of the ideas expressed in this keynote, even though I articulate them here in a somewhat basic and strategically simple way. I measure the success of the provocation in the context of the conference by the number of people (both scholars and artists) who came up to me in the campus bar to argue with me, share stories of their own experiences as artists, or to express appreciation of the issues I had raised. I wholeheartedly encourage strong responses from the reader as well.

Dear locos and locas: today, from my multiple repertoire of personas, I'm choosing to be the artist as theoretician, as speaking subject, "the mariachi with a big mouth," and my role will be to ask some hopefully incisive questions regarding the bittersweet relationship between artists and academicians – our mutual concerns, hang-ups and challenges.

First question: why is it that some of our closest colleagues are scholars, and some of our most formidable enemies are scholars as well? Often, when a critic confronts an artist who actively participates in contextualizing his/her work, a "savage" who doesn't just want to be passively photographed for the Benetton ad, so to speak, the critic often chooses not to write about the work because (they say) "the artists can do it themselves." Or else if they do choose to write about us, they criticize the hell out of us, perhaps because they secretly resent the fact that we can theorize about our own work rather than waiting for them to explain it for us. Isn't it a dated, modernist view to regard artists as passive objects of study? If, as artists, we decide not to be silent, unresisting subjects of research, can it be that the only options for scholars are either not to deal with our work at all, or to be emphatically nasty in their criticism? There has to be a third option, a possibility for another mode of relating – and perhaps even collaborating – in which both sides are critical and generous at the same time.

Generosity, what a corny term! Why have we gotten to a point where all generosity of spirit is seen as dated, eulogistic, or compromised? Note #1: when I talk about the spirit of generosity that I feel is lacking in critical writing, I don't see it by any means as something specific to performance studies – it's a malaise in academia and we have to fight against it. Note #2: I am fully aware that generosity comes with experience and recognition. Younger, more insecure, unknown scholars often tend to be less generous than their more established colleagues (though there are, of course, exceptions to this rule on both sides).

But let's return to the main subject of discussion: the epistemology and ethics of the relationship between artists and scholars. As artists, we don't want to be eulogized, but neither do we wish to be misunderstood or misrepresented. We always want to be given the opportunity to be part of the conversation and to enter into the debate around our work – to talk back, so to speak. But this rarely happens. Questions: at a time when it is hipper for scholars and critics to be fashionably nasty than to be generous, what platforms do artists have to talk back? Can anyone answer? (Pause.) And if we find such a platform, how can we problematize your view of us and of our work without triggering an even nastier response?

As artists, we are fully aware that we need to engage in an ongoing conversation with theorists and critics, but let's get it straight: we no longer depend entirely on you to explain us. Some of us have mastered the tools that allow us to be part of creating the context for our own work. And this should not be seen as an unpleasant inconvenience, but as an advantage. Together we can engage in a more complete and multifaceted analysis of the performance work – its context, sources, contradictions, connections to other fields, etc. But again, this rarely happens. Why?

A lot has been written about the artist's role in relation to society, but not enough about the position of unquestionable authority of the critic in relation to the artist, and the responsibility that ought to go with that authority. At a time when authority, both intellectual and artistic, has been (overly) "deconstructed" (auch, I bit my tongue), I ask: what are the scholar's ethical responsibilities towards us? What happens when the scholar examines me with binoculars, and I don't get to see their eyes? When I don't get to look back, or to refract his or her gaze? The Malinowskis of the 90s are certainly hipper than their predecessors, but much more difficult to hold accountable. In this sense, I feel a certain nostalgia for colonial anthropology, when the anthropologists used to sit with us around the bonfire, have a drink with us, mimic our dances and convince themselves that meant that they really understood us. At least when the armies came they got shot with us. Now they just sit in the back row once every decade with a jaded and aloof gaze, or else they rent one of our performance videos and go home to write a dissertation. I politely insist that there has to be a more enlightened and responsible way of dealing with us. Scholars need to do more research, more fieldwork, and take the time to talk with us before crucifying us in an essay, or deporting us back to Latin America or to oblivion with convoluted phrases meant to impress colleagues in their own field.

I suggest that artists form a review board to monitor the ethical behavior of theoreticians, since "you" (the scholars present in the audience) are constantly scrutinizing and making judgments about our ethical and political behavior. But before we take that fictional step, I need to ask: what would be the consequences of any sanctions we might place on you? Are we going to lose some gigs? Or will we just further increase your fear of writing responsibly about "us"? Please bear in mind that engaging in an intimate, ongoing dialogue with your research subject does not mean that you are going to lose your objectivity and impartiality. It just means that you will have better and more accurate information, and that maybe you'll be a little less likely to objectify us in your writing. The pertinent question here is: what are the possibilities for creating a more enlightened and symmetrical relationship between artists and theoreticians in the immediate future? This presentation is one possible example, since it is the result of a collaborative brainstorming session with my performance colleagues over coffee and cigarettes while doing Mexercise.

Intercut: I also wish to pose a challenge to my artist colleagues who hide behind irrational or bohemian notions of art. Can you *vatos* stop being so anti-intellectual once and for all? Can't you become more theoretically rigorous yourselves and less phobic about analyzing the implications of your work? Can you guys be less distrustful of theoreticians? Can't you make sure that your voices and ideas get heard, rather than complaining bitterly about invisibility or about being misunderstood? Write about your own work and politely but firmly question those who irresponsibly criticize it, instead of silently resenting their arrogance and authority. If many of us are embarked on this multi-leveled project of dialogue, there won't be any other option for scholars but to listen carefully to us, to respect our views and take our ideas into consideration.

As much as theoreticians need to make an effort to communicate with artists, we need to reciprocate with an even greater effort, and perhaps we can meet in the middle. Maybe, for the moment, Aberystwyth can become the neutral zone. On this exotic "isle" (the UK), and particularly in this minute post-colonial nation (Wales), hopefully we will all have the opportunity to join in creating a conceptual space that lies somewhere between New York City, London, Leningrad, Singapore, Calcutta, Mexico City and Sao Paolo – a virtual space equidistant from practice, theory and activism; a true space for interdisciplinary, transcultural dialogue, where the tough but necessary questions get raised in a spirit of generosity, and where we can disagree across disciplines and metiers and still get together for a drink.

There are other pressing issues I wish to raise: theory is sometimes like pop culture – one fad follows another, sometimes within a few months. One year it's cultural diversity, the next year it's border culture, then queer theory, the year after that cyberculture . . . What's next? Albino pygmy art? Cyber Chicano Butoh? Zapatista porn? We must acknowledge the importance of continuity, and face the fact that the fundamental issues that motivate these debates don't get resolved as quickly as theories go out of fashion.

This leads me to confront directly the problem of the Vietnam syndrome of multiculturalism in the era of "globalization." We are currently dealing with a kind of fashionable and fully globalized form of multiculturalism which assumes that all sensitive matters of race and gender are either passé, or that the conflicts and inequities inherent to intercultural relations have already been resolved. This new, de-politicized multiculturalism acritically celebrates extreme difference and marginality, and brings them to the "center" for immolation, conceptual cannibalism, and ritual sacrifice. Since now we know that to deal with sensitive matters of race, gender and ethnicity publicly and in a non-euphemistic way is likely to lead us to painful conflicts and self-defensive essentialisms, every time the political texts surface, everybody is ready to split. Why? Have we grown intolerant of real difference? Isn't there a new, more enlightened way to continue dealing with the genuine issues of difference and cultural diversity that all societies dramatically need to address, especially in this era of phony globalization, *que no*? We have to acknowledge that the debates about multiculturalism that have taken place up to now have resulted in no real change, and that a lot of work still needs to be done, no matter how difficult or painful it might be. The field of performance studies has always been at the forefront in articulating a politicized and socially responsible multiculturalism; you simply cannot drop the ball now, when these ideas most emphatically need to be heard.

Identity politics in the 90s has succumbed to self-righteousness and new essentialisms. Debates about identity are now getting framed as a wrestling match between compassion fatigue and a binaristic ultra-essentialism. There has to be another option. Can we develop more open-ended, fluid models for understanding identity, or are we going to abandon the project altogether and retrench either to a ground zero, a sort of identity meltdown (echoing the backlashes in mainstream politics and in the media), or to a kind of self-defensive neo-nationalism, à la Nation of Islam or the American militia movement? Don't we know by now that both these positions involve formidable risks?

The debates on identity politics and cultural diversity in America have become first and foremost a terminological battle – not a civil rights battle, but a battle of vocabulary. Both theoretical and public language have been corrupted. In this process of mapping the territory verbally, words have either become overused and emptied of meaning and specificity, or overly charged with dangerous connotations. As a result, "we," as a society, are unable to engage in polemical debates without hurting someone or getting hurt. To victimize someone, or else be victimized by someone, is the American way, *que no*? Parallel to this, we are facing new transitional and hybrid realities that demand new vocabularies. At a certain point we reached communication overload; the language-scape is totally saturated. Stalemate. Total collapse. Question: how are we going to overcome this acute crisis of communication? How can we continue to talk about sensitive matters of race and gender without hurting each other, or without leaving the conversation, fuming, when the first red flag appears?

We have become specialized to such a degree that no one understands our theories anymore. Intelligibility. Theory has become unintelligible to most people outside our hyper-specialized fields. Can we write for an audience of more than 500 people without losing the genuine complexity of our ideas? Can we be complex and yet accessible? How can we bridge the gap between unintelligible theory and anti-intellectual art? Between "being real smart" and being understood?

Two more crucial questions to end this provocation. One: how can "we" be rigorous and responsible, without taking ourselves as seriously as I seem to be taking myself right now? And two: to what extent is what I just said going to color your perception of our performance work in the coming days?

Now my dear colleagues, I must apologize, but we have a performance tonight and I've got to go to dress rehearsal. The mariachi transvestite almost broke her leg trying to get down from the crucifixion, our Grotowski-trained colleagues are having a hard time dealing with our democratic rehearsal process and Chicano-Brechtian performance techniques, and the naked Green Alien is catching a cold here in Wales, since he's used to more tropical climates.

"Waking up every day in a world without theory can be a disorienting experience. There's no sense of transcendence whatsoever. All we have left is fractured and ephemeral: friendship, temporary love (if we are lucky, and if not, mere anonymous sex), temporary health, and the ephemeral utopias of art, traveling and laughter. These small privileges can make life bearable, temporarily bearable, but as we know, tomorrow the earth might open again . . . or you can get deported back to Mexico . . . or you can get AIDS. Yes, my dear contemporaries, uncertainty rules in our fragile kingdom. And our art is an expression of this uncertainty."

FROM THE FILM *BORDERSTASIS*, 1998

"All roads essentially lead to the end of the World."

SIDHARTHA LOPEZ, TIJUANA DRUNK

Reflections on the Culture of Despair

(The following short texts were written at different times and for various contexts and venues. Consequently, they are stylistically quite diverse. What binds them together is an attempt to understand and articulate the philosophical and political complexities of this decade, and how these new complexities affect our ever-shifting notions of culture, art, community and identity at the much-touted end of the Millenium.)

A Post-democratic Era

(Opening remarks, town meeting, Washington DC, 1996)

We experience the end of the world . . . and the word, as we know them, and the beginning of a new era. Perhaps our main frustration is our total inability to envision the characteristics and features of the coming age. It's a bit like being drunk in the middle of an earthquake, and not having a language to express our fears. But who are *we* anyway?

We now live in a world without theory, without ethics, without ideology. Our spiritual metahorizons are rapidly fading, and so are our geopolitical borders. Nation-states collapse in slow motion before our swelling eyes. As they crumble, they are immediately replaced by multinational macro-communities governed by invisible corporate boards, "trading partners," and media trusts. Composed of cold-blooded technocrats and clean-cut neoliberals who position themselves at the center of the center of nothingness, the new political class believes – or perhaps pretends to believe – that free trade and a healthy economy are the solutions to all our problems, even the cultural and social ones. They have no (visible) blood on their hands. They simply press buttons and computer keys. They silently exchange and transfer capital, products and weapons, from continent to continent.

In this unprecedented "post-democratic era" (if I may call it that), basic humanistic concerns are no longer part of the agenda for these politicos. Civic, human and labor rights, education, and art are perceived as minor privileges, expendable budget items, and dated concerns. Both the politicians and the media seem to have lost (or willingly abandoned) the ability to address the fundamental issues and ask the crucial questions: with all their rhetoric of globalization, why are the US and Western Europe retrenching to isolationist and xenophobic positions, advocating nativist policies and criminalizing immigrants? Why do they advocate open borders from North to South, and closed borders from South to North? Why is Washington still bombing small nations in the post cold-war era? Why are all types of guns freely available to the citizenry of the US? Why does the death penalty still exist in certain so-called "First World" nations? Why are policemen so rarely punished when they engage in acts of brutality? Why are most educational systems bankrupt and dysfunctional? Why are the homeless living in the streets? Why have the arts been defunded? Why aren't these questions being asked in national forums?

In our crumbling post-democracies, humanism has become a mere corporate "interest" or "goal," a quaint topic explored by the Discovery Channel, a trendy marketing strategy for computer firms. In this new context, artists and intellectuals don't seem to perform any meaningful role other than that of decorators of the omnipresent *horror vacui* and entertainers of a new, more tolerant and cynical consumer class.

As far as I am concerned, we have no real government looking after the human being. The homeless, the elderly, our children and teens, and the newly arrived immigrants from the South are completely on their own. Alone and abandoned in the virtual jungle of advanced capitalism, it is entirely up to us to figure out what can be the new models of citizen collaboration and multilateral

39 La Bailarina Nuclear & El Tex-Mex Puñal; Iranian-American performance artist Carmel Kooros and Gómez-Peña perform the kinky intercultural desires requested by Internet users and gallery visitors.

cooperation, the new terms for a new social and cultural contract, the new artistic rituals to give voice to our rage, shape our eclectic spiritualities and our fragmented identities. In this sense, citizen responsibility, community action and the creation of a civilian *logos* have been for me the most crucial issues of the 90s. This presentation is a humble expression of a search for new metaphors and images to begin articulating our new place in a foreign world, as well as a humble call for community action. But the main question remains unanswered: who are the remaining *we*? Who is left to listen and respond to this call?

The "Alternative" Mainstream

(This text was originally conceived as a radio commentary for All Things Considered, a news program presented by National Public Radio, 1997)

One of the strangest characteristics of this extremely bizarre decade is that the instatiable and undifferentiated mass of the so-called "mainstream" has finally devoured all margins, and the more dangerous, "other," and exotic these margins, the better. In fact, *stricto sensu*, we can say that there are no margins left. "Alternative" thought, fringe subcultures, and so-called radical behavior have actually become THE mainstream.

The most obvious examples of this phenomenon of inversion can be found in fashion and pop culture. While white suburban teens have adopted the early clothing style and slang of "gangsta" rappers and Chicano lowriders, US Black and Latino teens are dressing in expensive sportswear and mimicking the Anglo upper-class. Freed from the moral constraints of critical multiculturalism and "political correctness," the young hipsters of the 90s have selectively borrowed elements from numerous third world "pet cultures," to create their own designer tribalism. From San Diego to Manhattan, white Apocalypse youth gather for post-industrial pow-wows in a desperate attempt to recapture a lost sense of belonging to a larger "spiritual community." They wear Rasta dreadlocks, Indian braids or shave their heads. They cover their pale, ex-Protestant bodies with Celtic, pre-Colombian, Native American and Maori tattoos, not knowing or even caring why, except that it makes them look more stylistically marginal, and sexier.

To pierce oneself is no longer a bold statement: fashion models, sugary pop singers, and sportsmen now wear their piercings ostentatiously, and so do weekend-Bohemian yuppies and upper-class students from Yale or Harvard – the very same affluent hipsters who have suddenly discovered lounge culture, transvestite bars, vampire Goth clubs, and porn.

In the porn industry, the kinkiest videos and hotlines are being marketed to average, middle-class persons with boring, unfulfilled lives. No biggie. Sexual fetishes, hard core S&M, and theatrical sex are regular subject matters on Cable TV, and Hollywood is making movies about exotic dancers, necrophilia, and the snuff film subculture. Prime-time TV has followed suit. America's afternoon talk shows have become more outrageous than any performance art piece I ever saw. Lonely housewives and senior citizens are daily spectators of a bizarre ritual confrontation between rapists, serial killers, white supremacists and their victims, relatives and fans. Just one more day in the life of middle America, where the tribulations of psychos like Tim MacVeigh and Andrew Cunanan are logarithmically more appealing than those of artists, intellectuals and visionaries. The logical result of this spectacularization of the bizarre is that the borders between "real life," performance and media have become completely indistinguishable.

In the millennial culture, words like radical, extreme, exotic, original and alternative have lost their meaning, and a performance artist like me is practically out of a job. I mean, in comparison to mainstream pop culture, we look and behave like altar boys. Because of this, my colleagues and I have been forced to redefine our objectives and strategies as practitioners of so-called "radical" behavior and "alternative" thought. The great question for us now is how to continue promoting meaningful forms of personal and cultural freedom and raising thorny issues that no one else is willing to discuss in a time when the stylized bizarre has become the norm, and people have a hard time differentiating between the Unabomber (now a cyber cult-hero) and Marcos, the Zapatista leader; or between Princess Diana and Mother Teresa. Poor Marcos, poor gothic vampires, poor sex workers, poor lowriders, poor nostalgic citizens of the dying margins of Western civilization; if they could only earn a tiny percentage of the profit generated by the appropriation of their images and activities by the insatiable mainstream.

Neo-puritanism and the Culture of Fear

(This text was originally conceived as a radio commentary for the National Public Radio magazine Latino USA, 1998)

The other face of the 90s culture of the stylized bizarre and high-resolution boredom is puritanism. Despite our alleged "alternative lifestyles," a new kind of puritanism has come to permeate every aspect of our lives in America, not directly as a result of parochial morality, but rather because of fear. We are suffused in a culture of fear, denial and prohibition, whether based on fact or vague and groundless popular mythologies. We have learned to fear sex, joy, mystery, madness and chance, and, strangest of all, we have learned to accept these fears as "normal." And when the state decides to legislate our fears, we offer no resistance whatsoever.

Verbigratia: our understandable fear of AIDS and other millennial illnesses has made us overly cautious in our sexual encounters; every potential lover is perceived as a potential aids carrier, and sexuality itself is either stigmatized, or seen as an act of revolutionary defiance against "responsible sex." Channel 41. Sex nowadays is mainly discussed in medical, legal, criminal, moralistic, or pornographic terms, but rarely in poetical or metaphysical ones, and flirting as a necessary expression of human sensuality has come to be viewed as suspect to such a degree that it borders dangerously on (real or imaginary) sexual harassment. Yes, my fearful listener, romance in the 90s can only be found in Hollywood movies and cheesy bestsellers.

Channel 10. Fear of crime, America's prime obsession, has effectively persuaded us that the mean streets of our cities are to be avoided, especially at night. The night is no longer ours. We've lost a sense of ownership of the streets. The outside world seems increasingly more chaotic and threatening, and often the only window through which we look at it is the kaleidoscope of mass culture. But by magnifying and stylizing violence, TV and cinema end up contributing to the mystification of fear.

Channels 5 & 9. Meanwhile, the anxieties created by our demanding, uncertain, and underpaid jobs have fumigated our desire to party. Partying can be scheduled, but only once or twice a week, and just for a couple of hours. Drinking, of course, becomes a crime if the cops catch you driving on your way back home. Scary, *que no*? And if you drink every day, then you are clearly an alcoholic! In which case you need a therapist, *que no*?

So where lies our redemption? Pop psychology? Religion? Cults? "Alternative" diets? Frantic exercise, perhaps? Our bodies seem to be the only territory left over which we can exercise total control. And the objective is clearly to control the body, not to enjoy it – or rather, to pretend we enjoy our body by controlling it. The cult of health and the fear of loss of health have made us hyperconscious of everything we eat, drink, smoke, or do. Exercising in an obsessive way has come to be seen as more necessary than hanging out with family and friends, taking a walk, going to the local bar or cafe, or engaging sensorially in the world. Just to say the phrase "engaging sensorially in the world" makes me feel corny, anachronistic, and excessively rrroooomantic.

Instead, we work, and work, and when we are not working, we retreat to our highly privatized lives, because we are tired. We ensconce ourselves behind the multiple locks, gates, alarms and security monitors of our well-defended homes. There, we pursue hobbies and take vitamins and herbal or chemical anti-depressants. We watch videos. We exercise more while watching a video, or we venture into cyberspace, where we feel safe and enjoy a mythical sense of belonging to a larger "community" – an invisible one, but a community nevertheless. In cyberspace, we are without fear. "There," wherever there is, we can engage in wild cultural tourism, virtual romance, cyber-sex and assume fictional identities without experiencing any social, cultural, or biological consequences, without getting ill or shot. And no one will know about it. Only our secret accomplices. One day we will work up the courage to meet them in person, and we will inevitably disappoint them.

Channel 14. We often engage in self-righteous condemnation of those who don't abide by the laws of this unspoken puritanism, of this culture of normalized fear and programmatic health. If "they" smoke and drink, eat decadent foods, have an active sex life, or are not enslaved to their 9 to 5 jobs, we perceive them as irresponsible or uncivilized misfits, but deep inside we envy them. We envy their capability to live as if they were not scared. We can't take our eyes off them on the Jerry Springer show or in a performance art piece at the local "alternative" space.

Despite the fact that some of our fears have an obvious basis in reality, I strongly believe in the need to disobey the laws of fear and exercise our sacred right to party, go wild, lose control, enjoy the risky pleasures of the body, and to do so as often as possible. Perhaps it's time to not go to work tomorrow, even if only for a day or two, and attempt to recapture "the mystery of being in the physical world" (another super-corny phrase). It is a dangerous world, true, but nevertheless a quite marvelous one. Or perhaps its time to show up to work dressed up as your favorite "cultural other," or as one of your ideal or darkest selves, and thoroughly enjoy the consequences of your transgression. Perhaps we can all became vernacular performance artists, and defy puritanism on a regular basis.

The Philosophical "Big Bang" and the Challenges of Building Community
(Opening remarks, town meeting, Berkeley, California, 1998)

Our Christian/Manichean universe has experienced a new Big Bang, and we are now floating randomly in the middle of the explosion. We feel understandably dizzy, existentially misplaced, with our compass erratically affected by a philosophical magnetic field. With the loss of ideological certainties, those of us determined to dissipate the fog of nihilism are having an increasingly harder time sustaining a clear political vision. Why? Binary models of understanding the world are no longer functional: us/them, right/wrong, progressive/reactionary, global/local, Third World/First World, alternative/mainstream, center/periphery, etc., are constantly shifting terms in an ever-fluctuating cultural and political landscape.

The debates on identity politics and cultural diversity that so profoundly shaped our work during the 80s and early 90s seem to have succumbed to self-righteousness and new essentialisms. Very few theoreticians or activists have developed more fluid and inclusive models of identity and community that truly speak to our times. "Righteous" humanistic causes such as Zapatismo, neo-Chicanismo and feminism are no longer temples of clarity and hope, but ever-shifting territories where simplistic positionalities must be questioned on a daily basis; this permanent re-examination and interrogation inevitably challenges our faith and committment to a cause.

I ask the audience politely: what must we do then to remain politically astute and uncompromisingly "radical"? Is it fair to say that for the moment all we can do is practice creative skepticism – question everything, at all times – in hopes that tomorrow the storm will be over and we will be able to see the horizon again? What if we don't get to see a horizon in our lifetime? What if we never land on solid ground? Should we turn our gaze inward and engage in hardcore self-reflexivity, or so-called "radical spirituality," as so many of our contemporaries are doing?

Turning the gaze inward carries its own risks. America is a prime example. A society that has chosen to favor the psychological paradigm over the social, and the personal over the historical, also happens to be the society with the highest rates of psychosis, sociopathic behaviour, mental illness and crime. The risk of looking at one's self too much is the loss of a social contract, of a shared sense of being and belonging. The possible consequences of such pseudo-esoteric narcissism include disconnection, loneliness, and isolation. But then, a creative skeptic may ask, aren't all shared senses of belonging artificial and deluded?

Paradoxically, in America, the land of loneliness and rabid individualism, "community" has become a conscious goal and a national obssession. "Building community" has become the great American project of the end of the century for both the left and the right, each side in their own terms, and a new, simplistic morality has grown out of this desperate need. Since everyone wants to "belong" (precisely because no one feels that they are organically part of any larger whole), in their quest for belonging, Americans are always ready to embrace those who are racially, sexually, religiously, or aesthetically like themselves, and therefore reject, exclude, or condemn those who aren't, and who are unwilling to be converted. This binary morality is completely out of touch with the times and excludes the possibility of builing a more complex and holistic sense of community.

In the current debates around "community," the elements that designate membership in an alleged community tend to be quite narrowly defined: age, race, sexual preference, hobbies of sorts, metier, geographical location, or a shared social illness or condition. Such monolithic definitions of community overlook the obvious facts that nowadays, we all are members of multiple communities, at different times and for different reasons. Most communities in the 90s are fragmented, ephemeral, dysfunctional, and insufficient. They can only contain and "include" selected aspects of ourselves.

Given these complexities, I ask you: what, then, are the binding elements and distinguishing characteristics that will help us to shape a new, more enlightened model of community in the twenty first century?

Let's begin the discussion.

Afterword: Postcards from the Border Zone
Lisa Wolford

Over the past two and a half years, I've been engaged in an ongoing dialogue with Guillermo Gómez-Peña and the artists of Pocha Nostra. It began as a strictly professional/academic conversation, with fragmented meetings in theater lobbies and airport bars, or walking through the antiseptic hallways of convention hotels. I've always believed, however, that if a scholar wishes genuinely to understand an artist's creative practice, then he or she must be willing to risk stepping outside the protected detachment of the researcher's conventionally assigned role. A way has to be found of entering into the creative process, a way of inhabiting the world of the artists' creation (or at the very least, sojourning as an attentive and respectful guest).

The landscape that provides the backdrop for Pocha Nostra's creative endeavors is a shifting territory that offers temporary sanctuary (and in some cases, long-term residence) for a marvelous array of brilliant eccentrics, utopian dissidents, and visionary outcasts. Allisonica, Guillermo's erstwhile assistant, described it as "Pocha World;" I call it "Guillermolandia," despite my awareness of the danger of placing too much emphasis on a charismatic, central personality. A microcosmic manifestation of what Gómez-Peña has described as the Fourth World, it is a space that privileges hybridity and calls into question ascribed boundaries of identity and community, a realm in which binaristic conceptions of self and other collapse and implode. Over the time since I first entered into dialogue with Guillermo and his creative accomplices, I have often traveled to and within this space – first as an observer, a performance antropoloca chronicling the myriad encounters set in motion by the artists' street interventions and interactive dioramas. More recently, my role in relation to this artistic community has become somewhat more complex, encompassing not only the traditional role of the scholar/ historian, but also literary consultant, dramaturg as devil's advocate (in the best Grotowskian sense), ad hoc assistant director, and on occasion performance guide. I have traveled with Guillermo, Roberto and their remarkable colleagues, taken notes during marathon technical rehearsals, and been part of conversations, script revision meetings, and creative brainstorming sessions that lasted until 4 a.m. Despite having a certain art-world glamor and cultural cache, Pocha Nostra operates with a surprisingly sparse infrastructure; performers characteristically double as lighting, sound and property designers, and competent labor is always welcome. It's a structure that's familiar to me, having worked for more than ten years with underfunded, experimental groups, and one in which I've become conditioned to contribute in whatever way I can make myself most useful, whether that be revising a text or helping a performer refine and polish a particular fragment of action. It's not the usual role of an academic researcher, but one which I imagine will be familiar to artists who have worked on collaborative projects in which the ambitiousness of the artistic vision pushed or exceeded the limits of available resources. Going on the road with Pocha Nostra is an intensely rewarding though by no means entirely glamorous adventure. I have memories of spartan dorm rooms, communal kitchens, inedible truck-stop food, and interminable bus rides made bearable by reflective conversation. I cannot deny – nor would I wish to – that I have come to regard these people as my friends, and that I hold a deep and profound affection for each of them. Over the past years we have come to know one another's faults and idiosyncracies, and to accept each other, as colleagues learn to do. Roberto's quiet dignity and unfailingly watchful perception, Sara's extraordinary compassion, Juan's improbable mixture of monastic wisdom and utter madness, and Guillermo's tireless creative energy and shatteringly open emotionality are all qualities that I have come to value deeply.

If certain aspects of this still-emerging artistic and human dialogue have seemed almost instinctive, fueled by intuition, strangely congruent goals and ineffable assumptions, there have also been aspects that were challenging and painful (though never unproductive). Traveling with these intercultural diplomats and performance provocateurs has prompted me to confront difficult questions, not only about the artistic practice that is the overt object of my research, but more significantly about how I position myself in relation to the world, and what my relative cultural privilege has allowed me not to see. Journeying with these companions, I am asked to negotiate the mined and gated territories of border zones not as a tourist, but as a witness – constantly aware of the extent to which I am implicated, called upon to share not only the pleasures of the journey, but also the risks. I have come upon certain checkpoints where I was denied entry, and have been forced to confront my own resistance and reactions to being excluded, an anger that gave birth to a strange, parthenogenetically produced cyborg, and eventually found its way into a script.

Hartsfield International Airport, April 1997

Although I had followed Guillermo's work for several years, I had never really had the chance to talk with him at length until we were introduced during a conference in Atlanta. When Guillermo asked whether I might perhaps know of a student who would be able to work with him and Roberto to process audience responses gathered during the course of their *Temple of Confessions* installations and by means of their various websites, I immediately volunteered myself. I was delighted when he accepted, as I knew that the 1,000+ pages of transcripts from (live and virtual) patrons of their provocative installations constituted a valuable source of information about US-Americans' attitudes toward cultural otherness. Conferences being what they are, however, I had little opportunity to speak with Guillermo or Roberto about the project after our initial conversation. Walking through Hartsfield airport on Sunday afternoon, waiting for a plane back to Ohio, I wondered how things would proceed and when I might have the chance to speak with them again.

I didn't have long to wait. Turning into the atrium, I saw Guillermo and Roberto walking toward me along a corridor. Wearing black leather pants and a vest embroidered with sequins, Guillermo was by no means inconspicuous, flamboyant as a rock star with his ever-present sunglasses and long hair hanging loose. Roberto was more casually dressed in jeans and a grey turtleneck, with his hair pulled back. Guillermo invited me to walk with them so that we could have at least a bit more time to talk about the *Temple of Confessions* project.

As we approached the battery of security checkpoints that separate the atrium from the shuttles to the Delta terminal, Roberto drifted away from us to join a shorter line. Caught up in conversation, Guillermo and I passed our luggage through the x-ray machine and walked through the metal detector without incident. Grabbing my bag from the conveyor belt, I heard Guillermo curse. "*Chingao*! They busted Roberto again!"

A guard had taken Roberto out of the line and led him to a sort of alcove marked off by a three-sided barrier, approximately four feet high. Roberto had removed his jacket and stood, arms outstretched, while the guard ran a metal detection wand over his body from head to foot. He remained passive, unresisting. Despite the fact that the search grew more invasive, he looked on with unassailable composure. The guard instructed him to unbuckle his belt, then to unfasten his jeans, then to lift up his shirt. Each time, the wand was passed more aggressively over his body. The stream of human traffic flowed on, unabated; travelers rushing toward the shuttle doors adjusted their course so as to keep distance from the barrier and the four of us standing there. No one questioned the proceedings, or even stopped to look. Over the head of the crouching guard, I caught Roberto's gaze and noted that he was smiling – a smile both beneficent and resigned, without anger or malice.

If there was anything I found more disturbing than the incident itself, it was the sense of recurrence, even ubiquity – the obvious familiarity these men display with scenarios of interrogation and infringement of their civil rights. (It is a scene I have since seen repeated several times in different airports and other cities.) I remembered a detail from two nights before: returning to an upscale hotel late at night after having gone out for dinner and drinks, Guillermo and Roberto paused to fasten their conference name tags before entering the lobby, while the others in the group (an Englishwoman, a Welshman, and myself) breezed through without the slightest hesitation, never thinking that we might be detained or asked to prove that we belonged there.

Never in my life had I been more acutely aware of the privilege granted by my apparent *whiteness*, the invisibility, in my body and skin, of my father's Native blood. I have never experienced police harassment. Not once in my life have I ever been detained in an airport, much less subjected to invasive physical search. In the hundreds of times I drove through the border checkpoints of southern California, I was stopped only once – and then because I was with an Armenian–American man whom the border patrol officer probably mistook for Mexican. The security guard interrogating the Chicano artist at the entrance to the Delta terminal did not see me as "other." With my light skin, inconspicuous hairstyle, and bourgeois dress, he did not see me at all.

At length, satisfied that he would find no evidence of guns or bombs or contraband, the guard informed Roberto that he was free to go. Roberto refastened his clothing, put on his jacket, gathered his bags, all the while maintaining the same air of unresisting patience and inviolable dignity.

Guillermo gazed intently over the rim of his dark glasses. "You see," he murmured in his distinctively rich, low voice (half speech, half incantation) "it is dangerous to travel with us, *esa.*"

Old Town, San Diego, June 1997

California suffers from a debilitating case of historical amnesia. Nowhere is this labor of incomplete forgetting more pronounced, more disturbingly visible, than in the border region that separates affluent San Diego from her neighbor to the south. For three years I lived here in a state of what I can only now describe as political obliviousness, a well-preserved naivety that allowed me (safe in the confines of La Jolla's university community, or passing from the Taoist Sanctuary to the trendy coffeehouses of Hillcrest) to overlook the turmoil of a city in denial of its Mexican past, and unwilling to acknowledge the extent to which its current prosperity is built on the underpaid labor of Mexican workers.

When I returned to San Diego after several years of living in the Midwest, I remember feeling a moment of *frisson* when I walked into a popular downtown restaurant and realized that I was the only Anglo in the room. After living in the relatively monocultural environment of Bowling Green, Ohio, this initial moment of recognizing myself as part of a cultural minority functioned as a kind of Gurdjieffian shock, a jolt of awareness. I cannot say that in that instant I was able to understand the xenophobic anxiety at the root of Anglo-Californians' Nativist sentiments and political policies, but I will acknowledge that I found myself responding to the people in the restaurant with the sort of containment and careful politeness I adopt when traveling abroad, hiding behind a book so as to avoid conversation.

When I had lived in San Diego several years before, my closest friend at the university was Yareli Arizmendi, a performance artist from Mexico City who was deeply involved with the border arts movement. It was Yareli who most effectively chipped away at the limits of my (a)political vision, introducing me to her friends and colleagues, leading me into a cultural milieu where I couldn't help but become aware of a different San Diego, infused with the vitality and urgency that characterized the work of the Chicano/a arts community. And it was Yareli who insisted that I go with her to a performance at an alternative space down-town which she assured me that I must not miss. Seated behind a simple table lit by votive candles, Guillermo Gómez-Peña – cross-cultural diplomat and agent provocateur – incanted the words of *Border Brujo.*

Actually, what I witnessed that evening was a combination performance/film presentation, showcasing Isaac Artenstein's film of Gómez-Peña's well-known performance piece. Seven years later, seated with Guillermo and Roberto at an outdoor restaurant in San Diego's Old Town, it struck me as somewhat . . . odd? serendipitous? . . . that the performance I witnessed was the last one he did in San Diego prior to returning with Sifuentes for a production of *Dangerous Border Game* in June 1997, co-sponsored by Sushi Gallery and Centro Cultural de la Raza. Along with two graduate student colleagues, Becky Becker and Leslie Bentley, I had traveled to California to see the performance and to talk with Guillermo and Roberto about possible research projects.

Guillermo had suggested that we meet "in kitschy Old Town." Despite hav-ing lived in San Diego for three years, I had never actually been there before, and found myself gawking at this colorful simulacrum of "rrrromantic Mexico." A maze of shops and restaurants in white brick and adobe beckons tourists with promises of tropical pleasures. Dark-haired women in flounced skirts and folkloric white blouses sell bouquets of paper flowers. Tiered fountains in the center of airy, sunlit courtyards become a display stand for exotic drinks in jewel-bright tones. The entire atmosphere is one of hedonistic indulgence, an invitation to escape into an erotic fantasy of otherness – a fantasy as carefully pruned and domesticated as the lush hibiscus and tuberose growing along the meticulously landscaped paths. It's a surreal combination of yuppie shopping plaza, living tourist ad, and exotic virtual reality program, made all the more strange and ironic by its proximity to the geographic reality of the Mexican border a few miles to the south.

Adjacent to the complex of restaurants and shops, buildings that once housed missionaries are preserved as a historic monument, complete with period furnishings. Seeing a woman in a heavy, dark nun's habit, I was uncertain at first whether she is an actual nun, or part of an *in situ* reenactment. Guillermo engaged her in conversation. She explained to him that she is was a "real" nun, but functioned as docent/tourist guide, providing information on the exhibit and the religious order for which it was built. Walking through the courtyard, we debated whether Old Town would work as the setting for a performance intervention. "It might," Guillermo commented wryly, "if the persona was friendly enough." At the request of one of my colleagues, he and Roberto posed for snapshots behind a sandwichboard sign with a smiling, cartoon figure of a Mexican, taco in hand. After touring the *Bazaar Del Mundo*, we waited for a table at one of the courtyard restaurants. We walked past a type of open kiosk near the kitchen, where a sign invited patrons to watch a woman rolling hand-made tortillas on a stone counter. Adopting the exaggerated tone and demeanor of a tourist guide, Roberto labeled it "an indigenous performance diorama."

Coco Fusco, citing the work of Celeste Olalquiaga, has observed that Anglo-Americans' primary mode of experiencing other cultures is through commodification and consumption. Such a dynamic, in which the experience of "crossing the border" is perceived to be about shopping or eating ethnic food, allows Anglo-Americans "to disavow the existence of radical otherness in their midst".[1] In such a dynamic, Fusco notes, "ethnicity and otherness become a vicarious experience of sentimentality and emotion, and a reassertion of power through the act of consuming".[2] Old Town, an alluring, Hollywood-movie-set version of Mexico, offers its affluent patrons a gratifying and easily digestible taste of cultural difference. Guillermo explained that the district had become a type of pilgrimage site for tourists who want to experience the "authentic Mexico" without risking a trip south of the border, and that rather than going to Tijuana or further south, they visit here for Mexican food and exotic souvenirs. I was reminded of anthropologist Edward Bruner's insights regarding tourist districts in Bali:

> Although the elite try to avoid the Other in First World cities, making a conscious attempt not to see, to overlook – an absence of sight – when they go to the touristic borderzones they do so with the specific objective of looking, for in tourism there is a voyeurism, an overabundance of looking, a cornucopia of visualization – almost a pathology, a scopophilia. [...] The Other becomes domesticated, reworked for the tourists, frozen in time, or out of time, in past time or no time, performing a Western version of their

---

1   Fusco, Coco and Guillermo Gómez-Peña, 1992 videotaped interview by Johannes Birringer (Chicago, 1992).
2   Sawchuk, Kim. 1992 "Unleashing the Demons of History", *Parachute* 67 (1992) 22–9.

culture, essentially as entertainers. In First World space the Other is dangerous, associated with pathology and violence, with bad neighborhoods and crime. Western peoples fail to see the joy and beauty of the Other in First World space, just as they fail to see the poverty and suffering of the Other in Third World space.[3]

In San Diego, where the so-called "Third World" collides dizzyingly with the "First," the sheer proximity of the sanitized tourist districts to the economically disadvantaged inner city neighborhoods invests these contradictory modes of perceiving otherness with an almost surreal quality. (To the aforementioned diagnosis of the city as suffering from historical amnesia, add an acute case of cultural schizophrenia.) In the low-income districts of downtown San Diego, the Mexican other is constructed as inherently violent and menacing. A five-minute drive away, in the confines of the upscale tourist zone, the "domesticated" Mexican (and it is by no means insignificant that the majority of staff in direct contact with the customers in the stores and restaurants of Old Town are Mexican/Chicana women) is a site of erotic pleasure, inviting colonial fantasies of languorous seduction. Old Town promises that the true California dream, Mexico without Mexicans, is still available . . . for a price. Or failing that, an illusion of Mexico in which Mexicans (primarily young, attractive and female) exist only as part of a silent and compliant servant class, pouring margaritas against a backdrop of tropical foliage.

LISA WOLFORD

---

3   Bruner, Edward M. 1996 "Tourism in the Balinese Borderzone." in *Displacement, Diaspora, and Geographies of Identity,* ed. Smadar Lavie and Ted Swedenburg (Durham, NC, 1996), 157–79, at 160–1.

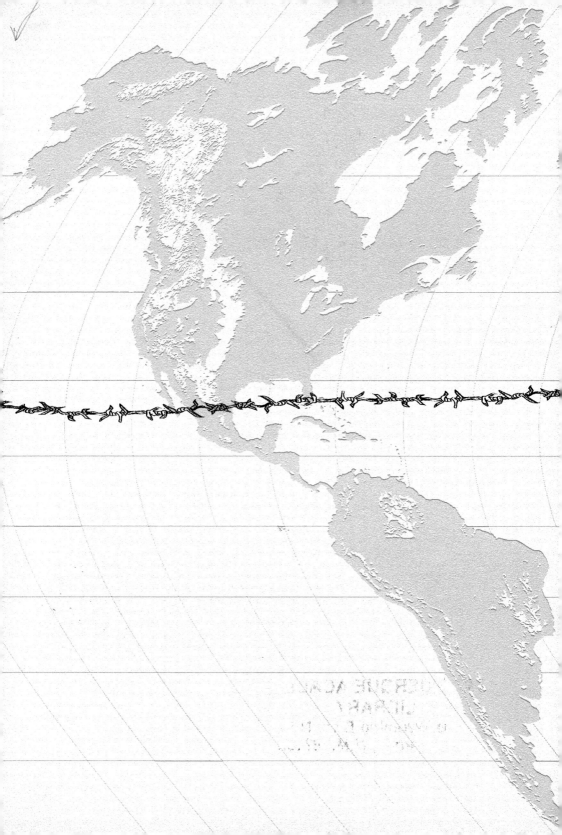